THE LIFE AND TIMES OF MAJ. GEN. WILLIAM HENRY SLEEMAN: ELIMINATION OF THUGEE IN INDIA

ISBN: 81-7835-020-3

Published in 2002 in India by
Kalpaz Publications
C-30, Satyawati Nagar
Delhi-110 052
E-mail: kalpaz@hotmail.com

Laser Typesetting at: Power Photocomposers
Printed at: Mehra Offset Printers

Contents

Preface

This book covers the years 1788-1856. It is not a tale of Thugs it is the story of the man who exterminated them, the professional and mysterious stranglers of the Yellow Scarf, who for five hundred years had infested the roads of India. His success earned him the sobriquet of 'Thuggee'. Thugee Sleeman was William Henry Sleeman, a Cornishman, an officer of the Indian Army seconded to the Indian Political Service and stationed for most of his life on what was then the frontier of India about Saugor, Jubbulpore, and Gwalior. At the end of his forty-seven years of service in India he was a major-general and honoured with the K.C.B.

Besides his great achievement in the campaign against Thuggee, he had to his credit the suppression of other violent crimes on a vast scale, the settlement of the native rebellion in Saugor and Bundelkhand, a record as a brillaint and progressive administrator both in British India and in the Native States, and the authorship of a considerable number of books and reports of the utmost value to the Government of India of his time and to historians of India of the present day. The least of his attainments was that he was a master of a formidable list of languages both European—classical and modern—and oriental. With it all he was a very human person with a great love of his fellow creatures. He and his colleagues, determined, honest, able, and courageous, and their successors of the same sort, will live in history long after their foolish travesties—the brain-children of novelists—have been for ever forgotten.

Sleeman takes his place in the history of British India prominent among those whom were Philip Woodruff in *The Founders styles* 'the Titans'; the company of Nicholson, Metcalfe, Edwardes, and the Lawrences. He preceded them by a few years, but his career overlapped theirs and he and a handful of other men of his calibre made possible the creative achievement of the Titans and the immense work of consolidaiton that followed upon them.

Historians generally agree that the annexation of Oudh by the Marques of Dalhousie in 1856 contributed, in greater or lesser degree, to the mutiny of those regiments which were mainly recruited from that kingdom. Many may consider that the greatest work of Sleeman's life was done in Oudh. With all his varied abiliities and his deep humanity he never succeeded in bringing into its native government the improvement that would have obviated annexation after he had left. No other man of his time could have done more, and only Outram, whom Sleeman recommended as his successor at the residency at Lucknow, could have done as much. Outram also failed. None the less the Indian Mutiny was a half-hearted affair, and it is in great measure due to Sleeman, who had enlisted to his side all men of goodwill in Oudh, that this revolt did not spread far and wide among the civil population and was therefore so local and so ill supported.

Modest men seldom come under the scrutiny of the biographer. Nicholson, Outram, the Lawrences. Brian Hodgson, Edwards, Malcolm, Hodson, and a score of others of the same sort as Sleeman have attracted writers' attention, but this man's career has never been made public. Yet his achievement in some ways transcended those of these others. To have rid the highways that wound those thousands of miles across the face of India and to have cleansed vast expanses of her country from gang of criminals and murderers was more than any man had ever done before was likely to do for generations after he had gone. But Sleeman was also a craftsman and did not thirst, as for instance did Outram and Malcolm, for the rewards of glory. He never paraded his successes before those who might have honoured him; in fact, in one instance he deliberately put the vital tasks on hand before the chances of his own preferment. Thus it is that one of the ablest and most respected men that Britain ever lent to India is likely to pass into oblivion except for a bare mention of his name in conneciton with the suppression of the Thugs. Few indeed realize how closely he came to averting the catastrophe of 1857.

Vincent Smith in his *Oxford History of India* has a portrait of William Sleeman and much more than a bare mention. He has encouraged me thereby to write this book, to put flesh on the bones, and to show what manner of man was William Henry Sleeman and to account for the deep and lasting impression that his many qualities made on the India of his day and left for the India that came after him. Few have had a greater influence in British India than this brilliant Cornishman.

It has until recently been the custom for writers and speakers in England to portray their countrymen in old British India as a people for whom Indians at large had much ill feeling. Of late, however, the many British newcomers to India and Pakistan have been pleasantly surprised at the warmth of the welcome they receive and at the good feeling there is for the British. They have wondered why this should be. This Life of William Henry Sleeman, so typical of his kind, may help towards explaining the existence of this fund of goodwill and may afford a useful introduction to the great country of India. Certainly those who in increasing numbers are leaving this island for that vast sub-continent would do well to read of the not so distant past when Britain and India worked together in the administration of India.

Francis Tuker

Cornwall, 1961

Acknowledgements

This book could not have been written without the constant and ready help of Colonel Sir James Sleeman, the grandson of Major-General Sir William Sleeman, K.C.B., the distinguished subject of my researches. It is primarily from documents and letters in his possession and from correspondence with him that I have reconstructed this account of Thuggee's life.

A list of Sir William Sleeman's own publications consulted by me includes:

Rambles and Recollecitons of an Indian Official
The Spirit of Military Discipline in the Indian Army
Analysis and Review of the Peculiar Doctrines of the Ricardo, or New, School of Political Economy
The Story of the Byza Bae
A Journey through the Kingdom of Oude, 1849-50
Illustrations of the History and Practices of the Thugs
Reports on Tusma Baz Thugs
Papers on Thuggee
Report on the Depredations Committed by the Thug Gangs of Upper and Central India
Report on the System of Megpunnaism
Report on the Budhuk or Bagree Dacoits

Sir James Sleeman's own book *Thug*, or *A Million Murders*, has been a valuable source of reference.

Mr Charles Lesley Ames, President of the Ames Library of St Paul, Minnesota, U.S.A., representing the officers and trustees of the library, has courteously and unreservedly placed at my disposal Sleeman's original proof of *The Byza Bae.*

My thanks are due to those publishers who have so readily permitted me to make use of their books, in particular to the Oxford University Press for the *Rambles and Recollections,* an indispensable contribution to my story; to W.H. Allen and Co. Ltd for *Illustrations of the History and Practices of the Thugs*; to Wm Blackwood and Sons Ltd for *Recollections of My life* by Sir Joseph Favrer; and to John Murray for Lady Login's *Recollections* and *India Under Lord Ellebborough.* A list of other publications is given at the end of the book.

Quotations from Lord William Bentinck's papers have been included with the kind permission of His Grace the Duke of Portland and Nottingham University.

I am indebted to many willing helpers: to Major V. Hodson, for information about Sleeman's early career and associates; to the librarian and his staff and to the Records Department of the India Office; to Dr C. Collin Davies, Reader in Indian History Gerald Fox, Town Clerk of Tenby, the Rev. T. W. Gilbert of Stratton, Prebendary John A. Durling of Bideford and the librarian of the R.U.S. Institution for information on Sleeman's family and on his early years; to Mr G. Ellis Flack of Nottingham University for correspondence which passed between Sir William Sleeman and Lord William Bentinck; to Messrs Grindlay & Co., Messrs Wilkinson, the celebrated sword-makers, and to the editor of the *Fishing Gazette* for clearing up certain problems for me; and to Mr W.H. Murray for quite indispensable help in preparing the manuscript for publication.

Lastly, in order to keep me quiet during a long illness, Miss P.M. Quin, the nursing sister who cared for me, herself wrote almost the whole of this book to my dictation—a meritorious service if ever there was one.

Francis Tuker

Introduction

If I were asked to name one policeman whose memory should have been preserved as an inspiration for future generations, I would unhesitatingly recommend Colonel Sleeman. I have always been infatuated by the remarkable career graph of Sleeman who served India with utmost sincereity and highest degree of dedication. I rate him as an outstanding policeman of the world. Today, we have not been able to catch hold of Veerappan, Ibrahim Dawood and a small time bandit like Dodua and ordinary criminals are roaming free and are flourishring. Is there any inspired policeman who can deal with the lawless lot with that sense of dedication which inspired Maj. Gen. W.H. Sleeman to pursue the thugs till they are totally eliminated? There are political thugs and mafias for dealing with whom we require men like Sleeman. Is there any taker? I have been prompted to get this book *''Yellow Scarf''* by Lt. Gen. Sir Francis Tuker KCIE,. CB, ASO, OBE reprinted through my publisher who is a connossieur of good academic works.

Students of modern Indian history would undoubtedly be aware of his invaluable role in the elimination of organised thuggery during the turbulent years following the collapse of Mughal rule from large parts of India. Long before the concept of modern policing had acquired shape, Sleeman, designated as the Superintendent General for the liquidation of thuggery, went about the job like a true professional. He did not seek refuge behind an equivalent of TADA or NSA. Nor did subterfuges like fake encounters and recourse to doctoring of statistics tempt him. Instead, the problem was studied and its ramifications understood by him. Based on this study, an elaborate plan of action, preceded by authentic documentation, was handed over for implementation to a dedicated team of known achievers. As a first step, they broke the network's secret code and succeeded in infiltrating the gangs. The gangs were effectively liquidated with the arrest, prosecution and public hangings of those proved guilty after speedy trials.

Early Life

This distinguished officer, whose career in India extended over a period of forty years, and whose services were highly appreciated by three Governors-General—Viscount Hardinge, the Earl of Ellenborough, and the Marquess of Dalhousie—evinced by their appointing him to the most difficult and delicate duties—was the son of Philip and Mary Sleeman, and was born at Stratton, Cornwall on, 8th August, 1788. In this early years he evinced a predilection for the military profession; and at the age of twenty-one (October, 1809), through the good offices of the late Lord De Dunstanville, he was appointed an Infantry Cadet in Bengal army, and was promoted successively to the rank of Ensign, on 23rd September, on 1810; Lieutenant, on 16th December, 1814; Brevent-Captain, on 24th April, 1924; Captain, on 23rd September, 1826; Major, on 1st February, 1837; Lieutenant-Colonel, on 26th May, 1843; Colonel, on 24th November, 1853; and obtained the rank of Major-General on 28th November, 1854.

Early in his career he served in the Nepaulese war. The value of his talents soon became known, and in 1816, when it was considered necessary to investigate a claim to property as prize-money arising out of that war, Lieutenant Sleeman was selected to inquire into it. The report was accordingly made by him in February 1817, which was designated by the Government as "able, impartial, and satisfactory."

Assistant to Agent

In 1820 he was appointed Junior Assistant to the Agent of the Governor-General at Saugur, and remained in the Civil Department in the Saugur and Nerbudda territories, with the exception of absence of sick certificate, for nearly a quarter of a century. Here he manifested that, if he had been efficient in an inferior position, he was also an able administrator in a superior post.

He distinguished himself so much by his activity in the suppression of the horrible practice of thuggism, then so prevalent, that, in 1835, he was employed exclusively in the Thugee Department; his appointment in the Saugur and Nerbudda district being kept open, and his promotion going on. The very valuable Papers upon Thuggism submitted to the

Governor-General were chiefly drawn up by Sir William Sleeman, and the department specially commissioned for this important purpose was not only organised but worked by him. In consequence of ill-health, however, at the end of 1836, he was compelled to resign this appointment; but on his return to duty in February 1839, he was nominated to the combined offices of Commissioner for the Suppression of Thuggee and Dacoity.

In 1842 he was employed on a special mission in Bundelcund, to inquire into the causes of the recent disturbances there, and he remained in that district, with additional duties, as resident at Gwalior; from 1844 until 1849, when he was removed to the highly important office of Resident at the Court of Lucknow. Colonel Sleeman held his office at Gwalior in very critical times, which resulted in hostilities and the battle of Mahrajpore. But for a noble and unselfish act he would have received this promotion at an earlier period. The circumstance was as under: Colonel Low, the Resident at that time, hearing that his father was dangerously ill, tendered his resignation to Lord Auckland, who immediately offered the appointment to Colonel Sleeman. No sooner had this occurred, however, the House of Caunter and Co, of Calcutta, in which Low's brother was a partner, had failed, and, in consequence, every farthing he had saved had been swept away. Under this painful contingency he begged to place himself in his Lordship's hands. This letter was sent by Lord Auckland to Colonel Sleeman, who immediately wrote to Colonel Low, begging that he would retain his situation at Lucknow. This generous conduct of Colonel Sleeman was duly appreciated; and Lord Auckland, on leaving India, recommended him to the particular notice of his successor, Lord Ellenborough, who immediately appointed Colonel Sleeman of Jhansi with an additional Rupees one thousand a year to his income.

Suppression of Thuggee

One of the first and not the least important administrative measures carried out by Lord William Bentinck was the strenuous and systematic effort to suppress the Thugs in their practice of murder for the purposes of robbery. The complete success which crowned the steps taken for this purpose in the first year of his administration, and which were maintained with equal energy and vigilance during its whole course, render the suppression of *thuggee* one of the most notable achievements of the

Governor-Generalship of Lord William Bentinck. The story of the proceedings taken against the Thugs is told in the fullest official detail in five volumes of manuscript records preserved in the India Office. Therein will be found not merely particulars of the capture of the different gangs, exact reports of the trials and sentences, and precise returns of the expenditure entailed, but also genealogical tables of the principal. Thugs, showing that their nefarious trade had become a family profession and secret.

Thug is the Hindustani equivalent for 'cheat' , and the name strictly translated gives no indication of their mode of perpetrating the dreadful crime that rendered them the terror of the Indian traveller. The less usual but more correct name of *phansi-gar* gives a clearer insight into their practices, for *phansa* means noose, the fatal rope or scarf with which they strangled their unsuspecting and defenceless victims. The *phansa* plays a prominent part in the Hindu mythology and is assigned to several gods and goddesses and their favourite weapon. The exact date at which highway robbers adopted it for the purposes of their vocation is uncertain or unknown, but the French traveller Tavernier, in the middle of the seventeenth century, mentions the stranglers of the highway as one of the dangers of travel in the dominions of the Great Moghuls. The troubles of the eighteenth century, when the destinies of India hung at the mercy of military adventurers and lawless hordes of plunderers, added undoubtedly to their number, and the whole of Central India from Haidarabad to Oudh, and Bundelkhand to Rajputana, provided a vast and profitable field for the display of their skill as secret murderers.

Their mode of proceeding may be thus briefly described. Having performed certain prognostications as to the result of their enterprise—for the fatalism which characterised their religious belief and gave fortitude to their proceedings was largely tinged with superstition—they set out along one of the main roads frequented by merchants and other travellers. To all they appeared to be a party of unarmed and harmless men, either pursuing their business as traders or returning to their native village from a pilgrimage. In those days of open highway robbery travellers were only too glad to meet with companions, and the Thugs never experienced any difficulty in picking up one, or more than one, unsuspecting wayfarer en route. There was nothing in their demeanour or conduct to excite suspension. At the well or the *caravanserai* their seemed like the most inoffensive of travellers, and the only ground for suspicion was that which least arouses it, a special cheerfulness of manner and a conciliatory attitude towards all strangers. Having once selected the victim, their patience in waiting for the most favourable moment to strike the blow was remarkable, and constituted the main secret of their power and protracted impunity. Sometimes they would deem it expedient to strike at once, but more often they would perform a journey of days and weeks together with their intended victim before they would deliver the fatal blow. But in nearly all cases it was done at a moment when the victim would be least prepared and most off his guard—either engaged in his prayers or at ablutions—and the noose was always used with such deadly precision that the murdered person never had a chance of raising an alarm. The larger proportion of victims were single individuals, but if the gang was sufficiently numerous, and sometimes the Thags travelled in bands of sixty or seventy, they would not be afraid to entice a considerable body of travellers, and to murder as many as a dozen at a single massacre. In all cases they resorted to every precaution to prevent surprise from interruption, and with such success that no instance of failure is recorded.

The younger members of the family or band served their apprenticeship as scouts, and it was only after many years of experience in this innocent capacity that they were allowed to so much as witness the perpetrating of the crime, while the act of throwing the scarf was always entrusted to the most expert and experienced Thug. Their skill in effecting the murder of their victims was matched by the secrecy with which they disposed of their remains, and sometimes the most conclusive evidence against a captured Thug was discovery of the skeletons of the murdered in an unlikely spot, revealed by the confession of a confederate. The strictness of the discipline was softened by the ties of family, and the secrets of the brotherhood were preserved by the invocation of religion as much as by the terror of the severe punishment meted out a treachery.

The disturbed condition of India during the whole of the eighteenth century added largely, as has been said, to the number of Thugs, whose reputation was greatly enhanced in the popular mind by the practical impunity with which their operations were carried on. If their own account of themselves might be accepted, they originally formed a special colony divided into seven tribes and located Near Delhi. In those days they were said to be all Muhammadans, but the beliefs and regulations of the caste were essentially Hindu of a corrupt kind, and when the Thugs were brought before British Courts of Justice the majority were found to be of Hindu race. It is probable from this statement that they were at first a local caste in the nighbourhood of the Mughal capital, where their enormities soon attracted notice. The Muhammedan Emperors were strong enough to banish the offenders to a feasible distance from their capital, but not to break up their organisation. They left Delhi, and scattering themselves throughout Central India and the Deccan found a more profitable arena for their exploits.

They were commencing the career of extended mischief which made them known throughout India when the French traveller, Tavernier, noted their depredations as one of the gravest perils to the traveller in peninsula. They flourished during the whole of the eighteenth century on the troubles of India, and in the absence of any central power or authority to call them to account. The officials of many of the smaller states, finding themselves unable to cope with the malefactors, made common cause with them, and for a share in the profits accorded them the protection that was provided by their own inertness and indifference. Their numbers and their success steadily increased, until at the end of the nineteenth century they were brought into contact with the British Raj. The annexations of Mysore and Chittor were followed by the dispersion of some of the most formidable bands, and the majority of the survivors withdrew into the native states of Malwa and Rajputana, where for another thirty years they enjoyed security and immunity from official pursuit. In the time of both Lord Hastings and Lord Amherst several bands were discovered and broken up, but such was the feeling of toleration or fear with which they were regarded by the native courts and officials, that the conviction of the prisoners was by no means the certain consequence of their capture, and it is correct to say that when Lord William Bentinck took up the matter nothing had been done to break up the Thugs as an organisation hostile to the community.

In 1829 specials orders and fuller powers were given to Mr. F. C. Smith, Agent to the Governor-General in the Narbada Territories—a division corresponding to the present Central India agency and central provinces combined—to proceed against all Thugs, and to put down their associations with the strong hand. Major Sleeman, whose name will always be honourably coupled with disappearance of this crime in India, was given a special appointment as his coadjutor and assistant. Other officers were at a later period entrusted with a similar task, when it was found by practical experience that the Thugs embraced too wide an area to be dealt with by a single officer or a local department, and among them it is only just that the names of Major (afterwards Sir John) Low in Oudh, Mr Wilson in Bundelkhand, and Colonel Stewart in Haridarabad, should be mentioned as among the most/energetic and successful.

The active operations of the Thugee department covered a period of six years, and during that time two thousand Thugs were arrested. Of these, fifteen hundred were sentenced either to death or to different periods of transportation. Although there had been no attempt on the part of the native governments to proceed against the malefactors, it was gratifying to find that once the British Government took up the matter the darbars of the principal States, such as Haidarabad, Oudh, and Gwalior, hastened to lend their hearty and useful co-operation. This was the more satisfactory and necessary, inasmuch as the headquarters of some of the largest gangs were to be found within the Native States. The readiness of the Native Governments to associate themselves within a work that was not merely beneficial to the community, but which might be termed essential from the point of view of humanity, was not however, imitated by the Native Courts, where the judges showed a tendency to deal too lightly with captured Thugs, and availing themselves of any deficiency in the evidence as to murder to evade the infliction of capital sentences. The possibility of administrative energy being neutralised by judicial timidity was averted by plenary judicial powers being conferred on Mr Smith, and the sentences passed on convicted Thugs.

End of Thuggee

The final result of these sustained and systematic efforts to suppress the crime was that all the principal bands were broken up, that the reputation of the Thugs was destroyed, and that the most formidable murder associaiton which India had ever known passed out of existence. Almost two centuries have elapsed since the labours of the Commission presided over by Mr Smith and Major Sleeman were brought to an end, and, although thore have been isolated cases, there has been no attempt to revive the old organisation. The family secrets and ties which constituted the strength of the fraternity have died out or been dissolved by the lapse of time, and it may be doubted whether the crime in its old from could be revived, were India to pass through another of those troubled periods which formed so large a part of her history, and from which she seems now happily to be rescued. Strictly speaking, the suppression of the Thugs was due to the active and energetic measures of the Indian administration rather than to the policy of Lord William Bentinck, but he vigorously supported the measures taken against them, and urged on his lieutenants to make a speedy end of these enemies of the public peace. It must also be noted to his credit that when he took up the reins of office the Thugs were more formidable than they had ever been before, and that when he left India they were shattered and practically annihilated.

Glorious End

Later in the year, General Sleeman went to the hills, in the hope of recouping his wasted health by change of air and scene: but the expectation proved vain, and he was compelled to take passage for England. But it was now too late: notwithstanding the best medical aid, he gradually sank, and, after a long illness, died on his passage from Calcutta, on the 10th February, 1856, at the age of sixty-seven.

His Indian career was, indeed, long and honourable—his labours most meritorious. He was one of those superior men which the Indian service constantly producing, who rendered the name of Englishmen respected throughout the vast empire of British India, and whose memory will endure so long as tales of British power shall remain in the East.

It is well known that Lord Dalhousie, on his relinquishing the Indian Government, recommended General Sleeman and two other distinguished officers in civil employment for some mark of the royal favour, and he was accordingly nominated K.C.B. on 4th February, 1856; of which honour his Lordship apprised him in a highly gratifying letter just before his death.

But, however high the reputation of an officer placed in such circumstances—and none stood higher than Sir William Sleeman, not early in the estimation of the Governor-General and the Honourable Company, but also in the opinion of the inhabitants of India, where he had served with great ability for forty years, and won the respect and love particularly of the natives, who always regarded him as their friend, and by whom his equity was profoundly appreciated—it was to be anticipated, as a matter of course, that his words and actions would be distorted and misrepresented by a Court so atrociously infamous. This, no doubt, he was prepared to expect. The King, or rather the creatures who surrounded him, would at all cost endeavour to prevent any investigation into their gross malpractices, and seek to slander the man they were unable to remove.

The following Narrative of a ''Pilgrimage'' though the kingdom of Oudh was written by the late Major-General Sir William Sleeman in 1851 (while a Resident at the Court of Lucknow), at the request of the Governor-General the Marquess of Dalhousie, in order to acquaint the Honourable Company with the actual condition of that kingdom, and with the view of pointing out the best measures to be suggested to the King for the improvement and amelioration of the country and people. On October, 1847, the King of Oudh had been informed by the Governor-General, that if his system of rule were not materially amended (for it was disgraceful and dangerous to any neighbouring power to permit its continuance in its present condition) before two years had expired, the British Government would find it necessary to take steps for such purpose in his name. Accordingly on the 16th September, 1848, the Governor-General addressed a letter to Sir William Sleeman, commissioning him to make a personal visit to all parts of the kingdom. Excerpts of the letter have been given as follows:

Indian Police-Its Defects and their Cause and Remedy

The police officers employed on our borders find it very convenient to trace the perpetrators of all murders and gang robberies into the territories of native chiefs, whose subjects they accuse often when they know that the crimes have been committed by our own. They are, on the one hand, afraid to seize or accuse the real offenders lest they should avenge themselves by some personal violence, or by thefts or robberies, which they often commit with a view to get them turned out of office as inefficient; and on the other they are tempted to conceal the real offenders by a liberal share of the spoil, and a promise of not offending again within their beat. Their tenure of office is far too insecure, and their salaries are far too small. They are often dismissed summarily by the magistrate if they send him no prisoners; and also if they send in to him prisoners who are not ultimately convicted, because a magistrate's merits are too often estimated by the proportion that his convictions bear to his acquittals among the prisoners committed for trial to the Sessions. Men are often ultimately acquitted for want of judicial proof, when there is abundance of that moral proof on which a police officer or magistrate has to act in the discharge of his duties. In a country where gangs of professional, and hereditary robbers and murderers extend their depredations into very remote parts, and seldom commit them in the districts in which they reside the most vigilant police officer must often fail to discover the perpetrators of heavy crimes that take place within his range is a matter of concern.

When they cannot find them, the native officers either seize innocent persons, and frighten them into confession, or else they try to conceal the crime, and in this they are seconded by the sufferers in the robbery, who will always avoid if they can, a prosecution in our courts, and by their neighbours, who dread being summoned to give evidence as a serious calamity. The man who has been robbed, instead of being an object of compassion among his neighbours, often incurs their resentment for subjecting them to his calamity; and they not only pay largely themselves, but make him pay largely to have his losses concealed from the magistrate. Formerly, when a district was visited by a judge of circuit to hold his sessions only once or twice a year and men were constantly bound over to prosecute and appear as evidence from session to session, till they were wearied and worried to death, this evil was much greater than at present, when every district is provided with its judge sessions, who is, or ought to be always ready to take up the cases committed for trial by the magistrate. This was one of the best measures of Lord W. Bentinck's admirable, though much abused, administration of the government of India. Still, however, the inconvenience and delay of prosecution in our courts are so great, and the chance of the ultimate convictions of great offenders is so small that strong temptations are held out to the police to conceal or misrepresent the character of crimes; and they must have a great feeling of security in their tenure of office, and more adequate salaries, better chances of rising, and better supervision over them, before they will resist such temptation. These Thanedars, and all the public officers under them are all so very inadequately paid that corruption among them excites no feeling of odium or indignation in the minds of those among whom they live and serve. Such feeling are rather directed against the government that places them in such situations, so much labour and responsibility with salaries so inadequate; and thereby confers upon them virtually a license to pay themselves by preying upon those whom they are employed ostensibly to protect. They know that with such salaries they can never have the reputation of being honest, however faithfully they may discharge their duties; and it is too hard to expect that men will long submit to the necessity of being throughout ecorrupt, without repeating some of the advantages of corruption.

Let the Thanedars have everywhere such salaries as will enable them to maintain their families in comfort, and keep up that appearance of respectability which their stations in society demands; and over every three or four Thanedars jurisdiction let there be an officer appointed upon a higher scale of salary, to supervise and control their proceedings, and armed with powers to decide minor offences. To these stations the Thanedars will be able to look forward as their reward for a faithful and zealous discharge of their duties.

He who can suppose that men so inadequately paid, who have no promotion to look forward to, and feel no security in their tenure of office, and consequently no hope of a provision for old age, will be zealous and honest in the discharge of their duties must be very imperfectly acquainted with human nature, and with the motives by which men are influenced in all quarters of the word; but we are none of us so ignorant, for we all know that the same motives actuate public servants in India as elsewhere. We have acted successfully upon this knowledge in the scale of salaries and gradation of rank assigned to European civil functionaries, and to all native functionaries employed in the judicial and revenue branches of the public service; and why not act upon it in that of the salaries assigned to the native officers employed in the police? The magistrate of a district gets a salary of from two thousand to two thousand five hundred rupees a month.

The native officer next under him is the Thanedar, or head native police officer of a subdivision of his district, containing many towns and villages, with a population of a hundred thousand souls. This officer gets a salary of twenty-five rupees a month. He cannot possibly do his duty unless he keeps one or two horses; indeed, he is told by the magistrate that he cannot; and that he must have one or two horses, or resign his post. The people, seeing how much we expect from the Thanedar, and how little we give him, submit to his demands for contributions without murmuring, and consider almost any demand trivial from a man so emplolyed and so paid. They are confounded at our inconsistency, and say, ''We see you giving high salaries, and high prospects of advancement to men who have nothing to do but collect your rents, and decide our disputes about pounds, shillings, and pence, which we used to decide much better ourselves, when we had no other court but that of our elders while those who are to protect life and property, to keep peace over the land, and enable the industrious to work in security, maintain their families, and pay the government revenue, are left with hardly any pay at all.''

There is really nothing in our rule in India which strikes the people so much as this inconsistency, the civil defects of which are so great and manifest; the only way to remedy the evils is to give a greater feeling of security in the tenure of office, a higher rate of salary, the hope of a provision for old age, and, above all, the gradation of rank, by interposing the officers I speak of between the Thanedars and the magistrate. This has all been done in the establishments for the collection of the revenue, and administration of civil justice.

Hobbes, in his Leviathan, says, ''And seeing that the end of punishment is not revenge and discharge of choler, but correction, either of the offender, or of others by his example, the severest punishments are to be inflicted for those crimes that are of most danger to the public; such as are those which proceed from malice to the government established; those that spring from contempt of justice; those that provoke indignation in the multitude; and those which, unpunished, seem authorized, as when they are committed by sons, servants, or favourites of men in authority. For indignation carries men, not only against the actors and authors of injustice, but against all power that is likely to protect them; as in the case of Tarquin, when, for the insolent act of one of his sons, he was driven out of Rome and the monarchy itself dissolved.'' (Para 2, chap. xxx) Almost every one of our Thanedars is, in his way, a little Tarquin, exciting the indignation of the people against his rulers; and no time should be lost in converting him into something better.

By the obstacles which are still everywhere opposed to the conviction of offenders, in the distance of our courts, the forms of procedure, and other cause of 'the law's delay,' we render the duties of our police establishment everywhere "more honoured in the breach than the observance," by the mass of the people among whom they are placed. We must, as I have before said, remove some of these obstacles to the successful prosecution of offenders in our criminal courts, which tend so much to deprive the government of all popular aid and support in the administrations of justice; and to convert all our police establishments into instruments of oppression, instead of what they should be, the efficient means of protection to the persons, property, and character of the innocent. Crimes multiply from the assurance the guilty are everywhere apt to feel of impunity to crime; and the more crimes multiply, the greater is the aversion the people everywhere feel to aid the government in the arrest and conviction of criminals; because they see more the innocent punished by attendance upon distant courts at great cost and inconvenience to give evidence upon points which seem to them unimportant, while the guilty escape owing to technical difficulties which they can never understand.

The best way to remove these obstacles is to interpose officers between the Thanedar and the magistrate and arm them with judicial powers to try minor cases, leaving an appeal open to the magistrate and to extend the final jurisdiction of the magistrate to a greater range of crimes, though it should involve the necessity of reducing the measure of punishment annexed to them. Beccaria has justly observed that "Crimes are more effectually prevented by the certainty than by the severity of punishment. The certainty of a small punishment will make a stronger impression than the fear of one more severe, if attended with the hope of escaping; for it is the nature of mankind to be terrified at the approach of the smallest inevitable evil; whilst hope,the best gift of Heaven, has the power of dispelling the apprehensions of a greater, especially if supported by examples of impunity, which weakness or avarice too frequently affords.

A robbery affords a rich harvest. Some article of stolen property is found in one man's house, and by a little legerdemain it is conveyed to that of another, both of whom are made to pay liberally; the man robbed also pays, and all the members of the village community are made to do the same. They are all called to the court of the Thanedar to give evidence, as to what they have seen or heard regarding either the fact, or the persons in the remotest degree connected with it as to the arrests of the supposed offenders the search of their house-the character of their grandmothers and grandfathers-and they are told that they are to be sent to the magistrate a hundred miles distant, and then made to stand at the door among a hundred and fifty pairs of shoes, till his excellency the Nazir, the under-sheriff of the court, may be pleased to announce them to his highness the magistrate, which of course, he will not do without a consideration. To escape all these threatened evils, they pay handsomely and depart in peace. The Thanedar reports that an attempt to rob a house by persons unknown had been defeated by his exertions, and the good fortune of the magistrate; and sends a liberal share of spoil to those who are to read his report to that functionary. This goes on more or less in every district, but more especially in those where the magistrate happens to be a man of violent temper, who is always surrounded by knaves, because men who have any regard for their character will not approach him-or a weak, good-natured man, easily made to believe anything, and managed by favourites-or one too fond of fields sports, or of music, painting, European languages, literature, and sciences, or lastly, of his own ease. Some magistrates think they can put down crime by dismissing the Thanedar; but this tends only to prevent crimes being reported to him for in such cases the feelings of the people are in exact accordance with the interests of the Thanedars; and crimes augmented by the assurance of impunity thereby given to criminals.

It is a common practice with Thanedars all over the country to connive at the residence within their jurisdiction of gangs of robbers, on the condition that they shall not rob within those limits, and shall give them a share of what they bring back from their distant expeditions.

They say the gangs go out ostensibly in search of service, on the termination of the rains of one season in October, and return before the commencement of the next in June; but their vocation is always well known to the police, and to all the people of their neighbourhood, and very often to the magistrates themselves, who could, if they would secure them on their return with their booty; but this would not secure their conviction unless the proprietors could be discovered, which they scarcely ever could. Were the police officers to seize them, they would be all finally acquitted and released by the judges-the magistrate would get into disrepute with his superiors, by the number of acquittals compared with convictions exhibited in his monthly tables; and he would vent his spleen upon the poor Thanedar, who would at the same time have incurred the resentment of the robbers; and between both, he would have no possible chance of escape. He therefore consults his own interest and his own ease by leaving them to carry on their trade of robbery or murder unmolested; and master, the magistrate, is well pleased not to be pestered with charges against men whom he has no chance of getting ultimately convicted. It was in this way that so many hundred families of assassins profession were able for so many generations to reside in the most cultivated and populous parts of territories, and extend their depredations into the remotest parts of India, before our system of operations was brought to bear upon them in 1830. Their profession was perfectly well known to the people of the district in which they resided, and to the greater part of the police; they murdered not within their own district, and the police of that district cared nothing about what they might do beyond it.

These are things of daily occurrence in all parts of our dominions, and the Thanedars are not afraid to play such "fantastic tricks" because all those under and all those above them share more or less in the spoil, and are bound in honour to conceal them from the European magistrate, who it is in the interest of all to keep in the dark. They know that the people will hardly ever complain, form the great dislike they all have to appear in our courts, particularly when it is against any of the officers of those courts, or their friends and creatures in the district police.

The annexation of Oudh to the British dominions followed, but not as a consequence of Sir W. Sleeman's report. No greater injustice can be done than to assert that he advised such a course. His letters prove exactly the reverse. He distinctly states, in his correspondence with the Governor-General, Lord Dalhousie, that the annexation of Oudh would cost the British power more than the value of ten such kingdoms, and would inevitably lead to a mutiny of the Sepoys. He constantly maintains the advisability of frontier kingdoms under native sovereigns, that the people themselves might observe the contrast, to the advantage of the Honourable Company, of the wise and equitable administration of its rule compared with the oppressive and cruel despotism of their own princes. Sir William Sleeman had profoundly studied the Indian character in its different races, and was deservedly much beloved by them for his earnest desire to promote their welfare, and for the effectual manner in which, on all occasions in his power, and these were frequent, he redressed the evils complained of, and extended the Aegis of British power over the affected and oppressed.

I would like to append a note of caution for readers. Throughout the quotations in this book I have as far as possible kept to the original spelling of names of places, regions and people and only altered them where they might possibly be unrecognizable to a modest reader. Thus the Oudh of today is shown as written by Sleeman—Oude.

CHAPTER 1

The Loom of Youth

The Siege of Lucknow had dragged on for nearly five months, right through the hot monsoon season of 1857, while the tiny garrison at the British residency—only a few hundred men with women and children—made a resistance unsurpassed for valour in British history. The end came on the night of 22nd November. Under cover of darkness they marched out from the battered defences. All were safely away when Colonel Ouvrey of the 9th Lancers bethought him of the battle-torn portrait of an old friend and a great man, 'Thuggee' Sleeman, which had hung on the residency walls and watched over them throughout that long ordeal. He could not bring himself to leave it there, at the mercy of the mutineers. So back he went through the night, through their encircling positions, into the deserted building. He cut the canvas from the frame and brought it away. Rolled around a soldier's musket it was carried to safety and sent to Thuggee's son, Henry.

A man who survives a fierce ordeal such as that of Lucknow, and has known the long-drawn strain upon the nerves is not immediately brought to sentimentalities, nor to risk his life for a trifle. Yet Ouvrey went back. It may be that the leaders of the garrison had found in the portrait a symbol of steadfastness. Certainly it must have had a value for which no lesser symbol can account.

Examination of the portrait does support that notion. The painting had been made by George Duncan Beechey in 1851, when Thuggee was sixty-three. At first sight it looks very much the official portrait: Major-General Sir William Henry Sleeman, K.C.B., aloof, as if resigned to those fetters of gold braid. Then we pay attention to the face and our estimate has to be revised.

Were it not for the braided collar, the face might be that of some eminent man of science, literature, or divinity. The head is egg-shaped, the forehead high, with auburn hair swept forward at the sides from back to front. The mouth is firm, as we might expect of a man we know to be one of India's great servants, yet also it is mobile, well able to express at need a haughty or a gentle mood, and to be stern or humorous at will. That mobile power is a key to the character. We notice it especially in the eyes, the most remarkable feature of all. They are large, wide apart, and beautifully shaped: omnivorous eyes, observant in seeking to understand, because wanting to act out a purpose. His intelligence, we can see, is brought alive by compassion. He is accustomed to take a resolve, to make a decision, to command. We begin to understand why Ouvrey went back. Firmness of soul, like sanctity, is infectious.

The painter has caught in the eyes a hint of sadness. Perhaps Sleeman had already guessed that his struggle to make his counsels prevail with the governor-general-and they would have saved India from the mutiny if they had—might in the end not be heard.

That final endeavour was to fail in the year he died. His more spectacular services remain, bearing the stamp of greatness; we see displayed in them the best side of the British administration. They sprang from an enlightened mind, and from the will of a man who had found his purpose in life and kept it simple, devoid of ulterior motive: to protect his fellow men from ill and so far as he was able guide them into good. In a disordered country the effects of a purpose so simple are quickly felt and feared by ruthless enemies, and the man who would act it out in political life (not just theorize) needs all the courage he can get. His way leads inevitably into strife and danger. If assassination does not end his life, heavy stresses shorten it. Such was to be Sleeman's fate. But his work lives on to our own day.

Long-lasting work is a fruit of robust human stock. William Henry Sleeman was born in 1788 at Stratton in Cornwall, the fifth son of Captain Philip Sleeman, then employed as Supervisor of Excise, and his wife Mary. The Sleemans were an old Cornish family, the name being also spelt Sleman, Selman, Slemman or Sloman as fancy or literacy took the bearer from generation to generation. As with all other Cornish gentry, the Sleemans had in the past held almost professional status in the smuggling of silks, laces and liquor. It was not pure coincidence that persuaded H.M. Excise to offer the retired Captain Philip a chance to prove himself as adept at prevention as his fathers had been at promotion. His wife Mary was a Spry, and the Sprys were of Place, the family seat near St. Mawes. Philip's and Mary's children were Cornish in blood and bone.

Along the high north coast of Cornwall the great winds roar in from the north-west across the wide mouth of the Bristol Channel; the trees are stunted by it, their heads bowed away and their branches streamed off with the blast as though swept by a vast broom. The main coastal road casually throws off a loop southwards into a fold of the hills. To its steep sides clings Stratton, a hamlet of grey granite houses and lime-washed cottages, clustered about the solid square tower of its old church. The traditional family seat was not here but at Pool Park, near St Tudy, where another Sleeman reigned, Philip's cousin Oliver. Thus it happens that all at Stratton can point the visitor to the old house where Anthony Payne, the Cornish giant, lived and died in the seventeenth century (a hole had to be cut in the roof to hoist out the coffin), yet no man can say where the Sleemans lived or William was born. Over great regions of India his memory is kept fresh. In history his name is secure. Yet here there is no smallest trace of him.

Philip Sleeman was a cheerful, robust, energetic man, a great friend of his sons and their stern critic. To him, who never knew what it was to tire or give up, nothing was ever too much for them to achieve. Mary shared with him many of these qualities, tempered by a motherly understanding of disappointments and difficulties.

The family was at Stratton until William was ten. By then it had grown apace to eight boys and a girl Mary. Mary, called Teeny by the boys, was beloved by them all, but her most devoted slave was brother Will, the next below her in age. These two and John followed the same pursuits, out on the moor with their rough ponies, sometimes over to Pool Park to cousin Oliver's shoots or to ride his horses, and sometimes, in summer, riding the pack trail down to Falmouth to spend a few days with the Furse family. Here young John Furse, a year or two older than Mary, and John Sleeman would spend their days in the harbour looking at, and sometimes looking over, the great West Indianmen when they rolled in before the rough sou'wester. This was romance. Both Johns were determined to go to sea. Will and Mary were more drawn towards Pendennis Castle where the artillerymen exercised with their heavy ordnance.

The drums would roll the Preparative and the gunners fire two rounds from the centre with a great roar and a reverberation round the harbour. At the first roll of the General the guns would cease like clockwork; the Flam beat and the teams unhooked the drag-ropes and fixed them to the draught rings; then the March, and forward went the pieces, the men at the drag-ropes, in one direct line. They would go through the whole exercise, firing, advancing, retreating and changing about, all on the drum signals.

Mary used to kneel with hands over ears, but entranced, while Will stood on one leg and thrilled to it all. Mary, for her part, had clearly made up her mind that her dearly beloved brother was to be a soldier, different from the others, all of whom seemed to take it for granted that they would follow their father to sea. But Will would be different. She looked at his eager face and into his very blue eyes, intense and sparkling. His sturdy little body would exactly and rightly be suited by a red coat and gold braid and the high hat—Will, sword in hand, leading the forlorn hope.

In 1798 Philip's work took him to Bideford in Devon. One by one his sons were thrusting out into the world; Thomas to Bristol into business, which finally took him to Tenby in Wales as a timber importer, James as a merchant in Reading, Nathaniel to study medicine in London, and later John, Philip and Lewis to sea. George the youngest, and William, both unswervingly bent on the army, remained with Mary at home. William divided his time between gun, rod and horse and a surprisingly willing study of his lessons under the Rev. Mr Richard Keats, French, German, Latin, Greek, poetry, literature, and, with it all, in his spare time an utterly absorbed study of the campaigns of Greek, Macedonian and Roman commanders. Mr Keats found him a handful, for he had one of those ever-fresh, questing minds that discovered interest in everything he read or saw. Perhaps Keats had himself to blame in telling the boy that nothing but 'a whole man' could be a good soldier. Young Sleeman had set out to be a whole man.

The following January the family went to nearby Appledore to see Lewis off on board the sloop-of-war, *H.M.S. Weasel.* John and Will felt a twinge of envy at Lewis in his naval rig, and honest Lewis did not conceal from the would-be soldier his pride in belonging to England's greatest fighting service. In high spirits they and Lewis said goodbye, Lewis heading out to sea and William and John returning home. The weather was rough and gusty and rising to a great storm. In a few days it had blown itself out and the green hills, battered and drenched, bared themselves to the warm Cornish sun.

One bright morning William and John were about to saddle their ponies for a ride up on the moor when they heard their father calling. Grey-faced and serious he came across the yard, a paper in his hand. 'Your mother and I thought you had better be told at once.'

The boys, startled by his gravity, stood silent, saddles on their arms. Philip put a hand on both their shoulders and looked from one to the other. 'The *Weasel* went down in that storm—in the Bristol Channel—with all hands. All lost. We'll not see Lewis again.' Slowly he took his hands away. Will drew in his breath. He looked away and said nothing. He was trying to let the shock soak into his young mind, to assimilate it and contain it. Sorrow was something unknown to him. It was new. His own brother Lewis—happy, confident, warm-hearted Lewis, to whom they had said goodbye only a few days ago—drowned.

Philip turned and walked away. Will took both saddles and hung them on the rack. John's lips were trembling, the tears were very near. Will threw an arm about his shoulders and walked him off through the yard and out on to the road. His own throat ached and he longed in his misery to go away, anywhere, by himself and cry it out. Instead he handed John the harness duster. 'Dry your eyes, Johnnie. Come, Johnnie. He died as a sailor should.' These words heartened him as much as his little brother, but with a sudden shock he realized that John too was destined for the navy, 'I mean . . .' he groped.

'Yes,' choked John, grasping his hand, 'like a sailor'. Then firmly through his tears; 'Like I should, Will.'

Never in his life did Will Sleeman forget the anguish of this first loss. Years later, John as a captain was to go down with his ship, and Will, letter in hand, was to repeat his brother's words to himself, the clear, hard fact of that January day aching in his memory.

Three short years later his father died. The family moved back into Cornwall to be near their relatives. This final catastrophe served as all other strokes of adverse fate served William Sleeman. It roused him. He was only fourteen but his mother soon learned to trust the steady wisdom of this staunch, cheerful son. Shc consulted him on everything. Soon all was arranged. They were poor but they were determined that every one of the sons should go into the profession of his choice. Philip and John were soon away as midshipmen. Will gave up his claim to enter the King's Army, for he had discovered that if he waited he could enter the Bengal Army in India and there not only live on his pay but gain promotion without purchase. He said nothing to his mother but redoubled his studies, widening them to include political economy—Hobbes, Ricardo, Adam Smith—while continuing his reading of military history—the campaigns of Turenne, Marlborough and Charles XII of Sweden. But he said nothing of India for fear of frightening her; besides, he had now to take George under his wing. Little by little the family saved for George, for George was to be a real soldier in one of His Majesty's regiments of the line.

Books and sport and the needs of the family took Will happily along to manhood. At last he was ready. At seventeen he confided his intentions to his mother: he would apply to the Honourable East India Company and enter their Cadet College at Baraset, near Calcutta.

CHAPTER 2

Joining the Bengal Army

Young Sleeman respected persons and their achievements; for good and ill fortune he had no respect whatever. So when Samuel Sleeman, a kinsman in London, wrote to say that the Company's college at Baraset was only a school for debauchery, he shrugged his shoulders and asked: 'Who says so?'

'Samuel has spoken to Indians on leave'. replied his mother, handing him the letter, 'I suppose Indians should know?'

'Indians? I see, he means officers home from India, in London.'

He knew then that he must wait till he was twenty and go direct to a Bengal regiment. Three years, four years? Well, he could study, so off he set to find a retired official of the Company's civil service, and was soon plunged in Arabic script and Hindustani and more and ever more military history.

In 1807 he joined Nathaniel in London and worked in a counting-house to learn book-keeping while the Sleeman and Spry families used their not inconsiderable influence to obtain his cadetship in the army of the Honourable East India Company. As a result young William stood one day before Lord de Dunstanville to be vetted. The nobleman was impressed with the boy's self-assurance and modesty and recommended him to the Board of Directors, whereupon, in the winter of 1808, Mrs Sleeman came to London and proudly accompanied her William to East India House in Leadenhall Street for an interview with Sir Francis Baring and Colonel Sweny Toone. There the lad was accepted into the Bengal Army as a cadet, his mother signed a statement that he was born on 8th August, 1788, the statement was pinned to his cadet papers, and the matter was ended. Mary returned by coach to Cornwall, and William, aged twenty, importantly stalked round London fitting himself out.

Remembering that his father had impressed on his boys the value of a really good sword which would not bend when it struck the bone of an adversary, he eschewed the tailiors' bodkins and betook himself to Mr. Henry Wilkinson's house on Ludgate Hill, where after much discussion and trial he bought the finest of swords and had it engraved with the family crest. Then he bought one of Joseph Manton's sporting guns, and a rifle (both the best modern flintlocks in the world), and a rod and tackle from Mr Bowness of the Fish and Bell in Temple Bar. Finally he registered himself with the East India Agents, Prinsep & Saunders.

He soon followed his mother to Cornwall. He set off on his pony through the pack ways to Truro, Pentire, Falmouth and the Est to say goodbye to relations and friends. Up to the hocks in mud, his night's needs in his saddle-bags, he urged the old pony forward on their last ride—a long ride of two months. Then home again to the agony so many of us know so well, of that first parting from our childhood's home. His mother and Teeny were sure they would never see him again; George was more philosophical. As he rode away the much-loved Teeny trotted at his stirrup for the first mile or two, then stopped and wept. To be a soldier—she who had urged him to be one, where had she sent him?

Back in London he seized a last opportunity to see *Macbeth* at the Haymarket. How long he was to remember that date, 11th March, when his idols, Kemble and Mrs Siddons, played the leading parts!

On 24th March, 1809 he stood on the quayside at Gravesend, baggage about him, with John, Nathaniel and Samuel Sleeman, all forcing some sort of cheerfulness, waiting to say farewell. Out in the stream lay the great East Indiaman, the *Devonshire*. In his cadre uniform—short red jacket, black hat and black feather—of medium height, strong and agile beyond his fellows, he was good to look upon. Here was 'the whole man' he had been told he must be. He dropped into the boat with the other passengers and, waving, was gone. They watched him up the ladder and turned away. It was a long way to India in 1809.

The *Devonshire* called in at Portsmouth, there to remain awaiting favourable weather until 26th April. William kept a diary of the voyage: a call at Madeira and the Cape, storms up the coast of Madagascar, dropping anchor in the Hooglie in October and then ashore at Calcutta, the heat and the throng on the quay, the chaos and shouting of coolies. Steady and unmoved in the confusion were the first Indian soldiers he was to set eyes upon, red-coated with yellow facings, white shorts, bare legs, shoes, and tall brimless round blue hats. Their officer came forward and singled out Sleeman.

'Sleeman?' William nodded. 'I'm Gilbert Cowper, Ensign, of the 15th. Where's your baggage? Right. These men'll see it to Fort William for you.' A trifle bewildered at the speed of things, William walked off with his new friends, the latter chatting away, asking about England. The newcomer sweltered in his thick uniform, the lighter-clad veteran keeping up a good round pace until he hailed a *garry,* took the jarvey's seat and drove the chariot at half a gallop, scaring palanquins and bullock carts, along the wide, dusty roads, through the great arch of Fort William, past the about-to-salute sentry, and came to rest with a jerk outside the orderly room of the 15th Native Infantry. Cowper chaperoned him in to the adjutant, Lieutenant Donaldson Turner, and Turner marched him in to the colonel's office. William gazed wonderingly across the table at a grey-haired ancient who seemed minute by minute to be shrinking deeper into the high yellow collar of his red jacket. As though in sorrow Colonel Litellus Burrell asked him all about himself. Finally he admonished the new entry: 'Sleeman, keep off two things out here—the liquor and women.'

'Yes, sir,' Will. He had little experience of the first, none of the second. Luckily for him and for many other English youngsters whose first sight of the wide world was a presidency city in India, he was a countryman and had come up the hard way with seldom two coppers to jingle together in his pocket. Tobacco he disliked and an occasional glass of ale at the ordinary was his limit. Captain Philip's school had been for more one of self-denial and control than of indulgence.

'Can you ride? Do you shoot?'

'Yes, sir.' That made an impression; Litellus Burrell sat up. 'I've got two of Manton's latest guns.'

'Good—good.' The old man was now looking brisker. 'Do you spear hog?'

'No, sir. There are no wild hogs in Cornwall.'

The colonel looked at him doubtfully. Then to the adjutant: 'Where's George Greene? Tell him to take charge of Sleeman. He'll be under the drill havildar for a month before he's posted up-country. Got to learn the language. Send him to the tailor for his uniform; now let's see these new guns of his. Here, orderly! Bring in the *sahib's* guns. Where are they, Sleeman?'

Will turned to the sepoy and with great care and precision spoke his first words in Hindustani.

'Born out here?' barked the surprised colonel.

'No, sir.'

'H'm. You'll be useful on a shoot. Right. Take him away.'

The adjutant walked Will out of the office and consigned him to the care of Ensign George Greene.

Day after hot day Sleeman and two other cadets could be seen drilling on the parade ground outside the fort. The presidency commander, Major-General Baillie, and his staff would ride by in the early morning, and once Lieutenant-General Hewett, the commander-in-chief, visited the parade and questioned the young cadets. Will's trouble was that some of the drill he had taught himself from Smith's Military Dictionary was out of date, so he had to forget before he could learn again. 'Poise your firelock! Cock your firelock! Present! Fire! Half-cock your firelock! Handle your cartridge! Prime! Shut your pans! Charge with cartridge! Draw your rammer! and so on. To young Sleeman it was great stuff: the real thing.

He and his colleagues soon came to know the cadets at Baraset—and to have nothing to do with them. They were little better than savages, gaming, smoking, drinking, fighting spurred gamecock, duelling, throwing their creditors into the pond and every evening galloping madly all the miles from Baraset for a night's debauch in the stews and dives of Calcutta bazaar.

In mid December posting orders came for Sleeman to join the 2/12th N.I. away up on the borders of the Kingdom of Oudh. Off he set by tonjon or palanquin, changing sometimes to budgerow, the country boat, up the Ganges, making for Patna and then Dinapore in Bihar. His tonjon set him down at the orderly room of his new regiment, the corps that in 1805 had thrice stormed the breach at Bhurtpore Fort and thrice planted British colours on top of the bastion. His four hundred mile journey had impressed him with he vastness of India—the green watery fields of Bengal and the dusty stubble plains of much of Bihar spanning out to the horizon on either side. Here and there he caught a faint gleam of the high Himalaya off to the east: to the west the dark hills of the Ranchi plateau. His tutor was now Ensign Davis, a humorous young officer who evinced a great respect for Will's learning, his library and his progress with the language. His colonel had been one of Lake's battalion commanders at Laswari in the Mahratta war and a fine leader in battle, but now so grey and old! He was Robert Bourke Gregory, whom Sleeman soon discovered to be a great character. He was a simple, just and kind man, who had never read a book of any sort but who held the affection of all in his regiment, for he had led the battalion with courage and determination through the late Mahratta wars and during Colonel Monson's disgraceful and costly retreat to Agra. At their first meeting the colonel impressed on him the need to be thoroughly conversant with the Urdu tongue—an attainment that he himself had completely neglected.

It used to be generally supposed that our forbears in India spoke the native tongues much better than we of the twentieth century. This is not so: we were far more fluent. Sleeman, for example, was placed under an officer known as the interpreter and quartermaster, who was expected to instruct him in Urdu. In fact, Sleeman was an exception, for very soon after joining he was as well acquainted with Urdu as the best of them, while as time went on and his absorbed interest in Indians of all sorts from sepoy to peasant increased, he added Persian and Pushtu to his list. Further, during the Nepal wars he learnt Gurkhali. He tells us delightedly of the mistakes made by military and civil friends in conversing with Indians. Colonel, later Major-General, Sir Joseph O'Halloran in 1815 led the 1/18th N.I. through the State of Darbanga on its way to the Nepal war. The Rajah came to visit the Colonel bringing many presents. O'Halloran would never permit anyone in his battalion to take anything from the local peasantry. At this time, he in his mess having run out of coffee, he asked the Rajah if he could kindly get him a couple of bags as he could find none in the Company's territory and would need it in the cold climate of Nepal. That evening a considerable party of the Rajah's followers arrived with six large sacks. They all carried varieties of matchlock guns and sporting equipment. The colonel at once came out to meet them.

'Here we are, Sahib, I have brought six sacks of them for you,' said the rajah's minister.

The Colonel thanked him grateful, whereupon he signalled for the 'sacks to be brought forwarded and opened.' Out on the ground were shaken six piles of rather mangy Indian crows.

'We will bring you some more tomorrow, Colonel Sahib.'

The mess butler, who was watching, burst into a discreet laugh and explained to the astounded Colonel that *kawa* was different from *kahwa*—the former meant a crow and the latter coffee. The minister, highly amused, thereupon sent a small boy to the bazaar near at hand to buy the mess two bags of coffee.

Another tale is of one 'Bean' Wilton of Patna, close by the cantonment. Wilton was one of the Honourable Company's opium agents. These agents prided themselves on their idleness and took offence if anyone thought they did any work, but, like Wilton, most of them in those early days piled up a fortune despite their laziness. Bean was in Calcutta where a friend of his, Prendergast, was taken seriously ill. Thinking him about to die, the doctor suggested that he take a river trip on the Ganges. The good-hearted Bean put him aboard his own boat and set off, well knowing that he might next day have to dispose of his remains. However, at dawn Prendergast was asking for a little meat, a piece of kid. So Bean, who had never learnt the language, told his butler to go ashore and fetch a *murdwa,* and to roast it for his friend. 'What, a whole one, your Honour?' 'Yes,' retorted the Bean sharply, 'of course a whole one. No less for my friend.'

That evening the stout butler came down to the river bank with a long procession behind him carrying a miscellany of joints and pieces. Bean and the patient, who was lying on deck, watched the advance of the procession led by the butler, beaming at the success of his mission.

'Sahib, here is the mare. I am sorry that I am late but it took some time to find a young one and much bargaining to buy it. But your friend can make a good meal off this.'

From Prendergast came a peal of laughter and, said the Bean later, 'this burst the abscess from his liver into the intestines and he was cured.'

Bean Wilton became a friend of young Sleeman and lavished upon him kindness and hospitality during his stay at Dinapore.

Our ensign soon made himself one of his new regiment. He much admired the trust between British officers and Indian soldiers and even admired some of his colonel's ways of encouraging this—ways which had inherent flaws, destined to contribute fifty years later to the Sepoy Mutiny. Promotion was by strict seniority, so that many of the Indian officers might well be so aged as to lack both the physical vigour required for field operations and the mental vigour essential to the handling of young and insubordinate sepoys. In Sleeman's time all was well because the Indian soldier had no cause of grievance, so they all fought valiantly and their discipline was willing and good. Again, in the Bengal Army to which he belonged the families were all left at the sepoys' homes, mainly in the Indian State of Oudh: those of the Madras and Bombay armies followed the drum. At first sight it might appear that the presence of families within the lines must be inexpedient, as impairing soldier's efficiency; but in the day of disaffection the absence of families gave hotheads and bad characters freedom to stir up trouble unhampered by the presence of hostages.

Sleeman's diary of later years records an illuminating talk with one of his odd Indian officers.

"The commanding officers seldom know enough of the men to be able to judge of the selections for promotion." said the old man.

Here the old Subedar who had been at the taking of the Isle of France (Mauritius) in 1810, mentioned that when he was the senior Jemadar of his regiment and a vacancy occurred to bring him in as Subedar, he was sent for by his Commanding Officer and told that, by orders from headquarters, he was to be passed over on account of his advanced age and supposed infirmity. "I felt," said the old man, "as if I had been struck by lightning; and fell down dead! The Colonel was a good man and had seen much service. He had me taken into the open air and, when I recovered, he told me that he would write to the Commander-in-Chief and represent my case. He did so immediately, and I was promoted and I have since done my duty as Subedar for ten years."

These were the methods of old Colonel Gregory and of many other regimental commanders of the Bengal Army. They were patriarchal and actuated by great affection for the interesting and attractive men of Oudh, both Muslim and Hindu, who so readily enlisted themselves under the company's colours. Sleeman had one fault in his make-up and that was an excessive kindness to all who served him, whether British or

Indian. He grew into a man of immense strength of character and never could realize that others could vacillate, change their loyalties, or give way to self-interest and self-indulgence. He paid them all the compliment of assessing their worth as equal to his own. Those who went with him, and most of them did so, became from his example as staunch men as he was himself. The few who failed him were treated with an uncommon patience.

At Dinapore he settled into regimental duties and thanked his stars that Burrell and Gregory had given him such a thorough grounding on the square before letting him loose as a junior commander. He was a fine shot at both small and big game, and a strong horseman with a spear after pig in the high grass country which stretched many miles, dotted with sugarcane patches, on both banks of the Ganges.

Late in 1810 the regiment moved to Barrackpore, fifteen miles from Calcutta. Sleeman hated the idea of that move. He loathed leaving the countryside and its splendid peasants. What was he to do in a town such as Calcutta?

CHAPTER 3

Calcutta

In Calcutta Sleeman found himself imprisoned in a life bounded by the parade ground and by guards of honour to high officials, in particular to the governor-general, Lord-Minto. While the ceremonial duties brought him into contact with military circles about his lordship, the lack of sport and open-air life was gall to his energetic soul; hence he searched for other interests and soon found them at Fort William in the school of languages and its library. The Colonel understood his predicament and enrolled him for a fifteen months' course at this school. William had already read Persian and Arabic literature, more especially Persian poetry, so plunged into these studies with immense zest.

Thus the abhorred move to town gave him the first clue to a mission destined to make his name famous. In the Fort William library, while furbishing his French, he picked up the moth-eaten old chronicle of a French traveller in India of the seventeenth century—M. Thevenot. As he turned the pages he found himself confronted with this passage concerning a sect of people of whom he had heard vague reports, a people called by the name of Thugs, a precise term meaning 'deceivers.'

"Though the road I have been speaking of from Delhie to Agra be tolerable yet it has many inconveniences. One may meet with tigers, panthers and lions upon it, and one can also best have a care of robbers, and above all things, not to suffer anybody to come near one upon the road. The cunningest robbers in the world are in that country. They use a certain slip with a running noose which they can cast with so much sleight about a man's neck, when they are within reach of him, that they never fail, so that they can strangle him in a trice. They have another cunning trick also to catch travellers with. They send out a handsome woman upon the road, who with her hair dishevelled seems to be all in tears, sighing and complaining of some misfortune which she pretends has befallen her. Now, as she takes the same way that the traveller goes he falls easily into conversation with her, and finding her beautiful, offers her his assistance, which she accepts; but he hath no sooner taken her up behind him on horseback that she throws the snare about his neck and strangles him, or at least stuns him until the robbers who lie hid come running to her assistance and complete what she hath begun. But besides that, there are men in those quarters so skilful in casting the snare, that they succeed as well at a distance as near at hand; and if an ox or any other beast belonging to a caravan run away, as sometimes it happens, they fail not to catch it by the neck."

Sleeman read this passage again and again. He must know more but where could he turn for information? All his inquiries led back only to Thevenot's account, as if to a dead end.

Of necessity, if not of choice, he took part in the gaieties of the city, where one lady alone, of all whom he met, made any lasting impression on him. This was the Begum Johnson. There were then a few ladies of the old school still much looked up to in Calcutta. She was one. She prided herself on keeping up all the old usages. She would dine in the afternoon at four or five o'clock, take the air in her carriage, then from her return till ten at night throw open her house in royal style to visitors. There were music and dancing for the young, cards for the old; those who had been specially invited stayed for supper. William often visited the old *begum* and there met 'the first people in the country, for all people, including the Governor-General himself, delighted to honour this old lady, the mother-in-law of a Prime Minister of England'. As a girl she had been captured at Murshidabad when Siraj-ud-daula marched from there at the head of the army that took and plundered Calcutta and threw so many Europeans into the infamous 'Black Hole.' Only because she was far gone in pregnancy was she saved from becoming a member of his scraglio.

Sleeman writes:

"She had been a very beautiful woman and had been several times married, the pictures of all her husbands being hung round her noble drawing-room in Calcutta, covered during the day with crimson cloth to save them from the dust; and uncovered only at night on particular occasions. One evening, Mrs Crommelin, a friend of mine, pointing to one of them, asked the old lady his name. "Really, I cannot at this moment tell you, my dear; my memory is very bad (striking her forehead with her right hand, as she leaned with her left arm in Mrs Crommelin's), but I shall recollect in a few minutes." The old lady's last husband was clergyman, Mr Johnson, one of the Presidency chaplains, whom she found too gay and persuaded to go home upon an annuity of eight hundred a year, which she settled upon him for life.

On reaching a more mature age Sleeman gave an entrancing account of the British way of life in the 1830's.

"Since those days, the modes of intercourse in India have much altered. Society at all the stations, beyond the three capitals of Calcutta, Madras and Bombay, is confined almost exclusively to the members of the civil and military services who seldom remain long at the same station—military officers hardly ever more than three years, and the civil hardly even so long. At disagreeable stations, the civil servants seldom remain so many months. Every new comer calls in the forenoon upon all that are at the station when he arrives and they return his call at the same hour soon after. If he is a married man, the married men upon whom he called take their wives to call upon his and he takes his to return the call of theirs. These calls are all indispensable and, being made in the forenoon, become very disagreeable in the hot season: all complain of them, yet no one forgoes his claim upon them, and until the claim is fulfilled, people will not recognize each other as acquaintances. Unmarried officers generally dine in the evening because it is a more convenient time for the mess, and married civil functionaries do the same because it is more convenient for their office work. If you invite those who dine at that hour to spend the evening with you, you must invite them to dinner even in the hot season, when a table covered with animal food is sickening to any person without a keen appetite and stupefying to those who have it. No one thinks of inviting people to a dinner and ball—it would be vandalism; and when you invite them, as is always the case, to come after dinner, the ball never begins until late at night and seldom ends until late in the morning!

With all its disadvantages, however, I think dining in the evening much better for those in health than dining in the afternoon, provided one can avoid the intermediate meal of tiffin. No person in India should eat animal food more than once a day, and people who dine in the evening generally eat less than they would if they glass of water, or soda-water, at two o'clock, and dinner after the evening exercise, is the plan I should recommend every European to adopt in India as the most agreeable. When their digestive powers get out of order, people must do as their doctors tell them.

Their is, I believe, no society in which there is more real urbanity of manners than in that of India—a more general disposition on the part of its different members to sacrifice their own comforts and convenience to those of others and to make those around them happy, without letting them see that it costs them an effort to do so. There is assuredly no society where the members are more generally free from those corroding cares and anxieties which "weigh upon the hearts" of men whose incomes are precarius and position in the world uncertain. They receive their salaries on a certain day every month, whatever may be the state of the seasons or of trade; tey pay no taxes, they rise in the several services by rotation; religius feelings and opinions are by common consent left as a question between the man and his Maker; no one ever thinks of questioning another about them nor would he be tolerated if he did so. Most people take it for granted that those which they got from their parents were the right ones and as such they cherish them. They remember, with feelings of filial piety, the prayers which they, in their infancy, offered to their Maker while kneeling by their mothers, and they continue to offer them up through life with the same feelings and the same hopes.

In the autumn of 1813 he set out with his regiment up the Ganges once again to Tara Mirzapore, a cantonment between Benares and Allahabad. Here he resumed regimental life, well spiced with sport, pig-sticking and big-game shooting, with the occasional day after partridge and blue pigeon. During these excursions he indulged his abiding passion for converse with the villagers and farmers and observation of their ways.

This was the cold weather and the leave season was ending. Sleeman was puzzled and a little alarmed that sometimes his furlough men failed to return to his company. He knew them all well and refused to accept the general opinion that the men had deserted to their homes, especially so when in the spring of 1814 his own batman, Jiwan Sing, a steady, trustworthy man, also failed to rejoin the colours. The adjutant and other officers told him not to worry because every seaon a few men would not return owing to home troubles or ceremonies in their families, but all William's inquiries from other sepoys gave no shadow of evidence that the men he had lost had any such troubles or commitments. They had either not reached home or had gone astray on their return journey. They had disappeared. In his usual persistent way he went on puzzling and inquiring. Any notion that they, and several million of their countrymen, had been murdered on the roads would at that time have been dismissed as utterly fantastic.

From time to time during 1814 news came of forays on the Nepal border by Gurkha bands operating round about Gorakhpore, a disputed area on the frontier claimed by the Company. Matters came to a head when one of the Company's police stations in Bhutwal was attacked and the policeman killed. Soon a call came from headquarters for an officer, well qualified in languages, to report at once to 2/25th N.I. at Dinapore.

Sleeman was now quartermaster and interpreter of 2/12th. With great reluctance Colonel Gregory had to select him for the appointment, much to the chagrin of his seniors. Hastily bundling up his kit, he was off travelling day and night to join his new regiment, which was destined almost immediately for operations against the Gurkhas.

CHAPTER 4

War With the Gurkhas

Sleeman detested tonjon travel except in one respect—he could look at the country; its people, its crops and its geological structure. He loathed the idea of human creatures being employed as load animals. However, there it was: there was no other expeditious mode of travelling night and day. And he was a young man in a hurry. Despite the haste, he closely scrutinized each knot of travellers whom he met or passed. A little ashamed at his own credulity, he had to confess to himself that he was looking for those Thevenot 'deceivers.' Hastening along over the plains through the bright green expanse of the young corn, with the dust whirling in the steady westerly breeze, hot and cramped, he pressed on using relays of carriers, anxious lest the war be started, or even ended, before he arrived at the 25th N.I. So many of us know the feeling of uncertainity in ourselves, of apprehension lest we do not behave in action as boldly as we should, wondering how far it may be accepted that we avoid the bullets without cowardice or face them without recklessness. All these doubts crowded into his mind during the long hours of darkness. But why? Had Lewis been afraid in that appalling storm? William wouldn't believe it—not of the brother he knew.

At Dinapore the 25th greeted him as a long-awaited reinforcement for their sadly attenuated officer strength, especially as he was about to be gazetted lieutenant and so was fitted to command a company. The highly individual young officer now found himself blessing the system of uniformity which ran through the army, for here he was falling easily into this slot in a strange regiment hundreds of miles from his own. All its ways and nearly all its customers were those he already knew well.

The battalion was part of General Marley's large force destined for the invasion of Nepal and the conquest of its capital, Kathmandu. But the ardent young Sleeman soon recognized that Marley was not the man for the job. With no opposition, forward went the great array across the Nepalese border and then dithered to a halt with three widely separated posts flung out in front. No Gurkha could restrain himself in such a situation. The three posts were wiped out at one blow. General Marley, to his horror perceiving a small but energetic enemy column making straight for him, felt this to be too much and beat a retreat, giving out that he must defend the Company's territory. On the steady advance of his opponent the general's nerve broke. Silently and secretly at dead of night he stole away by himself without breathing a word to any other soul.

In due course the leaderless army was taken over by Major-General J.S. Wood. In March 1815 the division advanced, to be soon opposed by a defended stockade, upon which the artillery developed a tremendous cannonade. The infantry then attacked. Young Sleeman led his company in from the flank, coming under close and heavy musketry fire. Here he was tasting the very thing he had feared, and knew now that the *elan* and confusion of battle and the heavy responsibility on himself deprived him of all sense of personal danger. His battalion fired volley after volley as they advanced, until at length he found himself, Wilkinson sword drawn, waving his men in with the bayonet. They clambered over and through the defences, hurling the timbers aside, only to find the enemy gone.

He was appalled at the slaughter wrought by cannon and musket but consoled himself that only thus could heavy casualties to his own men have been avoided. The battalion re-formed to continue the advance. But General Wood was against further advance: Kathmandu would be left safe and the defeated Gurkhas would go scot-free. On his orders the grumbling brigade turned about and headed for Nathpore on the Kosi river, there to spend the summer.

Here a fearful catastrophe befell them.

For protection from the sun and the heavy rains they built themselves shelters. Wherever earth was moved rain settled and mosquitoes bred, until a virulent malaria scourged the troops. Casualties were heavy and deaths a high proportion. Out of the ten officers in

Sleeman's mess four died, and he himself was delirious for many days. Only he and two others remained fit for service at the end, while three hundred of the men were so debilitated that they had to be sent home on leave.

As usual he searched for the cause of the disease. In those days nothing was known of malaria, the fever being always attributed to the poisonous vapours given off from the ground at evening time—the miasma. (The Gurkhas attributed the violent form of the disease which was rife in the Terai to the fumes given off by snakes.) He noted that the fever was confined to those who occupied the houses and huts of one encampment. 'My Regiment [once again the 12th N.I.] suffered most as it was stationed on the soil which had remained longest unturned and untilled. . . . I am myself persuaded that had the soil remained unbroken and the houses and huts been raised upon it over wooden platforms, to secure officers and men from the damp ground, there would have been little or no sickness in the Brigade.' He was right about the turning of the soil but wrong about the damp vapours. They were mosquitoes, not vapours, that rose of an evening.

During his convalescence he was put on the staff of the brigade. In February 1816 war with Nepal broke out again. The 2nd Battalion now replaced the first and Sleeman was posted to it, this battalion and H.M. 87th Regiment (later the Royal Irish Fusiliers) and 2/8th N.I. concentrating as the 3rd Brigade under Colonel Miller. The brigade in turn then moved off to assemble at Simalhasa under the redoubtable Sir David Ochterlony for an invasion of Nepal, directed on Kathmandu.

Young Sleeman was interpreter and quartermaster, but in view of his wide experience of war as evinced in one short, sharp action, he was to his great joy, given a company. To his tent came nightly his brother officers, their only regret being that his sword as still unsullied. His friend Lieutenant Medwyn wanted to know what it felt like going into battle, to which he replied in words no less applicable to an infantryman of today than to one of century and a half ago, tactical changes accepted.

'You feel you've got no stomach. And you feel pretty sick.'

'And then, Will ?'

'We get to the firing of volleys and what with dressing the line and ordering the volley as one discharge we forget everything else–bullets, cannon-ball, everything. But all this is good as long as we are the hunter.

Last year, with the 25th, we were hunted and not allowed to turn and fight. I was not so pleased with that....' And so on, for Medwyn had not yet proved himself and could not leave the subject alone.

The force advanced, passing through the parched Sal forest of the airless, soundless, flat land of the Terai, whence it emerged from the trees on to the banks of the Bichiakoh river. Here it camped for some days while reconnaissance patrols searched out a little-known route by which the column could turn the Bichiakoh pass, thus to assail the fortresses of Makwanpore and Harihapore high up in the hills. Ochterlony was too skilled a soldier to attempt to force the pass by the easy and normal route.

After dark, at nine o'clock on the I4th February, the 3rd Brigade left its ground, led on foot by the tall, spare figure of its great army commander. Sleeman found himself at the head of his company, his men in single file carrying a heavy load of ammunition and rations along a deep ravine, the Bhalukhola. For five miles they staggered at funeral pace among the boulders. The tall cliffs were clothed with trees, which in places met overhead and obscured the moon. The only sounds heard by the hushed column were those of their axes cutting through the trunks and branches that blocked the way. By three o'clock they were out of the ravine on to broken ground. They clambered up a steep hill. Silently the advanced guard deployed across the high ground and the rest of the brigade with its bullocks followed.

Ochterlony had cheated his enemy. Soon after dawn the Gurkha commander, taking alarm, drew his men back upon Makwanpore.

Sleeman was impressed by the men of the 87th, who, like his own sepoys, had out their axes and saws and promptly rigged up shelters for their officers and themselves. He thought this was good soldiering, as it was, and was glad to see a British Regiment doing it. The pioneers made up the road behind the column and the elephants of the commissariat joined the fighting men, so that by the twentieth the brigade marched again, and by the twenty-seventh was drawn up in the valley just below the fortress of Makwanpore.

A Gurkha force at once counter-attacked and for long the forward positions hung in the balance until a part of the 8th and the 2/12th came up at the double, William Sleeman leading his company forward. The artillery opened a hot bombardment on the ridge while the troops marched steadily on, deploying just below the crest. Then with a great shout the red line charged, driving the Gurkhas at bayonet point into the jungle beyond. This was a stubborn engagement which continued until nearly sunset when Brigadier Miller himself led the 2/8th N.I. past Sleeman's flank and the whole force rose as one man to the assault. Thrown back into the forests, the enemy kept up a constant musketry fire until darkness fell.

During the battle the gallant Lieutenant John Shipp of the 87th was challenged to personal combat in front of the whole force by the Gurkha commander, Kisnabahadur Rana, and these two fought it out between the two armies. Sleeman witnessed this, his men standing silent about him. The Gurkha chief, to cover the rallying of his hardpressed men, rushed at Shipp. He was a powerful man with one shield strapped about his waist to protect his thighs to the knees and another, larger, round shield on the left arm. Shipp's weapon ,was his sword which he called 'my old Twentyfourther which I had two or three days before put into good shaving order .' At first he was forced on the defensive, till he could catch his formidable opponent off guard, The chief cut, Shipp guarded: he thrust, Shipp parried. They went at it hammer and tongs, round and round and back and forth at a great pace, until Shipp's sword seemed likely to be hacked to pieces. He could drive in no thrust past his enemy's guard. Now the Gurkha showed signs of failing strength, so the tall Englishman leapt in, cut at his legs, and as his shield went down flashed his blade at the neck. The Gurkha threw his head back to avoid the point, but with a twist of his arm Shipp sent his thrust in under the chin and down fell his gallant foe. A cheer went up and British and Indians dashed into the assault.

Both Shipp and Sleeman pay tribute to the gallantry of their enemy, who must have lost over eight hundred killed in the fight, 'At Makwanpore I never saw more steadiness or bravery in battle. Run they would not: they had no fear of death though their comrades were falling thick about them, for we were so close that every shot found its target. As I walked over the ground after the action I could hardly step between their dead and dying.'

Sleeman's company had suffered heavily, but he himself had miraculously not a scratch, despite his boldness and the fact that he was so easily distinguishable, a mark among the sepoys. It had been a great victory. The whole force was up with the 3rd Brigade and ready for a further advance, only to be forestalled by the Nepalese Government, who sued for the peace which was now at last granted.

Lieutenant Sleeman was bitterly disappointed.

'Our troops under Sir David Ochterlony, having taken the fort of Makwanpore, might in five days have been before the defenceless capital, but they were here arrested by the romantic chivalry of the Marquis of Hastings. The country had been virtually conquered; the prince, by his base treachery towards us and outrages upon others, had justly forfeited his throne; but the Governor-General, by perhaps a misplaced lenity, left it to him without any other guarantee for his future good behaviour than the recollection that he had been soundly beaten. Unfortunately he left him at the same time a sufficient quantity of fertile land below the hills to maintain the same army with which he had fought us, with better knowledge how to employ them to keep us out on a future occasion. Between the attempt of Kasim Ali and our attack upon Nepal, the Gurkha masters of the country had, by a long series of successful aggressions upon their neighbours, rendered themselves in their own opinion, and in that of their neighbours, the best soldiers of India. They had, of course, a very natural feeling of hatred against our government which put a stop to the wild career of conquest and wrested from their grasp all the property and all the pretty women from Kathmandu to Cashmere. To these beautiful regions they were what the invading Huns were in former days to Europe, absolute fiends. Had we even exacted a good road into their country with fortifications at the proper places, it might have checked the hopes of one day resuming the career of conquest that keeps up the army and military spirit, to threaten us with a renewal of war whenever we are embarrassed on the plains.'

Headquarters selected Sleeman to settle the business of prize money. Thus he journeyed about from the eastern front right up to the hills above the Sutlej river, learning the Gurkha tongue as he travelled. Near Sabathu, below the dark forested mass of the Simla hills, which Nepal had now ceded to the Company, he met a former Gurkha enemy and began to argue that the *kukri* was a less formidable weapon than the sword.

'It may be so, sahib,' retorted the Gurkha soldier, 'but this is the weapon with which we cleared all the hills you see before you.'

'Yes, my friend, they are now bleak enough, God knows, and you must have swept away with your *kukri* a great many of their finest trees.'

'I do not mean the trees, sahib—I mean the soldiers, armed with other weapons, who tried in vain to defend themselves against us. They could never stand before our kukris.'

And there the matter ended.

In February 1817 the governor-general, Lord Moira, designated Sleeman's report as 'able, impartial and satisfactory.'

It was this long sojourn among the villages all by himself which finally captivated the young soldier and bound him by lasting bonds to the peasantry of India and the hills. This affection dominated his life even to the exclusion of his beloved Bengal Army.

William proudly pinned his first war medal to his coat.

CHAPTER 5

The Kingdom of Oudh

In December 1816 the 12th N.I. under its good shepherd, Colonel Gregory, marched for Pertabgarh on the way to Allahabad, by a road that took them through the Kingdom of Oudh where Sleeman saw how the tax collector set to work in an Indian State. The battalion had camped four miles from a mud fort, and all day long they could hear the Amil, or governor of the district, thunder on the walls of this fort with his cannon, which stood back at least two miles from the target. Some of the 12th rode over to see the fun. The Amil had brought a force of three regiments of infantry, a corps or two of cavalry and a good park of artillery, while the garrison—the taxpayers—were two hundred stout Rajput landholders and yeomen. Sleeman tells the story.

"In the evening, just as we had sat down to dinner, a messenger came to the commanding officer, Colonel Gregory, who was a member of the mess, from the said Amil, and begged permission to deliver his message in private. I, as the senior staff officer, was requested to hear what he had to say.

'What do you require from the commanding officer?'

'I require the loan of a regiment.'

'I know the commanding officer will not let you have the regiment.'

'If the Amil cannot get more, he will be glad to get two companies; and I have brought with me this bag of gold, containing some two or three hundred gold *mohurs*, (three hundred to five hundred pounds).

"I delivered the message to Colonel Gregory before all the officers, who desired me to say that he could not spare a single man, as he had no authority to assist the Amil and was merely marching through the country to his destination. I did so. The man urged me to beg the commanding officer, if he could do no more, merely to halt the next day where he was and lend the Amil the use of one of his drummers!

'And what will you do with him?'

'Why, just before daylight, we will take him down near one of the gates of the fort and make him beat his drum as hard as he can; and the people within, thinking the whole regiment is upon them, will make out as fast as possible at the opposite gate.'

'And the bag of gold, what is to become of that?'

'You and the old gentleman can divide it between you, and I will double it if you like.'

"I delivered the message before all the officers, to their great amusment; and the poor man was obliged to carry back his bag of gold to the Amil. The Amil is the collector of the revenue in Oudh, and he is armed with all the powers of government and has generally several regiments and a train of artillery with him. The large landholders build these mud forts, which are defended by Rajpoot cultivators who are among the bravest men in the world. One hundred of them would never hesitate to attack a thousand of the king's regular troops, because they know the Amil would be ashamed to have any noise made about it at court[1]; but they know also, that if they were to beat one thousand, that they would soon have ten. The Company provides for the maintenance of those who are wounded in its fight and for the widows and orphans of those who are killed. Their prince provides for neither, and his soldiers are in consequence somewhat chary of fighting. It is from this peasantry, the military cultivators of Oudh, that our Bengal native infantry draws three out of four of its recruits, and finer young men can hardly anywhere be found ... We do the soldier's work much better than it was ever before done with one-tenth-nay, I may say one-fiftieth part—of the numbers that were employed to do it by our predecessors, and the whole number of the soldiers employed by us is not equal to that of those who were, under them, actually in the transition state, or on their way from the place where they had lost service to that where they hoped to find it, extorting the means of subsistence either by intimidation or by open violence. Those who are in this transition state under us are neither armed, accoutred nor mounted; we do not disband *en masse*, we only dismiss individuals for offences, and they have no leaders to range themselves under. Those who come to seek our service are the sons of yeomen, bred up from their infancy with all those feelings of deference for superiors which are required in soldiers. They have neither arms, horses, nor accoutrements and when they leave us permanently or

1. See Appendix 1

temporarily, they take none with them . They never rob or steal, they will often dispute with the shopkeepers on the road about the price of the provisions or get a man to carry their bundles for a few miles, but this is the utmost of their transgressions, and for these things they are often severely handled by our police.

It is extremely gratifying to an Englishman to hear the general testimony borne by all classes of people to the merits of our rule in this respect; they all say that no former government ever devoted so much attention to the formation of good roads and to the protection of those who travel on them, and much of the security arises from the change I have here remarked in the character and number of our military establishments.

There is perhaps no part of the world where the communities of which the society is composed have been left so much to self-government as in India. There has seldom been any idea of a reciprocity of duties and rights between the governing and the governed; the sovereign who has possession feels that he has the right to levy certain taxes from the land for the maintenance of the public establishments which he requires to keep down rebellion against his rule and to defend his dominions against all who may wish to intrude and seize upon them, and to assist him in acquiring the dominions of other princes when favourable opportunities offer; but he has no idea of a reciprocal duty towards those from whom he draws his revenues.

In India, the difference between the army of a prince and the gang of a robber was, in the general estimation of the people, only in *degree*—they were both driving an *imperial trade*, a *'padshahee kam'*! Both took the auspices and set out upon their expeditions after the Dussehra, when the autumn crops were ripening; and both thought the Deity propitiate soon as they found the omens favourable; one attacked palaces and capitals, the other villages and merchant's storerooms. The members of the army of the prince thought as little of the justice or injustice of his cause as did those of the gang of the robber. The people of his capital hailed the return of the victorious prince, who had contributed so much to their wealth by his booty and to their self-love by his victory; the village community received back the robber and his gang with the same feelings—by their skill and daring they had come back loaded with wealth, which they were always disposed to spend liberally with their neighbours.

Sleeman was one day to have a much closer acquaintance with Oudh and its government, an acquaintance of which more will be said later in this book. Bare fields that could be fertile bore silent witness to violence and rapine : night after night from their mess veranda officers could see in the sky the glare ofburning villages. No peasant would roof his house for fear of such a visitation: the four walls back mud stood open to sun and rain till they crumbled away. The most prejudiced in favour of native rule could not term this 'government.'

As his staff officer Sleeman came to know his Colonel very well, with all his defects a most lovable old man. In 1817, shortly before the British conquest of Saugor, when a Mahratta army under the unscrupulous, marauding Iranian adventurer Jean Baptiste Filoze had captured Gurhakotah fortress, a visiting surgeon gave Gregory the news. As soon as this officer had left him the Colonel wrote off a note to follow him: 'My dear Doctor, I understand that fellow John the Baptist has got into Scindheea's [Mahratta] service and now commands an army—do send me the newspapers!'

Sleeman's account of him is kindly but one is astonished to learn that Gregory later became a major-general and was decorated with the C.B.

"At the only occasion I ever heard him speak on the subject of religion, he discomfited his adversary in an argument at the mess by 'Why, sir, you do not suppose that I believe in those fellows Luther, Calvin and John the Baptist, do you?' Nothing could stand this argument. All the party burst into a laugh, which the old gentleman took for an unequivocal recognition of his victory, and his adversary was silenced.

"He was an old man when I first became acquainted with him. I put into his hands, when in camp, Miss Edgeworth's novels, in the hope of being able to induce him to read by degrees and I have frequently seen the tears stealing down over his furrowed cheeks as he sat pondering over her pages in the corner of his tent. A braver soldier never lived than old Gregory, and he distinguished himself greatly in the command of his regiment, under Lord Lake, at the battle of Laswaree and siege of Bhurtpore. It was impossible ever to persuade him that the characters and incidents of these novels were the mere creation of fancy; he felt them to be trued, he wished them to be true, and he would have them to be true. We were not very anxious to undeceive him, as the illusion gave him pleasure and did him good. Bolingbroke says, after an ancient author, 'History is philosophy teaching by example.' With equal truth we say that fiction, like that of

Maria Edgeworth, is philosophy teaching by emotion. It certainly taught old Gregory to be a better man to leave much of the little evil he had been in the habit of doing, and to do much of the good he had been accustomed to leave undone!

"The regiment continued the march over the wide dusty plains, camping every evening among the little villages and nightly scenting the but not unpleasant smoke from their cow-dung cooking fires, and so down to Allahabad at the junction of the great Jumna and Ganges rivers. No more pleasant memory can live in the dreams of old soldiers retired from India than the freedom of these long marches in the champagne air of an Indian winter. As the regiment moves parties peel off to shoot the small game which abounds and some, mounted on their chargers, to spear a pig. To right and left over the level plain to the far horizons spreads the multitude of diminutive fields of wheat and barley, tobacco, poppy and tall pulse, dotted with mango groves dark about the hamlets. The sugarcane is being pressed out in the bullock mills, the cotton pickers are at work and there is heard the dip and splash of the sling-baskets throwing water out of stream and pool on the fields and into the narrow irrigation channels. So it was in British India, but not so in Oudh, in the days when Sleeman marched with the 12th. Fear of violent death kept the peasant from his land, where men might till but seldom reap and where there were few families who had never fled from the flames of their plundered and burning homesteads."

Our young officer had no particular love for the larger and gayer staitons of India:

"Allahabad was a large station, having all too many attractions for us officers. I once again emphasize that there is no question that a good tone of feeling between the European officers and their men is essential to the well-being of native army, and I think I have found this tone somewhat impaired whenever our Native regiments are concentrated at large stations. In such places the European society is commonly large and gay and the officers of our Native regiments become too much occupied in its pleasures and ceremonies to attend to their native officers or *sipahees*.

In Europe there are separate classes of people, who subsist by catering for the amusements of the higher circles of society, in theatres, operas, concerts, balls, etc. etc., but in India this duty devolves entirely upon the young civil and military officers of the Government, and at large stations it really is a laborious one, which often takes up the whole of a young man's time. The ladies must have amusment and the officers must find it for them, because there are no other persons to undertake the arduous duty. The consequence is that they often become entirely alienated from their men, and betray signs of the greatest impatience while they listen to the necessary reports of their native officers as they come on or go off duty.

"It was there that I formed a friendship with an attractive but pathetic native nobleman of the name of Mirza Juhangur, the favourite son of the Mughul Emperor of Delhie. In 1836 I visited this poor prince's tomb at Nizamodeen, near Delhie. In an enclosure formed by marble screens, beautifully carved, is the tomb of this favourite son, whom I knew so intimately when he was kiling himself as fast as he could with Hoffman's cherry brandy. 'This,' he would say to me, 'is really the only liquor that you Englishmen have worth drinking; and its only fault is that it makes one drunk too soon. To prolong his pleasure he used to limit himself to one large glass every hour, till he got dead drunk. Two or three sets of dancing women and musicians used to relieve each other in amusing him during this interval. He died of course soon and the poor old Emperor was persuaded by his mother, the favourite Sultana, that he had fallen a victim of 'sighting' and grief at the treatment of the English, who would not permit him to remain at Delhie, where he was continually employed in attempts to assassinate his eldest brother, the heir apparent, and to stir up insurrections among the people! He was not in confinement at Allahabad, but merely prohibited from returning to Delhie. He had a splendid dwelling, a good income, and all the honours due to his rank."

Here and elsewhere we should understand Sleeman's frequent use of the word native. To him India existed only as a descriptive term without political meaning: there were no Indian people or Indian citizens—they were Hindustani, Deccani, Pathan, etc. The word native was not intended to distinguish 'coloured' from white, but used in its true sense, as he himself could be called a native of Cornwall. In his day vast areas of India were thus said to be under 'native rule'—Mahratta, Sikh, Oudh, Mogul, and so on—and their kingdoms were called native kingdoms. The word Indian, if applied, would have to include the Company's territories as well as the native kingdoms of the time.

News from Cornwall was good, for Mary, his much-loved sister, had married John Furse, their old boyhood friend, so now he addressed his letters to her as 'Mrs Captain Furse.' The wedding took place at Mylor on the banks of the River Fal on 17th September 1816, Philip Sleeman obtaining short leave to give his sister away and to sign the register. Furse had proved himself a very gallant commander. In 1813 Mr C. Saverland, Packet Agent at Falmouth, had written to the Postmaster-General of the great fight that Furse and his ship, *Lapwing*, had made against the American privateer *Fox*, which carried a crew of 107 and 17 guns to *Lapwing's* 30 men and 8 guns. Furse had been twice wounded and half his crew were casualties. The mate surrendered. This had been off Barbados. The captain of the *Fox* had treated the British crew with great barbarity. However, they all managed to escape from jail in Barcelona, to seize a small schooner and, after a perilous passage, to make a British port in Jamaica. Later, in command of the *Chesterfield*, Furse had engaged another American privateer for many had suffered serious damage and casualties against a superior enemy, yet the victory was his. By working his ship and fighting its few guns he had thrown back a determined attempt to board him.

This was a man after young Sleeman's heart and he was overjoyed at the news.

And now at Allahabad he discovered a document which was to change the whole tenor of his life and to dub him among his friends and in the history of India as 'Thuggee' Sleeman. He was one day looking among some old books in the Collector's office, his friend the Collector having told him that somewhere there was a document written by Dr Richard Sherwood on a sect of stranglers called Phansigars. Eventually the young soldier lit triumphantly upon this very paper, borrowed it and took it home for study. Sherwood, a surgeon at Fort St George in Madras, had written this report as late as 1816. It was a long paper giving a fairly full account of a sect of assassins known as Thugs, Phansigars, Ari Tulukar, Tanta Kalleru and Warlu Wahndlu, all terms signifying the use of a noose, in this case on a yellow scarf. It appeared that Europeans were unaware of the existence of such criminals until shortly after the conquest of Seringapatam in 1799, when a gang of about one hundred were apprehended near Bangalore. There were also, however, records of this particularly revolting crime from Dehi down to Travancore in the south.

Perhaps the most valuable part of the report was a short vocabulary of a few words in the Thug jargon termed 'the language of dispatch or emergency.'

Sleeman had only a few days to browse on the report as the battalion was under orders to move into Oudh to hunt down a young bandit who was indulging in a favourite Indian sport termed *bhumewat*, from the *bhumea*, meaning a landed proprietor. It was a sporadic war over land of which the young man had been unjustly deprived. The Oudh Amil had sent a considerable force against this youth, who with the aid of friends had cleverly ambushed the Government's troops. The Amil had of course heavily bribed the local newswriter[1] to induce him not to report this disgraceful reverse at the court in Lucknow, but by devious ways the Amil's private enemies and rivals saw to it that the truth reached the king. Fearing a still greater reverse the king appealed for British help and Calcutta ordered the 12th to march. The rebel was pursuing the usual course in this sort of affair by killing anyone who tried to cultivate the land in dispute, laying waste villages and crops in the neighbourhood and driving off the flocks—all this with the object of forcing the Government to make restitution. These were methods which in the present day might well be applied in England were a farmer dispossessed under the Agriculture Act of 1947.

The 12th N.I feeling deeply sympathetic towards the rebel, chased him in leisurely fashion into British territory, where he was comfortably housed and looked after until, becoming restive again, he returned to his own country, was seized and many years later died miserably in jail.

So immersed was Sleeman in native affairs and in this new Thuggee discovery that he found himself tending away from his regimental life, especially since he had been denied the further chance of active service when the 2/12th N.I. crossed India to take part in the second Mahratta war of 1818. Nor could he foresee any likelihood of active service in the near future. He had been studying the geology of Oudh and the systems of land tenure, until he felt it to be almost painful that he should be taken from these interests. Furthermore he had now mastered Urdu, Arabic, Persian and Gurkhali and wanted to make use of his qualifications. On 22nd August he therefore applied to the commandant for appointment as a professor or instructor at the college at Fort William, being unable then to see how otherwise he could employ himself. Colonel Gregory sent for him and demanded to know why he had submitted such an application, saying that he would in any case refuse to forward it. Believing that he had offended him, William 'trade delicately' while at the same time explaining to him his position. 'Sleeman,' he replied, 'this is no sort of post for a practical man of your qualifications. Do you want to become a grey-bearded schoolmaster?

1. See Appendix 1

I will have nothing to do with it. Here is a pen, here is ink and there a table. Write out an application to be appointed to the Political Service. That is your future. I'll give you a strong recommendation. I hope you'll be successful. All of us will be sorry to let you go, but the less we think of that the better.'

He wrote out his application, made a copy for the adjutant and took his leave of Colonel Gregory. He tried to forget about his letter, being loath to leave the regiment for good, but at the same time hoping that his application might succeed. In his heart he now knew the Civil Service to be his final choice. For some months no more was heard and he was beginning to settle his mind philosophically to the idea of continuing as a soldier.

One morning in December of the year 1819 the adjutant rode into camp near Pertabgarh and sent for the European officers to tell them that the battalion was to load up its baggage and move to Jubbulpore the following February, then turning to Sleeman he said: 'Bill, you will come with us, and on arrival at Jubbulpore you will take up civil employment.' With that he handed him a letter from the office of the governor-general in Calcutta confirming this and appointing him as junior assistant to the agent of the governor-general in the Saugor and Nerbudda territories, at first as a seconded officer, virtually on probation as he interpreted the matter. He was astonished, but soon recovered himself when he became the butt of his companions, who chaffed him good-naturedly as soon as they were alone, calling him 'His Excellency' and by other mock titles. That night he had his first chance to think over this momentous change in his life, finally accepting it as the best news he had had since he came to India and determining, 'in so far as Providence permits, to use all my energies and abilities to prosper all those who should ever come into my charge.'

CHAPTER 6

Joining the Political Service

Sleeman rode into Jubbulpore with his regiment in March of the year 1820. With its low wooded hills, tiled barracks and bungalows it was unlike any other part of India he had yet seen. Here, as assistant to the political agent, he lived with his regiment and took part in the morning parades. 'The parade ground at Jubbulpore was in front of the Agent's house and often did I as a subaltern look up from the exercise at this large house, little imagining that in years to come I, as the Chief Functionary over all these Territories and many others added to them, would be looking down from it upon other subalterns performing their drills with other regiments.'

It has become the convention to decry the efficiency of the civil and military services of the old East India Company, 'John Company' as its employees called it. There were plenty of writers who criticized them in Sleeman's day and later. Even then it was not uncommon for an English tourist to spend a few months or a year in India and then return to England to spill his ink on many a page of comment on the Company's administration. Such a one was G. 0. Trevelyan, Macaulay's nephew, whose *Letters of a Competition Wallah,* appear in great part to be the outpourings of a visitor who has been snubbed by an official. Better authorities were men such as Sleeman and others of the services who impartially criticized and commended British and Indian rule alike. But perhaps one may properly quote the words of a Swedish nobleman writing in 1838, Count Björnsgerna, Envoy Extraordinary at the Court of St James.

'The body of civil officers, according to the opinion of all persons understanding the subject, is uncommonly well composed, and has scarcely its equal in any country in Europe. ...For the individual ...enters the Company's service . . . after a long course of preparatory studies, among which is the learning of those Oriental languages (the Sanscrit, Hindoostanee,' and Arabic).

'The army is as great phenomenon in the annals of war as the Anglo-Indian empire in those of the world!' Again, after enumerating the differences in customs and religion between the Indian sepoy and theBritish officer, 'British India . . . has an army composed of more than 200,000, whose unshaken fidelity, amazing bravery and great military proficiency, are proved by fifty campaigns, and by the experience of nearly a century.'

In the 1850's the governor of the Dutch East Indies came to Lucknow to stay with Sleeman and corroborated, from what he had seen, all that Björnșerna had written. It is as well, therefore, to set these independent witnesses against the evidence of any British authority. It is in any event hard to believe that highly efficient men such as Sleeman, Low, Outram and their friends would have tolerated the arrogant boobies that have been popularly supposed to have been their colleagues, subordinates and superiors. In fact, the story yet to be told will show how able were most of their colleagues and how they dealt with those whom they considered below the standard they set. Despite occasional lapses the Company's civil services were, until 1858 when the Crown took them over, a quite remarkabl y efficient body of men for their time. The Indian Army reached its lowest ebb in the 1850'S after the Sikh wars. It was a part of the Bengal Army which raised the Sepoy Mutiny and the basic cause of its failure was thc strict adhercncc to promotion by seniority of both British and Indian officers, whereby the higher ranks had lost the power to command and had become feeble and hesitant.

In December of the year 1821 Sleeman finally said goodbye to his old regiment, but not before his friend Charles Welland breathed his last, taken by cholera. The high proportion of British officers who for one reason and another never again saw the land of their birth once they had left it for India is quite tragic. Statistics given for the Bengal Army from 1796 to 1820 show that one British officer out of three died of disease or was killed in action and that the proportion of those who died to those who retired was 7 to 1 in the infantry and 6 to 1 in the cavalry. Thus the chances of an officer retiring at pensionable age and reaching England were small, smaller still when one recollected the perils and hazards of the Cape route in a sailing-ship.

While here at Jubbulpore he learnt that many of the Company's senior administrators had recorded their opinion that however vile the Thug atrocities might be, no widespread campaign should be waged against them because the profession was based on religion, and to crush it might injure religious susceptibilities. He regretted and severely criticized this view. In 1822 his apprenticeship came to an end when he unexpectedly received orders to take over independent civil charge of the district of Narsinghpore in the Nerbudda valley. He had now thirteen years' service and but two years of experience in political affairs when this important frontier district was thrust upon him. Its importance was that only a few years before the British had taken it over from the Mahratta power and little enough remained of the original land titles from the confusion and thriftlessness of the Mahratta rule. He stayed there two years and always referred to these years as by far the most laborious of his life. His was the truly herculean job of recording and adjusting the settlement of land, but he enjoyed the many days when he rode about on his pony among the farmers and peasants. Some of his most entertaining conversations with that quite charming individual, the Indian *ryot* (peasant), are narrated in these pages; if anyone would enjoy more of that entertainment he should read a copy of William Sleeman's *Rambles and Recollections*, first published in 1844.

He was lucky to be working with two most humane and highly efficient officers, Molony and Carvin Smith. The Company had shown great wisdom when it assumed the Saugor and Nerbudda territories from the Mahratta princes. Instead of introducing an enormous and ill-digested Code of Regulations and so inflicting an intolerable evil upon the country, imposing a wickedly expensive civil establishment and multiplying the work proportionately, it left Molony a free hand. He produced a remarkable system based on the principle of undivided authority from bottom to top. This system inspired every European officer with so keen a feeling of interest in the happiness and welfare of the people and zealous a spirit in the discharge of his duties, as to be unusual even in any of the 'regulation' provinces of that early time.

The young political officer was thus brought up in the best of all schools in which commonsense, humane nature and boundless initiative were predominant. He grasped the opportunity with both hands, so that his able report and recommendations on all facets of the local administration and agriculture were accepted by the Government, and his services commended by the Court of Directors. Nobody was more surprised at the compliments paid to him than Sleeman, for he was blessed with the qualities of the true artist. Like other men he could look back with gratification on work done but never found satisfaction in anything which he felt should have been done better.

For many weeks in the cold season he would move about his district pitching camp from day to day among his people and discussing and settling their troubles. This winter touring he kept up every year until his seniority prevented it. Of this period in a newly acquired territory he had some observations to make.

It was natural that, in a territory but recently taken over by the Honble Company, the natives should make comparison between the rule of the native princes and that of the Company.

A very learned Hindu once told me in central India that the oracle of Mahadeo had been at the same time consulted at three of his greatest temples-one in the Deccan, one in Rajputana, and one, I think, in Bengal—as to the results of the government of India by Europeans, who seemed determined to fill all the high offices of administration with their own countrymen to the exclusion of the people of the country. A day was appointed for the answer; and when the priest came to receive it, they found Mahadeo (Siva) himself, with a European complexion and dressed in European clothes! He told them 'that their European government was in reality nothing more than a multiplied incarnation of himself, and that he had come among them in this shape to prevent their cutting each other's throats as they had been doing for some centuries past; that these, his incarnations, appeared to have no religion themselves, in order that they might be the more impartial arbitrators between the people of so many different creeds and sects who now inhabited the country; that they must be aware that they had never before been so impartially governed and that they must continue to obey these their governors, without attempting to pry further into futurity or the will of their gods.' Mahadeo performs, a part in the great drama of the *Ramayana*, or the rape of Sita, and he is the only figure there that is represented with a white *face*!

I was one day praising the law of primogeniture among ourselves to a Mahomedan gentleman of high rank and defending it on the ground that it prevented that rivalry and bitterness of feeling among brothers which were always found among the Mahomedans, whose law prescribes an equal division of property, real and personal, among the sons, and the choice of the wisest among them as successor to the government. 'This,' said he, 'is no doubt the source of our weakness, but why should you condemn a law which is to you a source of so much strength? I one day,' said he, 'asked Mr Seaton, the Governor-General's representative at the court of Delhi, which of all things he had seen in India he liked best?' "You have," replied he, smiling, "a small species of melon called *phoot* (dissention): this is the thing we like best in your land." 'There was,' continued my Mahomedan friend, 'an infinite deal of sound political wisdom in this one sentence. Mr Seaton was a very good and a very wiseman: our European governors of the present day are not all the same kind of thing. I asked Mr. N., a judge, the same question many years afterwards and he told me that he thought the rupees were the best things he had found in India. I asked Mr T., the Commissioner, and he told me that he thought the tobacoo which he smoked in his hookah was the best thing. And pray, Sir, what do you think the best thing?

'Why, Nawab Sahib, I am always very well pleased when I am free from pain and can get my nostrils full of cool air and my mouth full of cold water in this hot land of yours, and I think most of my countrymen are the same. Next to these, the thing we all admire most in India, Nawab Sahib, is the entire exemption which you, and I, and every other gentleman, native or European, enjoy from the taxes which press so heavily upon them in other countries. In Cashmere, no midwife is allowed to attend a woman in her confinement till a heavy tax has been paid to Ranjit Singh.'

Narsinghpore lay on the highway across India. It was a busy place. Religious pilgrims streamed through it on their way to and from the important shrines of the country, while the ordinary commercial traffic crowded the roads and the bazaars. Sleeman and his police did the best they could to keep tabs on all newcomers who entered and left the town. Their control seemed to be efficient. However, in 1822 a party of about thirty travellers with nothing but walking-sticks in their hands passed his picket in the dusk of evening. On being challenged they said they were cowherds and that their cattle were following close behind. It was in the month of February when marriage processions take place every day in all large towns and the nights are long. The police guard in the town saw a fine blaze of marriage torches some twenty yards away among the usual noisy concourse. Ten minutes later a little boy crept out of a ditch, half dead with fright, and whispered to the picket commander that his house had been robbed and his father killed. The picket ran to the scene but only the dead body, the wounded and the burning houses bore witness to what had been done.

The dacoits (robbers) had walked up the street to the houses of the most wealthy merchants, set their torches ablaze by a sudden blow upon the earthenware pots containing combustibles, stabbed everybody who ventured to move or make the slightest noise, plundered the houses, and in ten minutes were away with their booty. Although Sleeman rode into the bazaar at once and tried to find some evidence of the culprits, he could not discover enough even to form a general idea of the sort of people they were. This was not the act of the Thugs, who were uppermost in his mind: this was something different. To his quest for Thugs he now added this new quarry. He never forgot.

He observed:

'Nothing more was ever heard of them till I got behind the scenes some twenty years afterwards and became acquainted with the whole Dramatis Personate of these fearful exhibitions. . . . . This was not all of which I was only half aware at Narsinghpore: there were other more fatal and secret activities about us and very close to us, which never came to my court, however blessed I was with a loyal and painstaking police force. So near was I to the life of the natives around, particularly in the country-side, that it seemed that no serious happening could evade my helpers and myself: yet, evade us it did."

CHAPTER 7

Ramasi

William Henry, thirty-six years old and eminently marriageable, should by now, if not long before, have been seeking a bride. In Calcutta and Allahabad he had had every opportunity, especially in Calcutta before all the best of what was unkindly termed 'the fishing fleet' was chartered by others on their way to up-country posts. He was not averse to the company of women, but they did find him something aloof. This was not because they wearied him. He had placed them on a pedestal. And they, knowing his reputation as a young man of great promise, felt shy in his presence and fearful of disclosing their own lack of learning. Everything he did he seemed to do well, yet he was the last to think so if they had only known. Aloofness on the one side and shyness on the other keeping Miss E—and Miss K—at arm's length (how exasperating was the Victorian diarist's addiction to these initials), his frequent letters to the beloved Teeny never disclose a name or an affair or anything approaching an affair. No, the main trouble was that young Sleeman was devoted to things, people, and affairs of his professional life and with their problems he stayed, day in and day out. He breathed in their atmosphere till they were part of his own life. Like a good soldier he could thus discuss 'the other side of the hill,' an almost prophetic quality that made him so formidable an enemy to those whom he selected for punishment. They could never escape: he knew them and their habits and movements without setting eyes on them. They feared him and inevitably bolted into his net. And so with women, attentive he was, but as though watching the fauna of jungle and field. He would study their habits, drawn by their beauty, yet allow them little part in his life. They walked outside the walls of his vineyard. He would often quote Pope, 'The proper study of mankind is man.' Man interested him, and the Begum Johnson interested him more than Miss E, or Miss K.

Against promiscuity his upbringing had proofed him. He had a feeling that women who stepped so low must have lost their very being. He was something of an Elizabethan, with his knowledge and love of the classics, his delight in poetry, the drama and good letters, his capacity for philosophy and meditation, his toleration and withal his energy, enterprise and love of action. It was almost pathetic the way he continually resurrected for himself the keen pleasure of that last performance of *Macbeth* which he had so enjoyed before going into exile in the exotic wastes of India. Perhaps he was the 'whole man' he had set out to be.

Launched now on his life's work, he had less time than ever to meet and know the other sex. And his flood tide was upon him. It came in unpretentiously with a posting on temporary duty to Jubbulpore. On arrival there he reported to Mr Molony one early morning near the *Kachheri* (the government offices).

'I'm glad you've come, Sleeman. We're hard-pressed here.'

'I had heard that, sir. What can I do?' Outside the magistrate's court there squatted under the peepal-trees a large concourse of Indians waiting a hearing.

Molony turned to his clerk, 'Babuji, I can find no evidence against these people. Send them away.'

Then to Sleeman: 'They'd a lot of goods that I think must have been stolen, but no one will come forward to claim the articles. So I must let them go. Well, well—will you go over to the court-house and start work there? There are many cases waiting to be tried. . . . You might even find a case of Thuggee,' said he with a sly smile. He had often chaffed Sleeman with his pet obsession—a passing idiosyncrasy in a practical officer. Sleeman grinned good-humouredly. He had 'lived with' his problem, so he said emphatically what he really believed, although from experience he knew it to be rejected by his colleagues.

'Well, sir, my theory is that the whole Thug system is one single tree spreading over India from the Indus to Cape Comorin. Find one branch, follow it and you will feel your way down the stem to the root. Cut it there and it will fall. You will ask if I have proof. I have non. . . . Yes, sir, . . . I deserve to be laughed at.'

Molony looked at him quizzically. 'Yes, you do. People do laugh at your Thug theories. But' (kindly) 'don't bother. We all think you're obsessed, and we wouldn't have you otherwise, my lad. Do you know that we call you Thuggee Sleeman?'

Sleeman laughed. 'No, I was not aware of that, sir, Thuggee—Thuggee,' he mused. He took his leave of Mr Molony and walked happily over to the court-room. Well, perhaps he was wrong—perhaps—perhaps. ... No, he felt he was right—a tree—even a family tree? He smiled to himself. Thuggee Sleeman? Right: he would earn that name.

His mood was, it proved, coincidental.

From the court-room window he watched the motley band that Molony had examined walking off on the Saugor road, their baggage on half a dozen pack ponies, chattering away cheerfully among themselves like any other party of travellers who had journeyed with one another for days on end and from far away. By mid-day he had gone through the files that the clerk had placed before him, then made off to his lodging for tiffin. He was walking along rapt in thought when a man, whom he at first took to be a petitioner, approached him *salaaming*. Sleeman glanced at him and the man turned and followed. He was accustomed to being thus accosted so continued on his way, expecting the stranger to tell him his business, but the petitioner walked silently along behind and followed him on to the bungalow veranda. Here Sleeman turned about.

'What is it?' he asked.

His visitor looked to right and left and through the window into the house where the servant awaited his master. Thuggee understood. He stepped to the window and told the servant to clear out as he would not be lunching that day; he was to leave some toast and soda-water on the table. He then quickly ushered the newcomer into his own bedroom.

'Who are you?'

'Kalyan Singh. You do not remember me, sahib?'

Thuggee looked him over carefully. 'Yes, I do. I sent you to prison for three months last year for stealing grain for your horse.'

'Yes, sahib. And you took care of my little son while I was in prison.'

'I'm glad to see you again, but not in such company. You'll be in trouble once more if you travel along with them.' The young political rose and went to the door as though to speed his guest. Kalyan Singh put a hand on his arm to restrain him.

'You know them, sahib?' Thuggee said he did, which was untrue and a bow at a venture.

'They are evil men,' said Kalyan. 'Their leader, Durga, is a cruel and unjust man.'

'Yes, he has treated you most unjustly—he has not given you your share of the loot. Come, come, speak out, or I'll send one of my men to tell Durga you are here.'

The man looked at Sleeman and smile broke over his face. 'The sahib is clever.'

'No, I'm not clever. I just know. Speak up and quickly too.'

'They are Thugs, sahib.'

Sleeman's whole body tingled at this. What wonderful news and what an opportunity! At last!

'I know that,' said he calmly, 'Come with me.'

He walked his man outside and shouted to a police sepoy who was sitting near the servants' quarters. 'Tell the *syce* to saddle my horse at once and you yourself come here.' Then turning to Kalyan: 'I shall put you in jail now. It's the only safe place for you. Here, constable, take Kalyan Singh by a back road to the jail and lock him in. Tell the Thanedar to march his detachment at once along the Saugor road till he meets me.'

The two walked off, the policeman wondering what was in the wind. Sleeman slipped on breeches and boots, picked up his whip, stuffed the toast in his pocket and hastened round to the stable to help the *syce* to saddle up. Mounting, he swung his horse round and trotted off as hard as he could for the cantonment. He was at the adjutant's bungalow in a cloud of dust and saw the officer jump up from his tiffin table to see what all the trouble was.

'Give me a troop at once, will you! I'm after dacoits. If you're quick I'll have them back by dark.'

The adjutant knew Thuggee and did not wait to argue. He sat down, wrote a note for the orderly officer at the lines and handed it to Sleeman. 'The emergency troop will turn out in ten minutes for you. Good luck!' He had to shout the last words as Thuggee vanished into another cloud of dust.

Was he off on another wild-goose chase—and to end as the butt of his brother officers? It had happened before. 'Well,' thought Thuggee, 'at any rate it's a fine day. Better be out here than stew in a court-room.' As he rode he sniffed the clean, sunlit air.

In a short time he was cantering out on the Saugor road at the head of troop of cavalry. They rode steadily forward, Thuggee half a mile ahead so as not to alarm the Thugs, who it turned out had made such good time that the pursuit only came up with them at Patan. Sleeman, taking his life in his hands, trotted past them and turned at their head holding up his hand for them to halt. The unsuspecting robbers who had so recently been released came to a stop, chattering unconcernedly among themselves. A leader came forward and asked what the sahib wanted. Sleeman engaged him in conversation, asking the way to this and that place, until in a few minutes the malefactors found themselves surrounded by cavalry, who steadily eased them off the road into a grove of mango-trees. Here Sleeman told them all to sit down while he addressed them. He told them that they had burnt and looted houses in Narsinghpore some months ago. A titter of derisive laughter greeted this. They had never been near Narsinghpore, they said, and Sleeman knew it, but he must keep them here until a detachment of foot police arrived as escort. He told them they must wait for his police to identify them before he could decide on arrest or release. Durga said this was a waste of time—the sahib's time, not theirs—for they were only travellers and in no hurry.

Thuggee sat by them, ostensibly to rest in reality to listen, his head bowed on his hands as though in sleep. Dr Sherwood's short vocabulary of Thuggee words, long since engraved on his memory, now opened like a page of print behind his closed eyes. The men remained silent perhaps anxious about the consequences and meaning of this fresh arrest. In time, quietly, they began to exchange conversation, speaking in Hindustani. Before long they broke into a foreign tongue, possibly a dialect of the Deccan, he thought.

'Samcani,' 'raclan,' and then one, a leader, told another to do something with the *curp.* He rose and started to remove the loads from the ponies. This was Ramasi, Thuggee slang! Sleeman sat on as though sleeping. The conversation turned again to *samcani* and *raclan,* hare and jackal—that is, to omens. He was seated by a gang of Thugs.

The police arrived and the gang set off along the road to Jubbulpore under escort. He sent the *sowars* on and himself rode carelessly along beside the party. The talk went on Ramasi so that the sepoys might not be expected to understand. For himself he could not follow it but could grasp the subject by a word or two here and there—*burce* for rupee, *setac* for gold, *Bhitu* for Hindu, *nyamet* for a rich man, and so on. William Sleeman always regarded this as the happiest ride of his life. What an extraordinary chance! He looked down proudly at his carefree little flock as a moorland shephered would look at his sheep. But not for worlds would he lose a precious one of them. Now, thought he, the good-natured banter of friends at his pet obsession would change to a confidence in the truth of what he had to say about this atrocious trade, this secret society of evil of which no man ever dared tell. His whole being raged against the ghoulish thing: it was vicarious fear, he thought, that spurred him on so relentlessly to destroy it. He looked with awe at those hundreds of hands that without remorse and in the name of a blood-glutted deity had shared in binding the cord around the necks of millions of innocent travellers throughout the centuries. Now at last he, a modest Englishman, was about to destroy the whole growth, root and branch. The heat of the moment was gone and he felt a cold, ruthless desire to annihilate the guild that for hundreds of years had defied all attacks on itself. He never lost this strange stony determination until he had broken the whole system. He lived as a man dedicated to one end.

They arrived at Jubbulpore jail where all was ready to receive them. William identified and removed Moti, Kalyan Singh's brother, and had him shut up separately by himself, the rest, happy in their innocence, remaining in the general cell, docile and singing hymns.

Thuggee returned to his lodging, well seized as to where he stood, on firm ground at the beginning of what he had sought through five years of ceaseless investigation. Later that night, under the full moon, he walked to the jail, where the jailer, Kalyan Singh and Moti were waiting for him under the Thanedar in the guard-room. The little party, with the Thug Moti at its head, escorted by a posse of constables carrying picks and shovels, moved silently off on the road to Lucknadaun. There Moti led them into a grove of tall dark mango-trees, whose stems striped with black the white of the ground beneath. Shadow and light flickered over the silent figures as they moved, slowly following the questing Thug. This then, thought Sleeman, is the *bele,* the quiet place of half a thousand years of death. Beneath his feet as he trod were men and women and even infants smothered through the years, calling him to the extirpation of a great wickedness.

Moti bent down, examined the soil and bade the sepoys dig. In a few minutes there appeared rags and then the freshly killed corpse of a man. Here and there the digging went on until the dead bodies of three strangled men and a boy, their necks broken, lay upon the hard-baked earth in the moonlight. Sleeman told his policemen to examine the corpses for signs of identity. Two they identified for certain. They placed the bodies on litters, and having restored the earth and marked other places at which Moti told them to dig, returned to the jail with their grisly burden.

Thuggee let them go ahead. For a time he stood quite still opening himself to the atmosphere of the place, recollecting those who for centuries had fouled it, and the frozen silence that hid the deed from the outer world. In his mind he saw the two *Beles* who chose the *bele* and dug the graves, walking cheerfully ahead of innocent travellers charmed by the *Sothas,* the Deceivers who accompanied them. He saw the murderous pair discussing the site for the deed, then one of them with the magic pickaxe digging graves for those who were even now sharing food and entertainment with friends who would kill them in a few hours' time. He saw the whole cheerful party enter the grove in the evening, set out their beds, light the fire and sit round it for song and story-telling. He saw Durga coaxing the travellers to sing a song of their native land: he heard them clear their throats and saw them throw back their heads to sing. He heard Durga give the *fhirni*, the call of the beast of blood; he saw the *Bhurtotes*, the stranglers, whip the *rumal*, the yellow scarf, each one to his right around his victim's neck. So was the deed done. When the voracious Thugs had rifted the bodies down to their meanest possessions, the *Lughas* bent up the knees to the chin, placed them carefully in their graves and drove their knives here and there through the bodies to prevent disturbance of soil by swelling. Earth covered them, bright sun dried the soil at dawn; the silence of centuries returned. This was the way his lost sepoys had gone, never to return.

Thuggee mounted his horse and walked it slowly back to his bungalow. No matter what the obstacles and no matter the danger, his course was set till its end.

Next day he sent for the relatives of the three dead men to identify them. All the booty from this bund had been listed and placed in a shed. one by one witnesses came forward from the town to claim the articles. The sickening process of digging went on. Thuggee's investigations brought twenty-eight Thugs to the gallows and seventy to jail. One gallowbird was a government messenger, another an inspector of police, revealing still another means by which the Thugs covered their crimes. Using this inspector's influence they had been able to prevail upon men of property and standing to give the gang protection—a protection, in those days, too often lent to any gang.

Now at last the native population was coming forward to incriminate the perpetrators of these atrocities. Jubbulpore knew Sleeman well. It was a personal tribute to him that the people trusted him to carry the campaign through to the end, and not to leave the work half done and the unlucky informers wide open to a deadly vengeance.

Sleeman spared Moti's life and Moti taught him the whole Ramasi tongue. For some weeks he stewed over it until he could speak it fluently. Ramaseeana, he termed it, in a book he had printed for all his officers to read and to learn.

One other thing that Moti taught Sleeman was the need for a reformatory, including a school of industry, to wean Thugs away from their trade. Moti ran straight for a few years thereafter, apparently cured, until suddenly he took to his old ways and finished on a gibbet for some particularly atrocious crimes.

Sleeman returned to Narisinghpore where he continued his heavy duties, to which were now added those of the suppression of Thuggee over a wide area of central India. The addition came in tribute to success, an over-heavy burden, it might be thought, for any junior political to carry. But to Sleeman the task was no duty. It was a mission peculiarly his own. He knew more about it than anyone else in India. He was slowly developing a system for the suppression of Thuggee and expanding it gradually by obtaining the appointment of officers and police to help him. Now, too, he started building up the remarkable reports, the geographical and family connections that grew in the end to a monumental work, without which the destruction of this cruel religio-criminal profession would never have become possible.

In recounting these beginnings Sleeman insists that such violent crime did not indicate any slackening in the law and order of the Company's rule, for the whole face of its territory was tranquil and men went about their lawful occasions without fear. At the time he himself and other European men, women and children were camping among an immense concourse of Indians attending fairs and celebrations on the banks of the Nerbudda river. About them a hundred thousand people were peacefully jostling to and fro and the British officers happily left their own families for the day to go shooting, confident that they could come to no harm whatsoever. He reminds us that during the mutiny of native troops at Barrackpore in 1824 the leaders bound themselves by solemn oath to injure no British woman or child, no matter what the occasion. He says that his friend, Captain Reid, used to allow his five children to go into the lines and play with the soldiers of the mutinous regiments, while not one of the thirty officers' ladies thought of leaving the place. Travel by women remained safe.

Mrs Colonel Faithful with her daughter and another young lady who had both just arrived from England, went in 1835 all the way from Calcutta to Lodheana on the banks of the Hyphasis, a distance of more than twelve hundred miles, in the palankeens with relays of bearers, and without even a servant to attend them. They were travelling night and day for fourteen days without the slightest apprehension of injury or of insult. Cases of ladies travelling in the same manner by dawk immediately after their arrival from England, to all parts of the country, occur every day and I know of no instance of injury or insult sustained by them. Does not this speak volumes for the character of our rule in India! Would men trust their wives and daughters in this manner unprotected among a people that disliked them and their rule? We have not a garrison, or walked cantonments, or fortified position of any kind for our residence from one end of our Eastern empire to the other, save at the three capitals of Calcutta, Madras and Bombay. We know and feel that the people everywhere look up to and respect us in spite of all our faults, and we like to let them know and feel that we have confidence in them.

Sir Thomas Munro has justly observed: 'I do not exactly know what is meant by civilizing the people of India. In the theory and practice of good government they may be deficient; but if a good system of agriculture—if unrivalled manufactures—if a capacity to produce what convenience or luxury demands—if the establishment of schools for reading and writing—if the general practice of kindness and hospitality—and above all, if a scrupulous respect and delicacy towards the female sex are amongst the points that denote a civilized people; then the Hindoos are not inferior in civilization to the people of Europe. The Bishop Heber writes in the same favourable terms of the Hindoos in the narrative of his journey through India, and where shall we find a mind more capable of judging of the merits and demerits of a people than his?

CHAPTER 8

Suttee

In the new provinces of what was then India's western frontier William Sleeman was now up to his ears in the work of land settlement. At the same time he laboured well into the night preparing and organizing his Thug campaign. But Thuggee was by no means the only social and mental aberration with which he had to contend. Witchcraft and superstition were rife, and among Brahmin women (women of high caste) suttee was then common practice. While the latter was a matter for anxious concern, all the ways of superstition had his sympathetic attention as giving insight into the minds of his subjects—so much is obvious from the gentle, level manner in which he writes of them.

A suttee is a widow who burns herself to death on her husband's funeral pyre. The suicide is voluntary, but is done for most part under mental subjection to custom, and to the pressure of a wrong-minded public opinion; as such the Company stamped it out by ordinance Lord William Bentinck secured the abolition by a regulation of 1829. But not all suttees are so easily condemned and Sleeman is able to illustrate their origin in human love and faith, however mistaken. In November of that year, before the prohibition was promulgated to the general public, he was faced with a difficult predicament over a suttee on the banks of the Nerbudda at a small village called Gopalpore. As the scene of this sacrifice imagine a broad, sluggish river with a sandy shore, blue under the bright sunlight or mysterious under the white moon, gently flowing through the immense plains of India, where only the black mango groves and mud-walled villages break the overwhelming landscape.

'One of the most extraordinary old ladies that I have ever seen burned herself in my presence in 1829. I prohibited the building of any temple upon the spot, but my successor, Major Low, was never I believe made acquainted with the prohibition, nor with the progress of the work, which, therefore went on to completion during my absence. As suttees are now prohibited in our dominions, and cannot often be seen or described by Europeans, I shall here relate the circumstances of this as they were recorded by me at the time, and the reader may rely upon the truth of the whole tale.

'British newspapers of 20th October 1954 reported that on 19th October the widow of Brigadier Jabbar Singh, comptroller of the household of the Maharajah of Jodhpur, committed suttee on her husband's funeral pyre. (The word 'suttee' means virtuous woman)

'On the 29th November 1829, this old woman, then abut sixty-five years of age, here mixed her ashes with those of her husband, who had been burned alone four days before. On receiving the civil charge of the district (Jubbulpore) in March 1828, I issued a proclamation prohibiting anyone from aiding or assisting in suttee and distinctly stating that to bring one ounce of wood for the purpose would be considered as so doing. If the woman burned herself with the body of her husband, any one who brought wood for the purpose of burning him would become liable to punishment; consequently the body of the husband must be first consumed and the widow must bring a fresh supply for herself.

'On Tuesday, 24th November 1829, I had an application from the heads of the most respectable and most extensive family of Brahmins in the district, to suffer this old widow to burn herself with the remains of her husband, Omed Sing Opuddea, who had that morning died upon the banks of the Nerbudda. I threatened to enforce my order and punish severely any man who assisted, and placed a police guard for the purpose of seeing that no one did so. She remained sitting by the edge of the water without eating or drinking. The next day the body of her husband was burned to ashes in a small pit of about eight feet square and three or four feet deep, before several thousand spectators who had assembled to see the suttee. All strangers dispersed before evening, as there seemed to be no prospect of my yielding to the urgent solicitations of her family, who dared not touch food till she had burned herself or declared herself willing to return to them. Her sons, grandsons and some other relations remained with her while the rest surrounded my house, the one urging me to allow her to burn and the other urging her to desist. She remained sitting upon a bare rock in the bed of the Nerbudda, refusing every kind of sustenance and exposed to the intense heat of the sun by day and the severe cold of the night, with only a thin sheet thrown over her shoulders. On Thursday, to cut off all hope of her being moved from her purpose, she put on the *dhujja* or coarse red turban, and broke her bracelets in pieces, by which she became dead in law and for ever excluded from caste. Should she choose to live after this, she could never return to her family. Her children and grandchildren were still with her, but all their entreaties were unavailing; and I became satisfied that she would starve herself to death if not allowed to burn, by which her family would be disgraced, her miseries prolonged, and I myself rendered liable to be charged with a wanton abuse of authority, for no prohibition of the kind I had issued had as yet received the formal sanction of the government.

'On Saturday the 28th, in the morning, I rode out ten miles to the spot and found the poor old widow sitting with the *dhujja* round her head, a brass plate before her with undressed rice and flowers and a coconut in each hand. She talked very collectedly, telling me that 'she had determined to mix her ashes with those of her departed husband and should patiently wait my permission to do so, assured that God would enable her to sustain life till that was given, though she dared not eat or drink.' Looking at the sun, then rising before her over a long and beautiful reach of the Nerbudda river, she said calmly: 'My soul has been for five days with my husband's near that sun; nothing but my earthly frame is left and this I know you will in time suffer to be mixed with the ashes of his in yonder pit, because it is not in your nature or your usage wantonly to prolong the miseries of a poor old woman.' 'Indeed it is not; my object and my duty is to save and preserve them and I am come to dissuade you from this idle purpose, to urge you to live and to keep your family from the disgrace of being thought your murderers.' 'I am not afraid of them ever being thought so: they have all, like good children, done everything in their power to induce me to live among them and, if I had done so, I know they would have loved and honoured me, but my duties to them have now ended. I commit them all to your care and I go to attend my husband, Omed Sing Opuddea, with whose ashes on the funeral pile mine have already been three times mixed.'

'This was the first time in her long life that she had ever pronounced the name of her husband, for in India no woman high or low ever pronounces the name of her husband—she would consider it disrespectful towards him to do so, and it is often amusing to see their embarrassment when asked the question by any European gentleman. They look right and left for some one to relieve them from the dilemma of appearing disrespectful either to the querist or to their absent husbands. They perceive that he is unaccquainted with their duties on this point and are afraid he will attribute their silence to disrespect. They know that few European gentlemen are acquainted with them, and when women go into our courts of justice, or other places where they are liable to be asked the names of the husbands, they commonly take one of their children or some other relation with them, to pronounce the words in their stead. When the old lady named her husband, as she did with strong emphasis and in a very deliberate manner, everyone present was satisfied that she had resolved to die. 'I have,' she continued, 'tasted largely of the bounty of government, having been maintained by it with all my large family in case and comfort upon our rent-free lands; and I feel assured that my children will not be suffered to want: but with them I have nothing more to do, our intercourse and communion here end. My soul is with Omed Sing Opuddea and my ashes must here mix with his.' Again looking to the sun, 'I see them together,' said she, with a tone and countenance that affected me a good deal, 'under the bridal canopy!' alluding to the ceremonies of marriage; and I am satisfied that she at that moment really believed that she saw her own spirit and that of her husband under the bridal canopy in paradise.

'I tried to work upon her pride and fears. I told her that it was probable that the rent-free lands by which her family had been so long supported might be resumed by the government as a mark of its displeasure against the children for not dissuading her from the sacrifice; that the temples over her ancestors upon the bank might be levelled with the ground in order to prevent their operating to induce others to make similar sacrifices; and lastly, that not one single brick or stone should ever mark the place where she died if she persisted in her resolution. But if she consented to live, a splendid habitation should be built for her among these temples, her children should come daily to visit her, and I should frequently do the same. She smiled, but held out her arm, and said: 'My pulse has long since ceased to beat—my spirit has departed—and I have nothing left but a little "earth" that I wish to mix with the ashes of my husband. I shall suffer nothing in burning and, if you wish proof, order some fire and you shall see this arm consumed without giving me any pain.' I did not attempt to feel her pulse, but some of my people did and declared that it had ceased to be perceptible. At this time every native present believed that she was incapable of suffering pain, and her end confirmed that opinion.

'Satisfied myself that it would be unavailing to attempt to save her life, I sent for all the principal members of the family and consented that she should be suffered to burn herself if they would enter into engagements that no other member of their family should ever do the same. This they agreed to and, the papers having been drawn out in due form about midday, I sent down notice to the old lady, who seemed extremely pleased and thankful. The ceremonies of bathing were gone through before three, while the wood and other combustible materials for a strong fire were collected and put into the pit. After bathing, she called for a *paan* (betel leaf) and ate it, then rose up, and with one arm on the shoulder of her eldest son and the other on that of her nephew, approached the fire. I had sentries placed all round and no other person was allowed to approach within five paces.

'As she rose up, fire was set to the pile and it was instantly in a blaze. The distance was about one hundreded and fifty yards. She came on with a calm and cheerful countenance, stopped once, and casting her eyes upward, said: 'Why have they kept me five days from thee, my husband!' On coming to the sentries, her supporters stopped. She walked once round the pit, paused a moment and, while muttering a prayer, threw some flowers into the fire. She then walked up deliberately and steadily to the brink, stepped into the centre of the flame, sat down and, leaning back in the midst as if on a couch, was consumed without uttering a shriek or betraying one sign of agony! A few instruments of music had been provided and they played as usual when she approached the fire, not, as is commonly supposed, in order to drown screams, but to prevent the last words of the victim being heard, as they are supposed to be prophetic and might become sources of pain or strife to the living.

'It was not expected that I should yield and but few people had assembled to witness the sacrifice, so that there was little or nothing in the circumstances immediately around to stimulate her to any extraordinary exertions; and I am persuaded that it was the desire of again being united with her husband in the next world, and the entire confidence that she would be so if she now burned herself, that alone sustained her. From the morning of the day he died, Tuesday, till Wednesday evening, she ate *paans* or betel leaves, but nothing else; and from Wednesday evening she ceased eating them. She drank no water from Tuesday. She went into the fire with the same cloth about her that she had worn in the bed of the river, but it was made wet, from a persuasion that even the shadow of any impure thing falling upon her when going to the pile contaminates the woman unless counteracted by the sheet moistened in the holy stream.

'I must do the family justice to say that they all exerted themselves to dissuade the widow from her purpose and, had she lived, she would assuredly have been cherished and honoured as the first female of the whole house. There is no people in the world among whom parents are more loved, honoured and obeyed, than among the Hindoos, and the grandmother is always more honoured than the mother. No queen upon her throne could have ever been approached with more reverence by her subjects than was this old lady by all members of her family as she sat upon a naked rock in the bed of the river, with only a red rag upon her head and a white single sheet over her shoulders. Soon after the battle of Trafalgar I heard a young lad exclaim: "I could really wish to have had a brother killed in that action." There is no doubt that a family in which a suttee takes place feels a good deal exalted in its own esteem and that of the community by the sacrifice. The sister of the Rajah of Rewa was one of four or five wives who burned themselves with the remains of the Rajah of Oodeepore and nothing in the course of his life will ever be recollected with so much pride and pleasure, since the Oodeepore Rajah is the head of the Rajpoot tribes.

'I asked the old lady when she had first resolved upon becoming a suttee and she told me that, about thirteen years before, while bathing in the river Nerbudda near the spot where she then sat with many other females of the family, the resolution had fixed itself in her mind as she looked at the splendid temples on the bank of the river, erected by the different branches of the family over the ashes of her female reations who had at different times become suttees. Two, I think, were over her aunts and one over the mother of her husband. They were very beautiful buildings and had been erected at great cost and kept in good repair. She told me that she had never mentioned this resolution to anyone from that time, nor breathed a syllable on the subject till she called out 'sut, sut, sut!' (pure) when her husband breathed his last with his head in her lap on the bank of the Nerbudda, to which he had been taken when no hopes remained of his surviving the fever of which he died.

'The following conversation took place one morning between me and a native gentleman at Jubbulpore soon after suttees had been prohibited by government.

'What are the castes among whom women are not permitted to remarry after the death of their husbands?'

'They are, sir, Brahmins, Rajputs, Banniahs (shopkeepers), Kaets (writers).'

'Why not permit them to marry now that they are no longer permitted to burn themselves with the dead bodies of their husbands?'

'The knowledge that they cannot unite themselves to a second husband without degradation from caste tends strongly to secure their fidelity to the first, sir. Besides, if all widows were permitted to marry again, what distinction would remain among us and people of lower caste? We should all soon sink to a level with the lowest!'

'And so you are content to keep up your caste at the expense of the poor widows?'

'No: they are themselves as proud of the distinction as their husbands are.'

'And would they, do you think, like to have the good old custom of burning themselves restored?'

'Some of them would, no doubt.'

'Why?'

'Because they become reunited to their husbands in paradise, and there are happy, free from all the troubles of this life.'

'But you should not let them have any troubles as widows.'

'If they behave well, they are the most honoured members of their deceased husbands' families; nothing in such families is ever done without consulting them, because all are proud to have the memory of their lost fathers, sons and brothers so honoured by their widows. But women feel that they are frail and would often rather burn themselves at once than be exposed all their lives to temptation and suspicion.'

'And why do not the men burn themselves to avoid the troubles of life?'

'Because they are not called to it from heaven, as the women are.'

'And you think that the women were really called to be burned by the Deity?'

'No doubt: we all believe that they were called and supported by the Deity, and that no tender beings like women could ever voluntarily undergo such tortures. They become inspired with supernatural powers of courage and fortitude! When Shoolee Sookul, the Sehora banker's father, died, the wife of a "Lodhee" cultivator of the town declared all at once that she had been a suttee with him six times before, and that she would now go into paradise with him a seventh time. Nothing could dissuade her from burning herself. She was between fifty and sixty years of age and her grandchildren and all her family tried to persuade her that it must be a mistake, but all in vain. She became a suttee and was burnt the day after the body of the banker.'

'Did not the Shoolee Sookul's family, who were Brahmins, try to dissuade her from it, she being a Lodhee, a very low caste?'

'They did; but they said all things were possible with God; and it was generally believed that this was a call from heaven.'

'And what became of the banker's widow?'

'She said that she felt no divine call to the flames. This was thirty years ago and the banker was about thirty years of age when he died.'

'Then he will have rather an old wife in paradise?'

'No, sir; after they pass through the flames upon earth, both become young in paradise.'

'Sometimes women used to burn themselves with any relic of a husband who had died far from home, did they not?'

'Yes, sir, I remember a fisherman, about twenty years ago, who went on some business to Benares from Jubbulpore and who was to have been back in two months. Six months passed away without any news of him and at last the wife dreamed that he had died on the road, and began forthwith, in the middle of the night, to call out "sut, sut, sut!" Nothing could dissuade her from burning, and in the morning a pile was raised for her on the north bank of the large tank of Hanuman, where you have planted an avenue of trees. There I saw her burned with her husband's turban in her arms and, in ten days after, her husband came back!'

'Now the burning has been prohibited, a man cannot get rid of a bad wife so easily?'

'But she was a good wife, sir, and bad ones do not often become suttees.'

'Who made the pile for her?

'Some of her family, but I forget who; they thought it must have been a call from heaven when, in reality, it was only a dream.'

The way of the suttee can be harder even than she bargained for; but she is mercifully spared the knowledge.'

CHAPTER 9

Witchcraft

Among his many friends Sleeman had three in particular who used to pass on to him a great deal of material regarding native customs and superstitions, his cronies whom he used to chaff unmercifully over their beliefs and who in turn would assail him over British ways. They were his Maulvi, the counsellor who worked alongside him day by day—they 'laboured together in the vineyard,' as he put it—the little Sureemunt (a local title, like squire), a minor chieftain of Saugor, and a most sporting rajah, chief of Myhere. From these three he gathered to himself a vast amount of entertainment.

An experience typical of those he met in his daily work occurred in the course of his journeys about the countryside near Narsinghpore, where he came upon a haunted village, Burkhara. One day in 1823 a peasant was cultivating a field on its border and inadvertently or dishonestly drove his plough some yards beyond into a field which was haunted by the spirit of an old proprietor of 'so forward and violent a temper that no man would hire the land.' Realizing what he had done, the ploughman fell on his knees and implored the pardon of the ghost. But in vain; not even a visit to the village temple could purge him of his sin of usurping half an acre of the spirit's land. That very night his only son was bitten by a snake and his two bullocks were seized with the murrain. The prayers of the priests saved boy and bullocks and there today stands the shrine that the peasant built in gratitude as witness to the well-founded belief.

No one would take a lease of the village for fear of snake-bite. The old governor, Gurba Pandit, had himself rented it and set forth courageously with many ploughs and oxen to prove the superstition unfounded. The ploughs went merrily to work and the governor reclined comfortably under a fine and spreading banyan tree smoking his *hookah*, reflecting on the follies and whims of men who deserted so beautiful a village with so noble a tree. Lazily he opened his eyes to look into this noble tree and observed an enormous black snake curled round a branch above his head, ready to pounce. Leaving *hookah* and cushions the governor gave one screech, leapt away and fled home on his horse. Bullocks and ploughmen galloped in his wake.

Sleeman's predecessor, Lindsay, also tried to remove the prejudice. Against local protests and warnings he set forth to measure its lands for revenue. This was a fearful temptation to the ghost. Consequently the new measuring cord burst apart at the first stretch on the first field, and poor Lindsay that morning was taken with fever, had to return to Narsinghpore and soon after died. Sleeman was told by villagers who saw it that the cord 'had burst into a thousand pieces.'

On Sleeman repeating the tale to the Sureemunt, the little man strongly opposed his friend's outrageous explanation that on a sodden plain snakes would naturally make their homs on the dry hill where the old village stood. He knew of many villages where the spirits of ancient proprietors had to be propitiated. Sometimes the villagers were bitten by snakes, sometimes possessed by devils and at others thrown down in a fit. Sleeman says:

'They feel little of our mysterious dread of ghosts—a sound drubbing is what they dread from them. . . . In August 1834, while engaged in the twenty-year settlement of the land revenue of the Saugor district, Mr Fraser was about to deliver the lease of the estate made out in the due form to the head of the family, a very honest and respectable old gentleman, who asked him, respectfully, in whose name it had been made out. 'In yours to be sure,' said Fraser, 'Have you not renewed your lease for twenty years?' The old man, in a state of great alarm, begged him to have it altered immediately, or he and his family would all be destroyed—that the spirit of the ancient proprietor presided over the village community and its interests and that all affairs of importance were transacted in his name. 'He is,' said the old man. 'a very jealous spirit and will not admit of any living man being considered, for a moment, as a proprietor or joint proprietor of the estate! It has been held by me and my ancestors immediately under government for many generations, but the lease deeds have always been made out in his name and ours have been inserted merely as his managers, or bailiffs. Were this good old rule, under which we have so long prospered, to be now infringed, we should all perish under his anger.' Mr. Fraser found, upon inquiry, that this had really been the case and, to relieve the old man and his family from their fears, he had the papers made out afresh and the ghost inserted as the proprietor! The modes of flattering and propitiating these beings, natural and supernatural, who are supposed to have the power to do mischief, are endless.'

As in all simple communities, great store was placed on the particular method to be used to placate the gods for their intercession in times of pestilence. In 1823 Narsinghpore and its neighbourhood suffered a terrible visitation of cholera. Naturally the awestruck inhabitants came to the magistrate for advice. Would a silent procession or a noisy one best placate the Deity? Thuggee, who valued his night's rest, strongly recommended a silent one, observing that in all his experience the quiet demonstrations were by far the most efficacious. The advocates of a musical contribution protested loudly, but the magistrate ruled them out of order and decreed that it must be silent. That night the procession glided like shadows through the town and, strangely, the cholera abated and Sleeman slept. But the opposition was not content: it must prove its theory. At one in the morning a few nights later Thuggee awakened to a hideous compound of noises from pots, pans, shells, pistols and muskets. Strangely, the cholera intensified. It followed its fatal course to the last and Sleeman Sahib became a much-respected prophet.

Sureemunt, on hearing this, went one better. He had, he said, in 1826 cast out a violent influenza epidemic from his capital, Pithoria. On that occasion he had the aid of a man learned in such matters. This man caused a small carriage to be made to his own design, harnessed a pair of scape goats to it, and amidst ceremonies drove it out of town to a wood, where the goats were let loose. From that hour the disease ceased in the town. The goats never returned. 'Had they come back,' said Sureemunt, 'the disease must have come back with them, so he took them a long way into the wood—indeed' (he believed), 'to make sure of them the man had afterwards caused them to be offered up as a sacrifice to the shrine of Hardaul Lala, in that very wood.' He had himself never seen a *puja* (religious ceremony) so immediately efficacious as this. Most of its success he attributed to the science of the man who had planned the carriage and driven the goats to the wood.

The Gonds, who were almost naked aborigines, had a great reputation for witchcraft. Among the stories Sleeman heard was one of a Gond woman's cockerel. His friend, Kehri Singh, told him the following story.

A *chaprasi* (office messenger) of Mr. Fraser's was sent out to Mundlah with a message of some kind or other. He took a cock from an old Gond woman without paying for it and, being hungry after a long journey, ate the whole of it in a curry. He heard the woman mutter something, but being a raw, unsuspecting young man he thought nothing of it, ate his cock and went to sleep. He had not been asleep three hours before he was seized with internal pains and the old cock was actually heard crowing in his belly! He made the best of his way back to Jubbulpore, several stages, and all the most skilful men were employed to charm away the effect of the old woman's spell, but in vain. He died, and the cock never ceased crowing at intervals up to the hour of his death.

'And was Mr Fraser convinced?'

'I never heard, but suppose he must have been.'

In 1831 Sleeman gained a tremendous name for himself as a sorcerer in Saugor when he noticed that during a disastrous infestation of rust fungus on the corn, the linseed grown near by was the first to be infected. He advised the peasants to tear out and burn the linseed plants, not knowing what else to advise and being always expected to advise something. To his astonishment the rust vanished. After long investigation he concluded that the rust came on an east wind and the wind must by lucky chance have changed to westerly. However, his name was made, and nothing he could say and no protest would ever lessen his fame. One doubt remained in the peasant's minds—that the pest might have been really due to the British habit of eating the flesh of the cow, the holy symbol, and to the immorality, mainly adultery, of the same ill-conditioned British.

The sporting Rajah of Myhere, an authority on the power of certain men to turn themselves into tigers, told him of many instances where the man transformed had neglected to apprise his family of the magic word to return him to human form. The neglect, it seems, usually led to the tiger eating a kinsman. These tigers were all man-eaters and could, if one had time to look, be easily identified because they had no tails. The Gonds of the jungle were prime magicians in this business. If one offered them twenty rupees they would build a little shrine and sacrifice fowls, goats and pigs every year, but even this was not very effective in the extreme case of men transformed into tigers. It was, of course, infallible where the spirit of a tiger's victim rode on the tiger's head to guide him to his prey.

One day Sleeman inquired if they were likely to find any hare in a shoot.

"Tut, tut, Tut!' said the rajah. 'You will never see a hare if you call him *khargosh* (ass-eared), because that is an insult. If you call him by the pleasant name of *lamkhana* (long-eared), you will never fail to find him.'

CHAPTER 10

From Australia to Ile de France

On 24th April 1824 Sleeman, as a reward for his outstanding services, was gazetted to the rank of brevet captain. He was then assistant to the agent of the governor-general in the Saugor and Nerbudda territories. Unfortunately he was this year struck down time and again by severe attacks of the malaria which had nearly killed him in 1815 at Nathpore. The doctor urged him to take a sea trip, so he applied for eighteen months' leave to New South Wales. In those days of small sailing ships, elementary navigation and uncharted seas this was an enterprising venture, no doubt suggested by the news that his brother George had sailed for Australia with his regiment as lieutenant in the King's 39th, later and Dorsetship Regiment.

His application was granted in April 1825 and Thuggee set out immediately. Next year the brothers met in Australia to their intense joy. No such wonderful thing had been expected, and more welcome still was the news that the 39th was bound for India as its next station. Before meeting George, William had taken boat to the South Seas, and from Tahiti had obtained seeds of a sugracane much superior to that in India. In September 1826 he was back at Calcutta and soon making his way with his previous seeds to Saugor, where he was burning to sow them and see the results. To anticipate, the results were beyond all expectation and earned him the applause of all his peasant friends and the commendation of the Government. He ruefully remarked that his enthusiastic *ryots* (peasants) would probably soon neglect the Tahiti cane, which would then deteriorate to the state of their present variety. Much as he loved them he had no illusion about their constancy as cultivators.

However, he was saved in due time by his discovery of a yet better cane from Mauritius and a still better commodity which came with it.

On 23rd September 1826 he was doubly promoted by being gazetted substantive captain and also advanced to civil charge of a vacant division in the Saugor and Nerbudda territories until given one of the larger districts.

Brother Thomas, in the timber trade at Tenby in Wales and chronically short of money, was all this while a financial burden on William. Before leaving for Australia, therefore, he had succeeded in obtaining a cadetship for Thomas's son, James, so that on 15th April 1826 James arrived in India to join the 46th N.I. later to transfer to the 73rd. Before long the boy came to visit his uncle at Jubbulpore. Uncle William was quite excited to see what sort of son Thomas had sired. This, he found, was a fewsh, simple youth of keen intelligence.

A few days in Uncle William's enthusiastic company, amused by his cheerful banter, a day after partridge, a ride or two among the squires and peasants, a day in the saddle with a spear after pig, and young James was properly afire. Convinced that not only was the Political Service the highest aim of any sensible young soldier of the Bengal Army, but that the extirpation of Thugs was the only ambition worth cherishing, he left Jubbulpore determined to follow Uncle William. He thought of him no longer as a parboiled nabob but as quite the highest type of human being. He sang his praises loudly to doubting relatives at home.

Sleeman was so impressed by his unexpected qualities that he recommended the young man to join his own superlative profession the Indian Political Service—and this in due course the zealous James succeded in doing.

In this year, 1827, there was dynastic trouble in the neighbouring Mahratta State of Gwalior. Sleeman, who was often there on the track of Thugs, wrote a careful account of the affair in a small book. *The story of the Byza Bae,* which he printed himself. Though his account is unique there is no space to include it here. There is, however, a need to give the bare outline, because Thuggee later had much to do with Gwalior's affairs.

The maharajah, Daulat Rao Scindhia, died in March 1827, leaving a widow, the Byza Bae, but no legitimate heir. The Byza Bae ruled as regent, and after much negotiation adopted as heir a young relative of her late husband. This eleven-year-old boy was entitled the Maharajah Jankoji Scindia. With the Byza Bae as regent the boy grew up at the court of Gwalior, and a morose, ill-conditioned, evil youth he became. To his hand lay an instrument of mischief in the always turbulent Gwalior army. Ever rebellious, menacing the peace of the State and the safety of its neighbours, it throve on plunder and marauding. Little by little its leaders worked upon the hatred that the young prince felt for his benefactress, the regent. Finally, in 1833, she detected Jankoji in collusion with the army conspiring to throw her out. Jankoji fled to the British Resident's house hard by—to Mr. Cavendish. The resident, instead of coming down four-square on the side of the Byza Bae and advising Calcutta to rusticate the prince for a period of several years, sent to ask the old lady to pardon him. This she did. So within twenty-four hours the rogue had set himself at the head of the dissidents of the army and she in turn had fled to the residency for refuge. Cavendish lifted not a finger to help her. The prince, knowing now that her life depended on him he, ordered her to leave the State. The unfortunate regent, deserted by the Resident on whom she relied, had to leave at once in humiliating circumstances as an exile for the south of India.

The young Maharajah soon had his army split in fractions about him. Already a match for all in cynical duplicity and intrigue, he set the leaders at loggerheads and exiled his enemies. The only man who came out of the affair with credit was Colonel Alexander, a British adventurer with the Gwalior army, who remained staunchly loyal to the Byza Bae and went with her into exile. He returned and inevitably drank himself to death.

Thuggee, meanwhile, the confirmed bachelor, was utterly engrossed in his Thug campaign and fast working himself to a standstill with this and the immense burden of his civil duties. In April 1828 he rode into Jubbulpore from the fields and the forests of his winter tour, all unaware of the momentious discovery he was about to make for Indian agriculture. From Gwalior and Saugor we must now turn to the Ile de France whence came the best of all sugarcanes.

At Conliege, Baillage de Lons le Saunier, Jura, there lived the ancient and noble family of the Counts Blandin de Chalain who owned estates about the family seat of the Chateau de Fontenne. In 1775 Count Marie Francoise Emmanuel sailed off to the Ile de France (Mauritius). In 1779, foreseeing the coming upheaval in his native land and appreciating the opportunities for a French nobleman in his new island home, he sold his estates in France. The count had a son, one Auguste Blandin de Chalain, who in middle age thought that he might find still further opportunities in India to rebuild his fortunes. He accordingly sent his daughter Amelie Josephine to spy out the land for him. She was very young: in 1828 she was only nineteen when she came to stay with an English family in

Jubbulpore. She found everything quite fascinating, in particular the crops that were grown and the methods the peasants employed, but she had no very high opinion of Captain Sleeman's Tahiti sugarcane. He rode about with her, inspecting his canes. He was disappointed, for she insisted that Ile de France canes were far superior. He asked her to get him some and she sent for the seed post-haste.

Her English was somewhat broken but she managed to make herself understood to the forty-year-old political officer, and he found little difficulty in talking French with her, an exercise that he had not had for many years. The difference in age did not seem in any way to hinder and so, on 14th June 1828, they married in the Jubbulpore church, much to the annoyance of a large drove of young and very eligible officers of all arms in the district. Thuggee proudly took his bride home to his great house with the large walled park where the spotted deer roamed at will.

Amelie was tall with very fair skin and dark brown hair dressed in ringlets. She had a Latin vivacity. That quick intelligence and charm made her a striking young person in any company. Thuggee, the 'confirmed bachelor' of forty, was for ever astonished that this engaging young girl had for one moment considered marrying him. Throughout her life she never really mastered the English tongue and made many a false step to the great amusement of her friends, no less than her own. The fault was partly her husband's for he would more often than not talk to her in his very fluent French and would buy her the latest books from France. When the Mauritius sugarcane flourished and her husband was complemented by the Government on all he had done for agriculture, she pointed out that she had not been such a bad bargain after all. With this William heartily agreed, but continued his industrious life as though there had never been a break in it.

As if to celebrate the great occasion he started to plant an impressive avenue of trees on both sides of the road for the eighty-six miles—as far as from Falmouth to Exeter'—from Jhansee Ghat on the Nerbudda river to Mirzapore on the Ganges. 'I had these planted in 1829; they were watered for twelve years and today (1841) they are fine trees of full growth. The fruit that they bear is every year left for the travellers to enjoy... the trees were planted and nurtured under my direction by former Thugs. They are none the worse for their upbringing.'

CHAPTER 11

Thuggee

Sleeman's Grandson, Colonel Sir James Sleeman, estimates from all reliable records that over a period of three hundred years, forty thousand victims fell annually to the yellow scarf.[1] The bare figures are sufficiently starting to reveal the magnitude of the task confronting Sleeman in 1826. In that year he was given the chief responsibility for tracking down and bringing to justice all Thugs over a wide region, but it was not until 1830, when he held civil charge of the Jubbulpore district, that the Government officially appointed him to prosecute the suppression of Thuggee over the whole of central India.

Until then, having no official authority for his campaign, he had run against manifold obstructions and difficulties. Among the worst with which he had to contend in these early days was the unwillingness of any witnesses to come forward for fear of terrible reprisals, and also because they might be sent to give evidence a thousand miles away in some remote magistrate's court, for Thugs seldom killed anywhere near their homes for fear of identification through the victims' friends and relatives. He succeeded in overcoming these obstacles, firstly by ensuring that he always had a good case and that the accused and his friends would hang or go to jail;, secondly by obtaining legal sanction for courts to try crimes committed in districts outside their jurisdiction and for written evidence, duly authorized, to be sent to distant courts; thirdly, and most important, by winning acceptance that proof of association with a gang of Thugs should warrant imprisonment for life.

Still another source of difficulty lay in the protection afforded Thugs by influential barons and landholders, who drew from them a fine income

[1]Colonel Sir James Sleeman in his book *Thug* gives a detailed account of this terrible profession.

in *douceurs* paid from the loot of the winter campaigns. But by slow degrees Sleeman's success in tracking Thugs and inducing informers to identify their patrons rendered those patrons impotent and brought them within the law.

Unexpected obstacles appeared in well-meaning Company officials, such as Sutherland in Rajputana, who resented the interference of Sleeman's tracking parties inside the territories of the Native States to whose courts they were appointed. These officials were soon brought up with a sharp turn through Sleeman's chief, the agent to the governor-general at Saugor, Carvin Smith, who took the matter straight to the Chief Secretary at Calcutta, Swinton, who in turn went to the governor-general—at that time Lord William Bentinck. It is interesting to note that the Hon. R. Cavendish, of whom we have previously heard, Resident at Gwalior, was also one who impeded the work of Thuggee's informers by well-meant but ill-advised attempts to protect suspects, even those who might give evidence and who had fled to or resided in Gwalior State.

Despite all these difficulties, Sleeman and his assistants had brought to book several hundred Thugs in the four years prior to his official appointment. In 1831 he was transferred from Jubbulpore to Saugor to be nearer the centre of his organization. Bit by bit the Government extended his field of operations. Seven years later it was to spread from Lahore to the Carnatic in the south. Only then was he relieved of all other duties.

By 1832 his system was completely organized over the area he then controlled; later he had only to extend it. The general principle on which he worked in backing his theory that the guild was one complete system was to keep under every officer's hand the latest and most completely detailed information that might link one man with another or one gang with another. Every title of this sort, such as a variation in Thug slang, some kinship or parenthood, was carefully recorded, by slow and painful steps affording the data from which he constructed a genealogical tree and a map showing the spots at which certain gangs had within living memory committed atrocities. Thus he and his men became able in time to forecast the movements of gangs with which they had never had contact into the hunting areas and to localities within those areas. His sepoys, troopers and armed irregulars were directed with a complete knowledge of their quarry's expected identity, strength and movements. Thuggee's early training as a soldier was of untold value. The Government printed from time to time his latest 'trees' and maps for issue to his officers. When one thinks of the almost insuperable obstacles in his way one stands astonished at the firmness of his purpose. Here was a murderous profession, hidden from public view for five hundred years, patronized by powerful men, widespread throughout the land for a thousand miles each way; and these vast regions being

'The legendary origin of Thuggee is this,' says Sleeman:

Kali, the goddess who presided over Thuggee, was worshipped also under the names or Bhowani and Devi. She was the wife of Mahadeo, or Siva, and first appeared on earth on the banks of the Hooghly, at a spot afterwards called, in memory of the event, Kali Ghat, now Calcutta. Here stands her most solemn rites her chief festival, the Durga Puja. They who address her with the greatest reverence style her Kankali, or the 'man-eater,' representing her as quaffing huge draughts of blood from men and demons. When alone, she is depicted as black and hideous of aspect: but in company with her husband she is ever fair and beautiful. Once on a time the world was infested with a monstrous demon named Rukt Bij-danav, who devoured mankind as fast as they were created. So gigantic was his stature, that the deepest pools of the ocean reached no higher than his waist. This horried prodigy Kali cut in twain with her restless demon. For some she went on destroying them, till the hellish brood multiplied so fast that she waxed hot and weary with her endless task. So she paused for a while and, from the sweat brushed off one of their arms, she created two men, to whom she gave a *rumal*, or handkerchief, and commanded them to strangle the demons. When they had slain them all, they offered to return the *rumal*, but the goddess bade them keep it and transmit it to their posterity, with the injunction to destroy all men who were not of their kindred.

A tradition is current among Thugs that about the period of the commencement of the Kali Yug, Bhowani co-operated with them so far as to relieve them of the trouble of tearing the dead bodies, by devouring them herself. On one occasion, after destroying a traveller, the body was, as usual, left unburied; and a novice, unguardedly looking behind him, saw the goddess in the act of feasting upon it, half of it hanging out of her mouth. She, upon this, declared that she would no longer devour those whom the Thugs slaughtered, but she condescended to present them with one of her teeth for a *pickaxe*, a rib for a knife, and the hem of her lower garment for a noose, and ordered them, for the future, to cut and bury the bodies of those whom they destroyed.

White and yellow being considered the favourite colours of their patroness and those in which she is arrayed, the cloths for strangling are of one or other of these to the exclusion, I believe, of all other colours.

The true origin of Thuggee is shrouded in obscurity, but it is said to have sprung from the Sagartii, who contributed 8,000 horses to the army of Xerxes and are described by Herodous in the VIIth book of his History.

These people led a pastoral life; were originally of Persian descent and use that language; their dress is something betwixt the Persian and Pactyan; they have no offensive weapons either of iron or brass, except their daggers; their principal dependence in action is on cords made of twisted leather which they use in this manner: when they engaged an enemy they throw out these cords, having a noose at the extremity; if they entangle in these either horse or man they, without difficulty, put them to death.

There is reason to believe that the descendants of these Sagartii accompanied a Mohamedan invader of India and settled in the neighbourhood of Delhi.

The earliest authentic Indian historical notice of Thuggee is the statement in Zia-ud-Barni's history of Firoz Shah, written in 1850, that about AD 1290 a thousand Thugs were captured at Delhi but that the Sultan with misplaced clemency, refused to sanction their execution, shipped them off to Lakhnaut, and there let them loose. No wonder Bengal was to become a hot-bed of Thuggee in later years! This places the antiquity of Indian Thuggee over five hundred years before it was suppressed. The next mention of Thugs refers to the reign of Akbar (1556-1605), when some five hundred were captured in the Etawah district, always notorious for crime.

Hindus and Muslims in India have for centuries been at enmity, the animosity stemming from the various Muslim conquests of India and the resulting oppression of the Hindus. The strangest aspect of the whole story of Thuggee is the complete burial of this hatchet among the members of the guild, the acceptance by Muslims of the Hindu deities as their spiritual patrons and of Hindu ritual to serve those patrons: on the other and, the ignoring of all Hindu taboos within the gang. The two creeds mixed in this ghastly trade.

The Thugs did not come into the public eye until the British extended their rule; nor, until Sleeman divided it purely by a process of reasoning from causes, was it ever suspected that these people belonged to a distinctive class of murderers and plunderers spread over the whole face of India. Before the British came the local potentates, on the understanding that pillaging and killing by Thugs were only committed in someone else's territory, not only took no notice of their existence but also exacted a commission on the spoils. The Thug spent his summer in ease and unemployment at his home. After the British came and displayed a conscience in these matters, the much aggrieved. Thug was compelled to masquerade in the off-season as a cultivator and frequently had to work as one. The patrons, with some difficulty, continued the protection of the local gangs.

The early Hindus were familiar with the use of the Naga-pasa, or "dragon noose." We find in the epics that the demons who fight with the gods were thus armed. In the Ellora cave-temple, which was constructed about AD 760, we have a Thug represented strangling a Brahmin who is worshipping the emblem of Siva, whereupon the God comes to his rescue and kicks down the Thug.' W. Crooke, *Things Indian*, 1901. See also Appendix 2 concerning the Ellora caves.

In a country such as India of those days it was easy for Thugs to prosecute their trade without discovery. Distances were vast, communications poor and habitation sparse, while their methods were designed especially to avoid detection. In strangling no blood was spilled. Usually no weapon was used other than the strap or handkerchief knotted at both ends to give a better grip for the strangler and his assistant. No intended victim was ever allowed to escape, for if he attempted to, as some did, the sentries standing by with concealed swords promptly cut him down. The gang, usually numbering from twenty to fifty men, moved along the roads in every way furnished as ordinary travellers and all members were carefully schooled to appear as simple but entertaining companions to their fellow passengers. Seldom did a gang kill or plunder within a hundred miles, or even more, of their own homes, so that the disappearance of victims should never be related to these cheerful, dustry travellers. Above all, the whole operation of killing and looting was organized with a meticulous care born of centuries of experience and practice. There is no instance of any European being molested, for the reason that Europeans were traceable. They were few and in positions of responsibility. Thugs did not deal in the easily traceable.

The sons of Thugs and their nephews were gradually inducted into the profession over a period of many years, the final killing being concealed from them until it was certain that they would enthuse over it and keep the secret. The whole ritual, starting long before the gang set out on its winter campaign, was essentially religious. It is hard to realize that the Thugs killed and the Thugs plundered because it was the right, moral, godly thing to do. Of recent times the atavistic atrocities and practices of Mau-Mau and of Nazi Germany illustrate the mentality and convictions of those who soak themselves in wickedness. These horrors impress us with the truth of the tradition of struggle for the soul of man which is supposedly being waged, day in, day out, between God and the Devil. The way of the Devil seems so easy, were man not supplied with some instinct tending him to good. Thus he will try to commit his worst sins in the name of Good. Said a Thug proudly to Sleeman: 'I am a Thug of the royal records. I and my fathers have been Thugs for twenty generations.' This was a royal profession.

Before going forth on their expedition the Thugs would make their oblations to the gods Kali and Bhowani (the goddess of smallpox of the Carnatic), the most object superstition being often associated with the deepest guilt. Omens were taken from the head of a dead sheep, the convulsive movements of mouth and nostrils being noted as propitious or not when a fluid was poured on them. Before they actually left, some of the gang would proceed in the direction they were to take to observe the flight of the birds and to listen to the chirping of lizards. If the omens were ill, then they did the same in other directions and chose the roads that portended the greatest success.

The following were favourable signs: a lizard chirping and a crow making a noise on a living tree on the left side. A tiger appearing was deemed rather a good sign. The noise of a partridge on the right side denoted that they would meet with good booty on the very spot and there accordingly they would halt.

These betokened misfortune: a hare or a snake crossing the road before them; a crow sitting and making a noise on a rock or a dead tree; an ass braying while sitting; an owl screeming; the noise of a single jackal. If a dog should carry off the head of a sheep which they had sacrificed, it a betokened no booty for many years.

As omens were also watched during the campaign itself, the occasional victim has owned his life all unwittingly to an adverse omen. It was unlucky to murder a female or a person of the Kamala caste, metal workers, carpenters, washermen, vagrants, stone-cutters, pot-makers and lepers, also the blind and mutilated or a man driving a cow or female goat. Many a party of travellers have owed their lives to one of these humble souls being among them. There was no difference made between rich and poor, for this was a religious duty and the Thug killed because he was instructed to kill by Kali nevertheless there would be some disappointment when, for instance, the gang went to the trouble of strangling a humble person whose bag contained nothing but the tools of his trade or a cooking-pot.

The method of killing and robbery was firstly for certain specially trained Deceivers (*Sotha*) to make friends with travellers going their own way. By their pleasant manners and their ability to sing and to play music they would beguile the weary miles until the victims had no suspicions and even sought their company. These gangs had immense patience: they would accompany their intended prey for days on end until the perfect opportunity offered for a successful and secret killing. On that day, from a certain point on the route, the scout and the grave-digger would be sent forward to select the *bele* and to dig the graves for their honoured companions of the road. When the whole party gathered around in the evening for a sing-song, the Thugs would place themselves suitably for the killing. It took two stranglers (*Bhartote*) to bind the *rumal* about the neck, and another one (*Chamillii*) behind to jerk out the legs and throw the victim on his face, another dealt him a blow in the most sensitive parts and with a jerk backwards the neck was broken. It all happened in a flash at the *Thirni* of the leader—the death call—usually '*Tamakhu Kha-lo*!' (Scorpion!)—tobacco).

It was necessary that the quarry should be at the time in a suitable posture for strangulation. For instance, it was most difficult to kill a man lying flat in sleep. To bring him into the best posture one of the gang would shout '*Bichu! Bichu!*' (Scorpion!) or '*Sanp! Sanp!*' (Snake!). The sleeper would at once sit up and the final act would take place. Singing, head thrown back, was a very much sought-after position, so Thugs were accomplished in the art and in encouraging others to exercise it.

The dead bodies were piled, then doubled up and buried. If the Thugs were interrupted they covered the dead with sheets and set up a wail for their poor friends suffering from a highly infectious disease. Thereafter, when a well. After burial the Thugs would sit about on top of the graves, continuing their sing-song or planning the next crime. They did not necessarily deal with single men; they would often kill a dozen at one time.

To demonstrate the tenacity, ingenuity and capacity for combination of the members of this strange profession, William Sleeman describes the incident of the murder of a Mogul, a Muslim nobleman and high official. On this occasion a Thug gang had encountered a Mogul officer of noble bearing and handsome countenance, mounted upon a fine horse and attended by numerous servants. A man of high courage and well armed, he considered he had nothing to fear from this party of seemingly respectable Hindus going the same road. They approached him in a respectful manner and attempted to enter into conversation, but the Mogul had heard of Thugs and, thinking it best for this reason to have nothing to do with strangers, ordered them away. Whatever efforts they made to overcome his suspicions the Thugs found unavailing. Recognizing the futility of persistence, they took their leave and dropped behind.

Next morning the Mogul overtook other travellers—this time Muslims like himself but actually Thugs—who impressed upon him the dangers of the road, and the necessity for travellers keeping together for mutual security. They expressed the hope that they might be permitted to take advantage of the protection of such a well-armed party which was going the same way. The Mogul, however, was determined to have no strange companions and made this perfectly plain, even to the extent of threatening them with his sword. As he also had a bow and a quiver full of arrows over his shoulder and a brace of pistols in his waist belt, the Thugs thought that discretion was the better part of valour and departed.

But nothing diverted these human beasts of prey, and that evening other Thugs lodged in the same *sarai* (native inn) as the Mogul, and this time succeeded in ingratiating themselves with his butler and groom. His march was resumed the following morning and his party soon overtook the very same Thugs who had shared the *sarai*, and who, with their usual cunning, had left before the Mogul's party. They began to talk with the traveller's servants. The Mogul took exception to this and ordered them away, but his servants interceded for them, stating that these were respectable men and that they needed company. Their plea proved unavailing, however, and the Thugs were compelled to admit defeat for the third time. But they were not easily daunted and had not only prepared for this contingency but had by now actually completed their arrangements for the murder, even to the preparation of the graves.

The following day, in the midst of a wide and uninhabited plain, the Mogul's party came upon five poor Muslim sepoys sitting weeping by the side of a dead companion—Thugs with a victim they had recently killed. They said that their companion had died from exhaustion—his grave was ready but they were poor unlettered men, unable to repeat the funeral service from the holy Koran. They requested that His Highness should perform this last office for them. Such an appeal from coreligionists could not be refused and the Mogul, dismounting, saw that all was made ready for the burial. As, however, it was improper to perform this solemn service while armed, he removed his weapons and washed his feet, hands and face that he might not pronounce the holy words in an unclean state. This done, he knelt and began to repeat the funeral service with a Thug on either side, and the others a few paces behind with the servants, ostensibly to see that they did not interrupt the Good Samaritan at his devotions.

All being now ready, the leading Thug gave the signal, the *rumals* were thrown round the necks of the victims, and a few moments later the Mogul and his servants were not only dead but lying in their previously prepared graves.

Sleeman makes his assessment:

What constitutes the most odious feature in the character of these murderers is that, prodigal as they are of human life, they can rarely claim the benefit of even the palliating circumstance of strong pecuniary temptation. They are equally strangers to compassion and remorse: they are never restrained from the commission of crimes by commiseration for the unfortunate traveller and they are exempted from the compunctive visitings of conscience, which usually follow, sooner or later, the steps of guilt. Thuggee, they observe with cold indifference blended with a degree of surprise when questioned on this subject, is their business which, with reference to the tenets of fatalism, they conceive themselves to have been preordained to follow. By an application of the same doctrine they have compared themselves, not inaptly, to tigers, maintaining that as these ferocious beasts are impelled by irresistible necessity and fulfil the designs of nature in preying on other animals, so the appropriate victims of the Thugs are men, and that the destiny of those whom they kill 'was written on their foreheads.' A Thug will never kill a tiger, and believes that no man who has violated this rule ever survived long. They believe that no tiger will ever kill a Thug unless he has secreted some booty or cheated some of the gang out of their just share. A mere tyro or under-strapper, they think a tiger may well kill, provided he be not of good Thug descent.

This state of moral insensibility and debasement is calculated to give birth to pity, while it aggravates the horror with which we contemplate their atrocities. It ought not to be forgotten that, unlike many who adopt criminal courses, the Thugs had not previously to divest themselves of upright principles to oppose their practice to their feelings; but that, on the contrary, having been trained up from their childhood to the profession, they acquired habits unfitting them for honest and industrious exertion; that a detestable superstition lent its sanctions to their enormities; and that they did but obey the instructions and imitate the examples of their fathers.

Many will wonder why Indians themselves never revealed this extraordinary trade. But we have seen that influential men were concerned to conceal it. It must be remembered too that besides Thuggee there were very many other ways by which travellers were meeting a violent death. These ways—or some of them—will appear in due course in these pages. They amounted to a widespread prevalence of violence on the roadways and in the countryside, which persisted in addition to the plundering armies of Mahrattas, Afghan chieftains, Pindaris, Rohillas and other freebooters. In such chaotic conditions no Indian prince would ever have thought of organizing a police force for his roads. As Sleeman points out, these rulers had no sense of duty towards their subjects. Between campaigns their disbanded soldiery took their weapons with them and went a-plundering. It must be recalled that even in the days of the great Emperor Akbar there was constant fighting over the face of India during the frequent violent rebellions. What was a little matter of Thuggee committed hundred of miles from home among all this chaos?

CHAPTER 12

Killers' Patchwork

Sleeman's campaign was now under way. From his first remarkable success he culled from his captives not only information but also a selection of spies or informers, whereby he started the building up of the 'family trees' and maps of slaughter places. With these spies he picked up the occasional small band of Thugs. He was taking his first bites out of the enemy forces, but he well knew that he was only nibbling at the edges until his 'trees' and maps were better filled. He and 'Sleeman's young men,' as they were termed, enthusiastically busied themselves on these two works. Gradually (to the crusaders, exasperatingly slowly) they took form.

In 1829 Captain Borthwick, the energetic political agent in Malwa, was summoned urgently to Rutlam State to look into the murder of five men by Bhil tribesmen. Borthwick rode hotfoot to Rutlam with one of Thuggee's spies at his stirrup, for the unusual atrocity of the crime gave him to think that the Bhil aboriginals had taken to new ways. He went straight to the scene, taking with him the police inspector from Rutlam. A glance at the scene of the crime near the main road at once convinced him that no Bhil had been concerned in this. Without wasting any more time he inquired from villagers as to who had passed that way. He learnt that seven days before a large body of pilgrims had travelled along the highway, returning to their homes after visiting a shrine in Gujerat. Borthwick reckoned that even at the leisurely pace at which they were travelling they must by then be at least one hundred miles on their way. He turned to the policeman and directed him to ride off after these wayfarers and arrest the lot.

'Sahib, what can one man do against hundreds You know we have no mounted sepoys here. I have only these three horsemen—irregulars!'

'You know your hob, inspector. Count on me for all support whatever you do. I'll write you a note now describing the gang and its leader—and here's an authority to requisition help from any village on the way.'

He wrote out the description from what the villagers had told him and, taking a roll of records from his saddle-bag, picked out the gang that he believed this to be and gave his inspector full particulars of its leaders. He pointed to the very shallow graves in which the bodies had been interred and said: 'You can see from this that these Thugs have for years let their murders be attributed to the Bhils. Possibly they're over-confident, so be bold.' The inspector took horse and Borthwick turned off the high road to Jaora, where he had another case to investigate.

As he trotted on the inspector turned the matter over in his head, knowing that only by a ruse could one man capture a hundred. Discretely, at village after village, he inquired of his quarry. Tenaciously he stuck to the scent through six days until, at Dekhola, a hundred and fifty miles from his start, he picked up information that the pilgrims were just ahead of him. This was only a hamlet and the headman could not supply him with any young men. Rather than appear with a few rustics armed with staves, the inspector resolved to challenge the Thugs himself, armed with the Company's authority. Recalling that the Government had established a strict monopoly of opium over the district, and that Borthwick had posted enforcement troops at important defiles, he had already made up his mind how to act. He trotted on and found the travellers sheltering from the midday sun in a mango grove.

He drew up alongside the little group, which he knew to contain the leader, his heart bumping somewhat as he saw the danger in which he had placed himself.

'Salaam,' he cried.

Umrao, the leader whom Borthwick had designated from Sleeman's records, returned the greeting with cordiality.

'I am an inspector of the Opium Prevention. You have contraband opium in your possession and troopers from Bhulwara have been ordered to take you back there.'

'We're pilgrims! But here you are—here's all our baggage. Search it—see for yourself.'

'Maybe. But for all that you'll have to come back to Bhulwara, otherwise the British agent will send out cavalry to bring you in. You'll be in trouble then for evading the Customs, whether you've opium or not. So pick up your bundles and come.

The courageous inspector now had before him a two-day march in company with this bloodthirsty gang. His one assurance was that if he went missing the whole of the Company's resources would be mobilized to hunt down his murderers. This the Thugs knew also. That night he slept in a village headman's house and no harm befell. The gang (and he) knew well that they were innocent of opium traffic, but their leaders were very willing to be given a clean bill from a British officer. It would later safeguard them on their way.

The policeman rode ahead into Bhulwara and there alerted the detachment. On the gang's arrival it was at once surrounded. He now decided boldly to play his last card. Confronting them, he openly charged them with being Thugs and said he must take them to Captain Borthwick. They loudly protested their innocence, their leader pushing under the inspector's nose a passport which gave him British protection as a traveller. This was daunting at first, but the inspector put his trust in Borthwick and marched them off. Very soon one of them straggled behind. A constable accosted him, then brought him to the inspector. This man whispered the truth—they were all Thugs. He had lost confidence and turned approver. At the next village, the inspector having procured him a horse, the two rode off away from the gang and then hard for Jaora where the prize was delivered to Borthwick.

The approver's appearance acted like magic. Before long he was taking the political agent and local villagers to all the belles round about. Bodies were being identified and the whole gang incriminated by this man, Khaimraj, a blacksmith by trade. In this unfinished season alone the gang had killed close on eighty people. This one haul sent Sleeman's investigations and plans forward in one great leap, and better still proved to himself and his assistants that his careful documentation would yield remarkable results. From utter darkness they had voyaged through into the twilight.

In the white bungalow at Saugor, with his messengers going and coming, Sleeman was not yet confident of success. It was 1830, the cold weather had gone, the intense heat of spring was past, the rains had broken in full pelt and all around him the parched, cracked earth was soaking up the moisture and clothing itself in a bright garment of green.

The trees shone fresh and the blossom broke out in the forests. Thuggee sat at his table with scraps of paper scattered about him. He was fitting together the season's reports.

Somewhere in the great oceans and in the deep lakes there are monsters of whose existence every now and then some shadowy rumours reach the outside world. In the ocean of crime that he was searching there appeared every now and then the mistry form of some man who was at the centre of the whole wickedness in central India. For months Thuggee had been puzzling his head over this personage and he was now tracking him through the papers. He was somehow convinced that if he could bring this criminal down the whole structure would collapse over a wide area. He had felt along the branches and his hand was on the stem, perhaps on one of the roots. And now every morning before he started work he would continue this search in the records. The rains were half gone when he took a clean sheet of paper and on it wrote:

Rai Sing, an impecunious landowner, owed 18,000 rupees in taxation. Residing at his house was a kinswoman, of Brahmin caste, then in an advanced stage of pregnancy. To compel payment from the recalcitrant debtor a native regiment, officered by Europeans, was sent to seize him. Rai Sing had put his house into a state of defence, garrisoned by his own tenants and by all unemployed rogues for miles around. The house was assaulted, taken and burnt and his kinswoman prematurely gave birth to a son. In biblical fashion she named the child Feringheea, in memory of the Feringhees or Europeans of the attacking force.

Feringheea is therefore a man of high birth and of means and has no need to pursue the profession of a Thug for a living. He is of attractive personality, fine intelligence, soft voice, debonair and handsome. This is the man whom you are to hunt until he is brought to the gallows. His influence is great and with his capture central India will be cleared of Thugs. I believe that we came close to seizing him last autumn and again this spring, but we have never had a sight of him.

He handed the document to Amelie. 'At last I know who my enemy is.'

She glanced at it and begged him to be careful of his own life. But the hope she had was small.

The hunt for Feringheea was now Sleeman's own and he pursued him with that extreme tenacity and certainty of success with which he assaulted every task he undertook. But this one was particularly his own, to be fulfilled without ruth or mercy. He passed his note to the clerk to copy and to send out to all his officers.

Between and weaving across the hunters and the Thug quarry were a variety of other murderous organizations which continually threw Sleeman and his men off the scent. Paradoxically, it was the very peace and order brought by the British to India that for a time encouraged and increased these malefactors. On the one hand, the better roads and the security from freebooting troopers led to many more of the inhabitants enjoying the new freedom to visit far places and distant relatives; on the other, the disbanding of the armies and of the bloated civil establishments of chieftains great and small, as the Company's power advanced, left numbers of men without employment and sent them to seek enlistment with violent gangs or to wander harmlessly with their families looking for work from place to place along these same roads.

Here is Sleeman's account of a crime committed by a family of Daturias, the highway poisoners, on an old *faqir* (ascetic) and his little son at their hut beside the humble shrine that he tended.

'I sent for him (the old *faqir*) and requested him to tell me his story, and I might perhaps be able to trace the murderers. He did so and a Persian writer took it down while I listened with all the coldness of a magistrate, who wanted merely to learn facts and have nothing whatever to do with feelings. This is his story literally:

'I reside in my hut by the side of the road a mile and a half from the town and live upon the bounty of travellers and people of the surrounding villages. About six weeks ago, I was sitting by the side of my shrine after saying prayers with my only son, about ten years of age, when a man came up with his wife, his son and his daughter, the one a little older and the other a little younger than my boy. They baked and ate their bread near my shrine and gave me flour enough to make two cakes. This I prepared and baked. My bow was hungry and ate one cake and a half. I ate only half a one for I was not hungry. I had a few days before purchased a new blanket for my boy and it was hanging in a branch of the tree that shaded the shrine, when these people came. My son and I soon became stupefied. I saw him fall asleep and I soon followed. I awoke again in the evening and found myself in a pool of water. I had sense enough to crawl towards my boy! I found him still breathing and I sat by him with his head in my lap, where he soon died. It was now evening and I got up and wandered about all night picking up straws—I know not why, I was not yet quite sensible. During the night the wolves ate my poor boy. I heard this from travellers, and went and gathered up his bones and buried them in the shrine. I did not quite recover till the third day, when I found that some washer-women had put me into the pool, and left me there with my head out in the hopes that this would revive me; but they had no hope of my son. I was then taken to the police of the town, but the landholders had begged me to say nothing about the poisoners, lest it might get them and their village community into trouble. The man was tall and fair, and about thirty-five; the woman short, stout and fair, and about thirty; two of her teeth projected a good deal; boy's eyelids were much diseased.'

'All this he told me without the slightest appearance of emotion, for he had not seen any appearance of it me or my Persian writer, and a casual European observer would perhaps have exclaimed: 'What brutes these natives are! This fellow feels no more for the loss of his only son than he would for that of a goat!' But I knew the feeling was there. The Persian writer put up his paper and closed his inkstand; and the following dialogue, word for word, took place between me and the old man.

'What made you conceal the real cause of your boy's death, and tell the police that he had been killed as well as eaten by the wolves?'

'The landholders told me that they could never bring back my boy to life and the whole village would be worried to death by them if I made mention of the poison.'

'And if they were to be punished for this they would annoy you?'

'Certainly. But I believe they advised me for my own good as well as their own.'

'And if they should turn you away from that place, could you not make another?'

'Are not the bones of my poor boy there; and the trees that he and I planted and watched together for ten years?'

'Have you no other relations? What became of the boy's mother?'

'She died at that place when my boy was only a child and he has been poisoned for the sake of the blanket.'

(Here the poor old man sobbed as if his heartstrings would break, and I was obliged to make him sit down on the floor while I walked up and down the room.)

'Had you any children before?'

'Yes, sir, we had several, but they all died before their mother. We had been reduced to beggary by misfortunes and I had become too weak and ill to work. I buried my poor wife's bones by the side of the read where she died, raised the little shrine over them, planted the trees, and there have I sat ever since by her side, with our poor boy in my bosom. It is a sad place for wolves and we used often to hear them howling outside; but my poor boy was never afraid of them when he knew I was near him. God preserved him to me till the sight of the new blanket, for I had nothing else in the world, made these people poison us! I bought it for him only a few days before when the rains were coming on, out of my savings—it was all I had.' (The poor old man sobbed again and sat down while I paced the room, lest I should sob also; my heart was becoming a little too large for its apartment.) 'I will never,' continued he, 'quit the bones of my wife and child, and the tree that he and I watered for so many years. I have not many years to live; there I will spend them, whatever the landholders may do—they advised me for my own good, and will never turn me out.'

'I found all that the poor man stated to be true; the man and his wife had mixed poison with the flour to destroy the poor old man and his son for the sake of the new blanket which they saw hanging in the branch of the tree and carried away with them. The poison used on such occasions is commonly the *datura*, and it is sometimes given in the *hookah* to be smoked, and at others in food. The intention is almost always to destroy life, as 'dead men tell no tales'; but the poisoned people sometimes recover, as in the present case, and lead to the detection of the poisoners.'

The impunity with which this crime was everywhere perpetrated, and its consequent increase in every part of India, were among the greatest evils with which the country was at this time afflicted. These poisoners were spread all over India and were as numerous over the Bombay and Madras presidencies as over that of Bengal. There was no road free from them and throughout India there must have been many hundreds who gained their subsistence by this trade alone.

Much more could be said about the Daturias, but Sleeman's personal experience tells the essence of all.

Megpunnaism was the Anglo-Indian term for the murder of parents in order to steal the children. The original term derives from *nekh*, a peg, and *phansna*, to hang.

In November 1833, the British chaplain at Delhi, Mr Everest, was out for his morning ride when he came upon the bodies of three men and two women tied up in bundles and lying on the bank of the Jumna river. Delhi was at this time under native rule with a lacing of British in the administration. Everest rode back and told the assistant magistrate, Lawrence, who gathered up some police and rode out to examine the bodies, taking with him one of Sleeman's Thug informers. This Thug at once disclaimed any responsibility for the dead on behalf of his fraternity. 'It was,' he said, 'altogether too clumsy and must have been done by men new to the trade and very awkward. For instance, the bodies would never have been left exposed and in such a position: the strangling cords would not have been left about the victims' necks nor such clumsy knots have been tied.' Lawrence rode round inquiring, and decided that a gang of people called Bauris who had passed that way the day before must have done this. He sent the Thug with a party of Sleeman's sepoys off on one road and the police on another. The native officer with the latter, when passing through nearby Paharganj soon after dark, heard a faint cry for help from someone by the side of the road. He jumped into the bushes and felled a man who was holding a young girl in his arms, trying to silence her. His police secured the man.

The girl led them a short distance off the road where they surrounded a gang of eight men who had with them six children, most of them two to three years old. On the ground lay two dead women. One of the kidnapped children was a boy of fourteen, so the whole story came out. The families had fallen on hard times and these men had come to their parents and offered to escort them to Kurnaul where employment was to be obtained. By night they murdered the parents and stole the children, whom in good time they were going to sell or else to use as their own mistresses.

When the gang was finally rounded up there were women among them, and these very women had in the past been abducted as girls and kept by the men. The most gruesome aspect of the case was that these women, whose parents had been murdered by those men, were now their accomplices in similar murders. Sleeman questioned them himself and gives their replies.

'Where were your parents murdered?'

Radha: 'Near the village of Dunkari in the Bulandshahr district.'

'How many Thugs were present on this occasion?'

'Between forty and fifty.'

'Did you witness the murder of your parents?'

'No, they were murdered during the night and I and my two young brothers were entrusted to the charge of the female Thug, and we were offered for sale a few days afterwards to some gypsies, who would not give a sufficient sum for me, and I was subsequently adopted by Salga Jemadar, a relation of Khema.'

'Have you ever heard anything of your two brothers since the murder of your parents?'

'No.'

'You have been in the habit of accompanying your adopted husband on Thuggee since you have been living with him?'

'Yes. I have been on three or four expeditions with him.'

'A poor Faqirni woman was murdered in your house at Jonli eight or nine months ago; did you feel no compunction in taking charge of her children during the time your husband was employed in strangling her?'

'I was compelled to obey the orders of my husband, who directed me to prevent the children from making a noise.'

This simple interrogation is enough to indicate the ways and objects of Megpunnaism. It is astonishing that one of these guilds of which we have thus far spoken was aware of the existence of still another, the Tasma-Baz Thugs, whose criminal activity was invented by an Irishman. Sleeman is again the best authority:

'The Tasma-Baz Thugs were the fruit of European civilization grafted on the Asiatic stock. At the commencement of the present century one Greagh, a private in an English regiment stationed at Cawnpore, initiated these natives of low degree into the mysteries of an art formerly practised by thimble-riggers in England, and known as "pricking the garter." The game, designated Tasma-Bazi by his Hindu disciples, was played in this manner: A double strap being rolled and folded, a bystander was requested to insert a stick between any two folds. When the ends were pulled, the strap either came free or was held at the double, this deciding loss or gain. Greagh's apostles speedily became the leaders of gangs. Their first act was to conciliate the police, which was effected by payment of one-fourth of their profits. Freed thus from risk of molestation, they would meet as if strangers to one another at some frequented spot and begin to play. A crowd would gather and someone or another was certain to try his fortune.

At first he was, of course, allowed to win, but he rarely escaped being fleeced of his last coin. They did not solely rely on sleight of hand. When opportunity offered they added murder to robbery. Their ordinary method was by means of medicated sweetmeats pressed upon the unwary who ventured to play. The drug mostly used was expressed from the seed of the *datura* plant. The name Thugs was a misnomer, for they had none of the religious motives and rites of that ancient fraternity. They were simply organized bands of worthless characters, who preferred fraud and murder to labour. Their detection must have occurred earlier had not the police been bribed to connive. Needless to say their practices were no sooner discovered by the British magistrate than their occupation was gone.'

With all these gangs of killers operating across, among and over the tracks of the real Thugs it is hardly surprising that Sleeman and his small band were heavily overworking themselves in the pursuit of the main quarry. Little by little, from captures such as that at Delhi, they became able to disentangle quickly each thread from the others and to reveal the whole web of iniquity.

CHAPTER 13

Feringheea

All through 1830 thuggee and his men were fast on the trail of their devil incarnate, Feringheea, the Prince of Thugs. Now that all knew for whom they were searching they concentrated their resources purposefully on this one end alone, their spies working out every possible approach that their opponent might take. Sleeman looked back through his records during that rainy season, to find that only once had the name of Feringheea been mentioned and that too by a Thug from the deep south. It was down there his search had been directed—misdirected, hc now knew. But though he had been striking there at a phantom, he also knew that the many small captures had knocked chip after chip off the real man's age-old organization and that so elaborate a system could not be repaired in a day. If he could not tear the whole of Feringheea's structure to bits and dig him out as one dug out a queen white ant from the nest, all naked and shivering to the light, he could at least whittle away the colony. His men had already dealt blow after resounding blow; they must not rest satisfied, the strokes must be swifter, heavier and more frequent. These were his orders. They went out to his officers. He hated, loathed the beast he was chasing with such inexorable energy. The annual bouts of fever that the rains brought he brushed aside as a mere passing nuisance, not to be allowed to delay him by one minute.

By early November reports were passing between watchers that the Thugs were on the move. Sleeman shifted his headquarters to Jubbulpore, 'more centrical,' as he termed it, for his operations. Early one morning an agent came in to him in a breathless hurry to report that Feringheea had come with his family to a village not far away; apparently to organize the coming season of Thug incursions. Thuggee sent the agent with a mounted orderly to warn the nearest police post to move off that night, surround the house where Feringheea was known to be sleeping and bring him in. 'And remember this,' said Thuggee, 'the family is almost as important as the husband. Get me them, if you, can't get him, and I will have him in jail before winter's gone. Go out after him but don't miss them !'

Sleeman doubted whether he ought not to have gone himself but he had urgent administrative work on hand, so he resolved to put confidence in his Indian subordinate. Two days later there appeared at his office a small cortege of two palanquins and an escort. He took a glance at the group. This wasn't Feringheea. He went out into the sun.

'Sahib,' said the policeman, saluting, 'Feringheea's mother, wife and child. The Thug escaped us.'

Sleeman's inquiries showed him that the guard had been clumsy. They had reached the house where Feringheea was sleeping precisely at midnight, but being mainly new men and *najibs* or irregulars, they had started whispering among themselves. Before the patrol leader knew, Feringheea was out and away by the backdoor. When the *najibs* entered his bedroom they found lying on the bed an English blunder-buss and pistol, both loaded. The patrol commander was almost in tears at his failure, but Thuggee, who was confident that persistence would win the day, simply congratulated him on securing the family. The political officer thus made another loyal retainer .

'Have we not got Jhurhu, Feringheea's foster-brother, still here? Tell him that his mother is here,' Sleeman ordered.

Jhurhu was a Thug leader whom Sleeman had condemned to death along with ten others for particularly atrocious crimes. He was due to be executed the next morning. Just before going to the scaffold, therefore, he saw his foster-mother and the interview took place in Sleeman's presence.

'He fell at the old woman's feet and begged that she would relieve him of the obligation of the love with which she had nourished him and the care with which she had cherished him from infancy, as he was about to die before he could fulfil any of them. She placed her hand on his head and his brow and said she forgave him all and bade him die like a man.'

Feringheea's family were comfortably ensconced in the jail. It was quite certain that the Thug chief would not go far while those so dear to him were in jail at Jubbulpore or Saugor. And so it proved. Thuggee moved the family to jail in Saugor and went there himself.

One fine morning, after a stealthy stalk, a patrol disguised as travellers sighted the gang they were looking for about ten miles from Bhilsa, and lay in observation while they sent back for reinforcements. They recognized this platoon of forty men as Feringheea's own bodyguard, probably now moving to link up with other parties before lighting out on the serious operations of the season. The patrol stopped and took position on a little hillock overlooking a stream which flowed through bushes not far from the highway. The Thugs had made off the road here and were now bathing themselves, washing off the dust in the cool, clear water. The patrol commander thought he could single out the tall, swashbucking figure of the leader.

Feringheea entered the stream and with his *lotah* had begun bailing the water over his shoulders when he heard what he thought must be the call of the *chiriya* (the owlet) from a tree above his head. He looked up and listened. He heard it again but not a third time. He resumed his, bath with one eye on the chief augur, Kurhora, who was towelling himself on a patch of grass on the sandy bank, gazing intently up into the tree, a hand to his ear. Suddenly he tied his towel round his waist and ran to Feringheea.

'The *chiriya* has called, master! The *chiriya*!' He pointed into the tree. 'We cannot stay here, we cannot stay!' His voice rising in fear, 'We must turn back at once, back to our homes! Come, master! Summon the Thugs !'

'Quiet, Kurhora! Don't alarm the men. Don't rush. For the sake of Devi we must not abandon our work. We have eight innocents here and much *bunji* (booty). We can't abandon these! We must have them!'

'Master, no! We must run! Never ignore the *chiriya:* it is a terrible omen!'

'Away with you, Kurhora! The call of the *chiriya* was for the future, not for today. Let us go on to Saugor. By then we will gain touch with our other friends and then we can alter all our plans. This I have done before and have had great success.'

The augur hesitated and then with resignation and fearing to rouse the sharp temper of his leader replied' As you will, roaster, but I am not happy.'

The cheerful band ended their bath, packed up and straggled along towards Saugor taking their hostages and their *bunji* along with them, followed at a respectful distance by another party of travellers.

They had not gone far when they halted at the village of Marri for the evening meal. Laying their bundles on the ground, they stripped down to the loin-cloth to eat their food in the warm evening. Feringheea, still mindful of Kurhora's warning, bethought him to walk over, half dressed as he was, to find out from the village headman if there were any danger to be feared in these regions, for he was already feeling a little sensitive while in the neighbourhood of the man he most hated, his relentless persecutor Thuggee Sleeman. Bold as he might wish to appear to his followers, he had no desire to thrust his head into the Lion's jaws, although he fully realized the immense prestige he would gain throughout all India by singeing the lion's beard. He had enough conceit to believe that he could do this with impunity. Twice before he had snapped up his prey and twice got away from the white sahib's grasp.

He tied his horse to a tree hard by the gang and sauntered off to the *Patel's* house. Here he engaged the good man in a casual conversation about affairs of the countryside, asking if any parties of murderous vultures such as Thugs had passed that way and why the Saugor sepoys were not out to look after the roads. Suddenly he heard a great uproar and saw his horse galloping through the village. He ran back towards his men. Then he spotted the foot police in among the gang, laying about them and trussing his Thugs up like chickens. With his usual presence of mind he chased after his horse and away from the *mellee*. Out beyond the village he called it and caught it, mounted and was off, half naked as he was, for the wide countryside and the broken ravines.

He rode all that night fast and far, away from Saugor, making towards Jhansi for a Thug rendezvous of misfortune. He was now the hunted, no longer the one who preyed upon the helpless: he now was the helpless. Turn where he would, there was no succour. He was being strangled by that white devil away in Saugor who had his wife and children at his mercy. This morning he had been sure that he and his men could bribe or terrify their way into the jail and recover the innocent hostages. Now? A bare dribble of demoralized refugees one by one straggled into his rendezvous; that was all—twelve out of forty and these twelve a pack of whining pariahs. He told them so and he left them to forage alone. Undaunted but without hope, he left by himself on foot to be near the cage where his birds were imprisoned. Somewhere he might come upon another band that he could lead. If he could not rescue his dear ones, he could kill and kill and kill; he would seek a revenge on his enemy such as had never before been seen and none would ever see again. Feringheea's vengeance would be remembered for ever. His handful of wretches had clamoured against him: almost, his life had been threatened, but they dared not act; he had tried to laugh away the disaster but the laugh had been hollow and his throat dry. They were no longer his. Racked with anxiety for his dear ones he strode steadily on, alone—no, not quite alone—he could not even be alone. Sleeman's eyes were on him. He left the main road and took to by-lanes leading to a litter of villages where he had relatives. From, there he could spy out the land and recruit a new band, a band of men, not slaves and cowards as he knew most of his former companions to be.

Sleeman's finger wandered over the map towards Bhilsa. 'No, he would not stay there,' he said to the police inspector beside him. 'We, will make our next cast towards Jhansi, to that Thug assembly place on our map. Ride off and collect a strong patrol from Jhansi and visit the rendezvous. On the way leave a couple of approvers—the Thugs Dhan Sing and Soghar—with a runner to watch and report, at that, group of villages just here, dabbing a finger on the map. 'If Feringheea has left the rendezvous, move on to these villages and watch.'

Off went the policeman, and Thuggee walked quickly across to his court-room to try a small gang of his particular pests. A Thug, Amir Ali, leaves this record of him: 'A tall noble-looking person he was, and from the severe glance he cast on me I thought my hour has come, and that very night I should cease to exist.'

Feringheea walked swiftly on until he came to the village of Kisrai, not far east of Saugor, where he would find sanctuary. Thuggee had warned his patrol commanders that this Thug never spent more than two successive nights in any village. The police inspector and four men followed hard on the trail, for the runner had told him that Feringheea was in one of a close group of five villages. The approver, Dhan Sing, met the police at a village eight miles short of the group and the party set out directly after nightfall for the first village. Here they drew a blank, so seized and bound the headman, left him under two sentries and hastened on two miles to the next. Drawing another blank they did the same thing to this headman. The inspector had thus expended his four men as sentries, but continued two miles farther with Dhan Sing until they picked up Soghar, the second approver, with whom they passed to the fourth village, Kisrai, whither Soghar had tracked Feringheea a few hours earlier. This was their last chance, for the alarm would spread to the fifth VIllage at day-break, and day-break was near.

Soghar indicated the house. He and Dhan Sing crept up, charged the door down and fell upon Feringheea. The inspector had not yet arrived. The tough Thug could have strangled both these youngsters with no trouble at all, but he was so confounded that he made hardly any resistance and by the time the inspector came up they had him :- bound and helpless.

Bound and helpless, he was delivered into Sleeman's hands at Saugor jail in December 1830. All that waited him now was the process of trial: the certainty of sentence and the gallows. In a solitary cell he lay for a few days, Sleeman completely ignoring his existence.

One bright morning in January 1831 there was a concourse of curious people standing round the great tree in the Saugor court compound. Among a group of armed police there stood a tall man, shackled ankles to wrist. He was the centre of interest. He appeared very tired but he maintained his dignity, while some quality within him seemed to keep the crowd silent and at a distance. A police inspector broke away from the group and walked into the court-room where Captain Sleeman was sitting.

'Your Honour, I have brought Thug Feringheea. Shall I march him in?'

'Yes, bring him in,' and turning to his clerk: 'Now you will see Shaitan (the Devil] himself.' Sleeman picked up a thick file, placed it before him and started to study it.

The guard marched the prisoner in.

'Sahib, Thug Feringheea,' announced the inspector.

Sleeman went on reading as though this prisoner were of no account. The minutes ticked on till at last the British magistrate looked up at the man before him. With a slight start Thuggee realized that this limb Satan, whom he loathed beyond all things, had dignity, self-possession, and commanded attention. Looking casually out of the window he asked the Thug in Hindustani why he had come—what he wanted. Feringheea replied evenly that he had come to demand the release of his family whom Sleeman held unlawfully, and to tell him that he himself, an innocent man, had been seized by the police and dragged to Saugor by force.

'Yes,' said Sleeman, 'your family is indeed in my hands.'

He then turned on Feringheea and, using his own Ramasi slang, accused him of his crimes, exactly enumerating them deed by deed and by place of commission. For half an hour the prisoner stood before him dumbfounded as Sleeman talked. He then sent his staff from the room; alone, he offered Feringheea his life if he would turn approver. Putting his watch before him, Sleeman gave him one minute to reply.

With a feeling of repulsive wonder the Englishman gazed for that one minute at the strong, delicate, wicked hands that had dealt out death to so many harmless, innocent, even good people. Was he right in granting this man his life on any terms at all? Only if it meant as it did the obliteration of his ancient guild and the saving of thousands of other men's lives.

As Sleeman was about to call the guard in, Feringheea gave way. The game was played and ended.

As with a Japanese soldier, so with him: he at once became the loyal servant of his captor. No approver was more eager to betray his comrades, none more zealous to disclose the secrets of his trade, than Feringheea, Brahmin, one-time Prince of Thugs.

In his last expedition Feringheea and his gang had in a few weeks killed one hundred men and five women. But this was not exceptional. Twenty Thugs admitted to having taken part in an average of two hundred and fifty-six murders each during their career, and those careers, be it remembered, had been cut short by the anti-Thug police.

Sleeman, after hard bargaining with the Government, obtained a pardon for Feringheea and later made full use of him, particularly in Jaipore. At this time William and Amélie Sleeman were encamped at the village of Selohda, about thirty miles out of Saugor, for he was on tour in his district. Feringheea offered to show Sleeman straight away the honesty of his professions, so he was escorted out to the agent's camp. Sleeman writes:

'I was about to pass on my tour of the district, and he would [he said] show me his ability inclination to give me correct information. My tents were pitched where tents usually are, in the small mango grove. I reached them in the evening and when I got up in the morning he pointed out three places in which he and his gang had deposited at different intervals the bodies of travellers. A Pundit and six attendants murdered in 1818 lay among the ropes of my sleeping tent, a havildar and four sepoys murdered in 1824 lay under my horses, and four Brahmin carriers of Ganges water and a woman murdered soon after the Pundit lay within my sleeping tent. The sward had grown over the whole and not the slightest sign of its ever having been broken was to be seen. The thing seemed to me incredible, but after examining attentively a small brick terrace close by and the different trees around, Feringheea declared himself prepared to stake his life upon the accuracy of his information. My wife was still sleeping over the grave of the water-carriers, unconscious of what was doing or to be done. She has often since declared that she never had a night of such horrid dreams and that while asleep her soul must consequently have become conscious of the dreadful crimes that had been perpetrated.

'I assembled the people of the surrounding villages and the Thanedar and his police, who resided in the village of Korae close by, and put the people to work over the grave of the havildar. They dug down five feet without perceiving the slightest sign of the bodies or a grave. All the people assembled seemed delighted to think that I had become weary like themselves and satisfied that the man was deranged, but there was a calm and quiet confidence about him that made me insist upon their going on, and at last we came upon the bodies of the whole five, laid out precisely as he had described. My wife, still unconscious of our object in digging, had repaired to the breakfast tent, which was pitched at some distance from the grave; and I now had the ropes of her tent removed and the bodies of the Pundit and six companions, in a much greater state of decay, exhumed from about the same depth and from the exact spot pointed out. The water-carriers were afterwards disinterred, and he offered to point out others in the neighbouring groves but I was sick of the horrid work and satisfied with what he had already done. The gangs, which were concentrating upon Jaipore were pursued and, in the end, the greater part of them taken and Feringheea's life was spared for his services. It was afterwards found that the proprietor of the village of Selohda near by connived at all these murders and received the horse of the Pundit as a present. Some of the Thug gang actually resided in this village and the rest used to encamp in this grove every year in passing and remain there for many days at a time feasting, carousing and murdering. Yet the people of the village and of the surrounding country knew nothing of these transactions, which shows how cleverly the secrets of Thuggee were kept.

'While I was in charge of the district of Narsinghpore in the years 1822, 1823 and 1824, no ordinary robbery or theft would be committed without my becoming acquainted with it, nor was there a robber or thief of the ordinary kind in the district with whose character I had not become acquainted in the discharge of my duty as magistrate, and if any man told me that a gang of assassins by profession resided in the village of Kundeli—not four hundred yards from my court—and that the extensive groves of the village of Mundesur—only one stage from me—were one of the greatest *beles* or places of murder in all India, and that large gangs from Hindustan and the Deccan used to rendezvous in these groves, remain in them for many days together every year and carry on their dreadful trade along all the lines of road that pass by and branch off from them, with the knowledge and connivance of the two landholders by whose ancestors these groves had been planted, I should have thought him a fool or a madman. And yet nothing could have been more true. The bodies of a hundred travellers lie buried in and around the groves of Mundesur and a gang of assassins lived in and about the village of Jundeli while I was Magistrate of the district, and these men extended their depredation to the distant cities of Poona and Hyderabad.'

William Sleeman's cousin, Dr Henry Spry,[1] who was medical; officer in charge of the special prison built for Thugs at Saugor, remarks that about the time of Feringheea's capture there were 583 Thugs under arrest and that cartloads more were arriving every day. He goes on:

'Sentence of death was pronounced in a very impressive manner, by Captain Sleeman, on different parties of Thugs executed during my residence in Saugor. The criminals, drawn up in a semicircle round the

---

[1] Mrs Fanny Parks stayed with the Sleemans in Jubbulpore and herself witnessed a similar scene at Saugor which she described in her book, Wanderings of a Pilgrim in Search of the Picturesque.

bench on which he, as Judge, was seated, were surrounded by a strong guard of musketeers and dismounted cavalry. The warrants were placed before them and each name, as called out by the court, was repeated by the *sheristhadar* [sheriff's officer]. At the conclusion of this ceremony, Captain Sleeman addressed them in the Hindustani language, in a few sentences, which may be rendered thus:

'You have all been convicted in the crime of blood; the order from the Calcutta Council therefore is that, at tomorrow's dawn, you are all to be hung. If any of you desire to make any further communication, you may now speak.'

'Few answered; those who did merely requested, as a dying favour, that their bodies on being taken down, might be burnt. One hardened villain, however, as he was turning round to leave the court, disturbed the solemnity of the scene by muttering: 'Ah, you have got it all your way now, but let me find you in Paradise, and then I will be revenged!' [One can only guess at the effect of this remark on Sleeman!]

'The night was passed by these men in displays of coarse and disgusting levity. Trusting in the assurance that, dying in the cause of their calling, Bhowani would provide for them in paradise, they evinced neither penitence nor remors. Stifling their alarm with boisterous revelling, they hoped to establish in the minds of their comrades, who could hear them through the wall a reputation for courage, by means which at once proved their insincerity and belied their fortitude. Imagine such men on the last night of their existence on earth, not penitent for their individual errors or impressed with a sense of the public mischiefs to which they had contributed, not even rendered serious by the dismal ordeal which in a few hours was to usher them into an unknown world, by singing, singing, in the condemned cell, and repeating their unhallowed carols while jolting along in the carts that conveyed them to their gibbets!

When morning came, numerous hackeries drew up at the gaol door, taking five men in each. They looked dreadfully haggard. As one cart was laden after the other, it was driven away, surrounded by sepoys with fixed bayonets and loaded muskets. The place appointed for the execution was on the north side of the town of Saugor, about a mile and a half from the gaol. 'Ruksat, Doctor Sahib,' 'Salaam, Doctor Sahib'—meaning 'Adieu, Doctor Sahib,' or 'Compliments to Doctor Sahib'—

were the salutations which I received as I rode by the wretched tumbrils which were jolting them to their execution. The gibbets were temporary erections, forming three sides of a square. The upright posts which supported the cross-beams were firmly fixed in stone masonry five feet in height. From either side of these walls footboards were placed on which the unhappy criminals were to land on reaching the top of the. ladder. The cross-beams were each provided with ten running halters equidistant from one another. As each hackery load of malefactors arrived, it was taken to the foot of the respective ladders, and as one by one got out he mounted to the platform or footboard. Their irons were not removed. All this time the air was pierced with the house and hollow shoutings of these wretched men. Each man as he reached the top of the ladder, stepped out on the platform and walked at once to the halter. Without loss of time he tried its strength by weighing his whole body on it. Everyone having by this means proved the strength of his rope with his own hands—for none of them were handcuffed—introduced his head into the noose, drew the knot firmly immediately behind the right ear, amid terrific cheers, jumped off the board and launched himself into eternity! Thus in the moment of death we see a scrupulous attention paid to the preservation of caste. To wait to be hung by the hands of a *chamar* (leather-curer) was a thought too revolting for endurance. The name would be disgraced for ever and, therefore, rather than admit to its degradation every man hung himself.

The creed of Thuggee had three important effects on the minds of men who practised it.

Firstly, these men knew only one highest virtue, to kill their fellows and to live on the plunder of murder. The source of this 'knowledge' was religion, if one can so term their preversion. For them evil was good. In the world there have been in the past, and will be in the future, men who reverse the hard-won beliefs of the wise. For many of these wrongdoers there is no hope in this life: they are dammed. The Thugs' faith was reinforced by the great lie, that all whom they killed in sacrifice to Kali must by this act itself pass to Paradise. Once accepted the idea was dynamic: to kill was to do good—a triple good, in service to Kali, to the victim and to themselves.

Secondly, compassion they had none, except where the victim was one of their own guild, who of all living creatures least deserved it.

Lastly, in devotion to a wrong idea of good, a Thug involuntarily grew a 'religious' shell of ruthlessness. Greed and lust, self-generated, then flourished within, but the outer shell was impenetrable by any of those feelings of pity, generosity, humility and kindliness known to civilized men and women. Men of some other creeds, persuaded that they are religious beings, grow similar shells, but never, perhaps, ones so armoured by corrupted minds that they have no chinks.

Note: The reader who wishes to probe more deeply into the attitude of the Thugs to their profession may refer to Appendix 2.

CHAPTER 14

Sleemanabad and Famine in Saugor

Thuggee Sleeman was not the man to rest content even with such great success as that which he achieved by 1831. His campaign had to be carried on to its end, the total destruction of Thuggee, which entailed the creation of a new way of life for the children of Thugs. In 1835 he was made General Superintendent for the Suppression of Thuggee, with his headquarters fixed at Jubbulpore. The net of his organization had by then expanded to embrace the whole of India, and men trained under him were working as civil administrative officials in all districts under the chief officials of these regions. An assessment made in 1840 showed that up till then, 3,689 had been committed for trial, of whom 466 were hanged, 1,564 transported for life, 933 imprisoned for life, 81 confined for different periods, 86 set free under security for good bahaviour, 97 acquitted and 56 admitted as approvers. Twelve escaped and 208 died a natural death before sentence was passed. Sleeman insisted that all these executions and all these punishments were his sole responsibility as the chief officer charged with the suppression. He felt certain that no more lenient means could have freed humanity from this inequity.

He quotes the words of a powerful *taluqdar* (baronial lord) of Hyderabad, previously an avowed opponent of the British, in a letter that this chief wrote in 1840 to Sleeman's assistant, Captain Malcolm:

'Seeing that the best arrangements have been made in this matter, the whole of the inhabitants of the country and travellers have been emancipated from the fear of Thugs; day and night they raise their hands in prayer to state that in the days of kings bygone no such peace and comfort existed. Thanks to Almighty God, the power of conferring this great boon, a source of great renown has been reserved for you from the beginning of the world, in order that this matter should be so arranged.

Where are the murdered men? How can there be any, when you do not even hear the slightest allusion to Thugs? The whole world is giving thanks for this.'

'It must be confessed, however, that there was some slight exaggeration in the worthy *taluqdar's* congratulations, for in the course of the next seven years 531 more Thugs were apprehended and committed for trial and in 1848 a further 120 were committed. Since that year Thuggee appears to have quite died out. In 1853, indeed, some cases occurred in the Punjab, but vigorous measures under Thuggee's nephew, Captain James Sleeman, suppressed the outbreak as soon as it occurred.

On the constructive side of his campaign, Thuggee founded schools of industry at Jubbulpore and Saugor for the purpose of teaching the sons of Thug approvers some trade or craft by which they might earn an honest living. The parents were at first, as one might expect, lustily opposed to their offspring demeaning themselves by any sort of consistent honesty, but as soon as the rupees flowed in from the sale of their children's handiwork, the moaning ceased and the approvers sought places in the school for themselves. Brick-making, building, cleaning, making lac dye, sealing-wax, blankets, druggets, clothes and taper wicks, knitting and carpet-weaving were all taught in these establishments, which, in the end, became so famous that Queen Victoria demanded that a carpet should be made for Windsor Castle. Sleeman's Thugs wove for her a great seamless carpet of 80 feet by 40 feet, weighing about two tons, for the Waterloo Chamber.

That event marked the end and climax of the anxious, bitter and finally rewarding campaign waged by Captain Sleeman against an evil and devastating guild of highway murderers.

Sleeman acknowledged with gratitude the help he had had from Captain Reynolds south of the Nerbudda, from Wilson between the Ganges and the Jumna, from McLeod in Rajputana, Malwa and Delhi. Captain Borthwick was later a prominent aide, and later still James Sleeman was his right-hand man and successor as General Superintendent. For so great a service to mankind these men deserve to be remembered. If this were all that they and their contemporaries had ever done for the country they ruled, it might have been considered enough.

More than one attempt was made on Sleeman's life during this time, but how and when, he has left us no particulars. Of the three attempts he does record at any length, all were made after he left central India, and he has apparently only written of them because he was interested in the men who made them, the methods they employed, the cause of failure and their reasons for attempting. So now we can tell of more pleasant things in the year 1832, and of Sleeman's old friends, the Indian peasants and their landlords.

In 1937 Colonel Sir James Sleeman and his son, the grandson and great-grandson of William Henry Sleeman, made their way to a little village near Jubbulpore to visit a most sacred shrine. Father and son were given a boisterous welcome from young and old. In that shrine in that village they found a lamp still burning brightly, and in the hearts of the people of that village they found the memory of William Henry Sleeman as green as on the day when it was first planted.

In 1832 William and Amélie had already been married four years, but they had no children, and that, to an Indian peasant, was the darkest calamity. So when he and Amelie were touring and the holy Brahmin of this village heard of their approach, he came to meet them and conducted them to a shrine. 'This village,' said he, 'is yours because you made it, but the shrine is very, very old and all who come to this holy place will have the blessing of a son.' They walked on to the shrine, followed by most of the village who were interested witnesses of the pilgrimage. They made their offering, and Thuggee told the old priest that if he were blessed with a son he would of course give to the *malguzar* (landlord) a substantial sum of money for the temple funds.

Behold! On 6th January 1833 Amélie gave birth to a son, whom they called Henry Arthur.

When they were next that way they again visited the shrine to express their gratitude and to make their present to the *malguzar* and his priests. But this was not all. From that day on the village prospered and expanded so that the inhabitants renamed it Sleemanabad and ordained that at the shrine a lamp was to be kept burning for ever to commemorate Sleeman's association with the village and its holy place. The lamp burned in 1937. Perhaps it burns today also.

In a sense it was Thuggee who created this village by obtaining from the Government ninety-six acres of land and there settling some landless peasantry, close by the tiny old hamlet. From this the community expanded into a prosperous village which always treated its benefactor as an honoured guest. With the children in particular the redoubtable Sleeman was always a great favourite.

Suttee, the burning of widows, and Thuggee were now on the way to extinction. The man who had decreed the end of suttee and who had lent to Sleeman his powerful and vital support against all doubts, derision and obstacles—the governor-general, Lord William Bentinck—was in December 1832 touring the frontier regions. Through Captain Benson, his military secretary, he had been in close touch with both Carvin Smith and Sleeman from the beginning of Thug operations. He now took the opportunity to hear a first-hand report from the man himself and to congratulate him on the unexpected success that he had attained in so short a time. Sleeman accordingly rode out to meet him and to camp with him as he passed through the Jubbulpore district.

Thuggee knew of a fine collection of tombs at a place called Behrole built over the ashes of suttees who had burned themselves on the pyres of their husbands. Thither he guided Lord William by the road that passed the tombs, for he was intrigued to remark what impression they made on him.

Lord William asked what these tombs were, for he had never seen any of the kind before. When I told him what they were he said not a word, but he must have felt a proud consciousness of the debt of gratitude which India owes to the statesman who had the courage to put a stop to this great evil, in spite of all the fearful obstacles which bigotry and prejudice opposed to the measure. The seven European functionaries in charge of the seven districts of the newly acquired territories, were requested, during the administration of Lord Amherst, in 1826, to state whether the burning of widows could or should be prohibited; and I believe every one of them declared that it should not! And yet when it was put a stop to only a few years after by Lord William, not a complaint or murmur was heard. The replies to the Governor-General's inquiries were, I believe, throughout India, for the most part opposed to the measure.

Later writers have sought to belittle Bentinck's work in India. William Sleeman's recorded opinion is one of genuine admiration for this able proconsul's vision and determination, and it is an opinion worth regarding: Thuggee was a discerning critic with the best of qualifications. Moreover, ever since he rose to responsible position in his service he knew personally every one of these dignitaries. Bentinck at least had no doubt that the Bengal Army was losing efficiency, nor did he hesitate publicly to say so. It is a pity that his warning went unheeded.

The governor-general passed on his way and Sleeman took the road back to his headquarters at Saugor. It was not long before serious trouble faced him of a sort that he had not before encountered and of a nature most unwelcome.

There was famine in Saugor.

The fatal results of famine showed themselves with dismal suddenness. As was usual in India, so many of the population lived on a bare subsistence that any shortage brought immediate collapse. Every village had its dead and dying and the roads were strewn with bodies, but the worst effects were seen in the big towns and in the civil and military stations. European and native communities met together to raise funds for relief, but Sleeman knew that such help could bring no long-term cure. He also knew something which no one else seemed to realize: that although the traders still had considerable secret stores of grain, they would never open these if they thought that the authorities would requisition the contents. By threats he might have some of them opened, but the others would remain shut and concealed and never be found.

He was now put to the severest test of his whole life. Everyone demanded that he should break open the stores by force. Major Gregory, the commissariat officer at contonments, rode in to implore Sleeman; his Colonel followed him, swearing that the troops would mutiny within a week as food was giving out; Amélie in tears and almost on her knees brought starving swollen-bellied children to him to demand that he do something; famine-stricken natives thronged about his house; and the police inspector declared that the lives of his police would be no longer safe unless the grain pits were searched for and forcibly opened. Sleeman was regarded by all and sundry as a pig-headed, callous fool, if not a knave. He was shunned wherever he went, a grim strained figure.

To the Colonel he replied that he would permit him to buy freely whatever grain he could find in the city. To all others he declared firmly that he would never permit any man's granary to be forcibly opened. To this effect he issued a proclamation, stating further that anyone could keep his grain and sell it wherever and whenever he pleased and at whatever price he could get. Within a few days the traders came to him to ask him to protect their stores. His reply was that he would do so with his police provided that all, even the most secret stores, were disclosed to him. Within a few hours there was a constable on every single grain-pit in the area, the doors were flung open and the grain flowed out on to the markets, attracted by the high price, whereupon the traders forthwith sent messengers into Malwa for great convoys of grain to be brought into Saugor to catch the good market. The flood of wheat brought the price down at once and the famine was over.

When he was at the worst extremity he had a note from Captain Robinson in Hyderabad describing the terrible conditions in Elichpore, where the breaking in of the grain stores had only brought a temporary relief. Sleeman advised him to issue the same proclamation as he had issued: that would cure the trouble. And it did cure it.

Sleeman's diary reads:

"In the morning the bazaars of Saugor were all supplied and every man who had money could buy as much as he pleased. The troops got as much as they required from the city. Major Gregory was astonished and delighted; the Colonel, a fine old soldier from the banks of the Indus, who had commanded a corps of horse under the former government, came to me in amazement; every shop had become full of grain as if by supernatural agency. *'Kala admi ka akal kahan talak chale ga,'* said he 'How could a black man's famine serve him in such an emergency!"

It may well be imagined that Thuggee's heart had been deeply moved by the fearful sufferings he had witnessed and by the abuse he had met from all those for whom he cared. But his recompense came when all, even the old Indian colonel, came to thank him. Perhaps his worst experience had been the wounding of his beloved Amélie's feelings and her inability to understand what he was doing. For the first time since his marriage he had had to carry a burden without being able to share it with the friend who had most right to share, and whose moral support meant so much to him.

His move from Jubbulpore to Saugor had been made on his appointment as Principal Assistant in the Political and Criminal Department. Commendations from the Government and from the Court of Directors for his work in suppressing Thuggee were now showering upon him. The Court, he writes, further expressed itself as 'being much pleased with the exertions I had made "for improving the cultivation and manufacture of Sugar in the Nerbudda Territories," considered "my settlement of the Revenue of Jubbulpore as very creditable to me," and "perused with satisfaction the reports of Mr Smith and Captain Sleeman, and considered the account given by the latter officer of the character of the people, the fertility of the soil, and the general resources of the country as an access of information very creditable to the Collector.'

During the rains of the summer of 1834, Thuggee's bouts of fever became increasingly violent and frequent. No amount of sweating or dosing with quinine had any effect and it seemed that only time would bring any remedy. Amélie at last begged him to apply for a transfer to some other more healthy place, a thing he had persistently refused to do while his war with the Thugs was undecided. Now at last, with victory in his grasp, he felt that he could leave the exploitation and final pursuit of the enemy to his trusty and efficient lieutenants, so he wrote direct to Lord William Bentinck, who replied by his own hand to the writer, a compliment that few men in William Sleeman's position have ever been paid up a governor-general in similar circumstances. Bentinck offered him the commissionership of Arakan; but pointed out that the climate there might be no better than that of central India for his impaired health, and might well be worse. He ended his letter:

You will be a great loss to the country, in the administration of which you have had so great a share, and I know not how you would be replaced in that work so important to humanity of the extirpation of the Thugs, which has been successfully carried on towards its complete accomplishment under your especial direction. Believe me with great esteem and respect.

Very truly yours,
W.H. Bentinck

Ootacamund,
July, 18, 1834

The *dak* (mail) orderly handed the letter to Thuggee before he left for the office. He opened it, read it and sat looking out of the window for a time. His fever had left him for the past day or two, but although he was back at work he felt weak and, most unusual for him, depressed. In his weak state the death of his brother Johnnie came near to flooring him. He was ill, and moreover his little son seemed to be getting frailer every day. This was a problem. That evening he wrote in his diary that he longed for the *'otium cum dignitate* of life at Falmouth with my family and my sister and John Furse,' for he felt himself 'growing weary, sadly weary, of Indian customs.'

That evening, after little Henry had been put to bed, he and Amélie sat over the letter, with the oil lamp flickering under the punkha, discussing all sides of it. Amélie, the fond wife and mother, urged him to retire to England and there restore his broken health.

'But,' said he, 'we've had the sad loss of Johnnie, and so long as his widow and son are in straightened circumstances it lies with me to find the means to provide for them. George has just repaid me the three hundred pound loan that I made him. I'll send that to Philip for the upkeep of the widow and little Johnnie. But they cannot live on that for ever. And then there's this letter from the governor-general which shows us both that I must at any rate stay on in India until the Thugs are finished. No, Amélie, I must stay and I must in some way find the health to stay.'

Whether it was the heat, the monsoon humidity of the night or the collapse of the *punkha-wala* and the consequent invasion of the lamp by every variety of flying insect, Amélie late that night at last gave way. With this settled, and with the inspiring opinion of his governor-general to urge him on, Thuggee found a new peace of mind and a new courage, to raise his spirits and defend himself against his illness. Gradually, with Amélie's care, his health improved.

CHAPTER 15

A Year's Leave

The Year 1835 opened propitiously. On 10th January Sleeman was appointed General Superintendent of Thuggee operations with his headquarters at Jubbulpore and was at last relieved of his other duties, so once again off the family set to do the hundred and twenty miles in palanquins in three nights' journey. After them went nephew James, who seemed to have found a place in his uncle's good books, having risen to the appointment of interpreter and quartermaster in the 73rd. His uncle records James's arrival.

'James Sleeman had arrived on a visit of six months only a few days before we left Saugor, much improved in every respect by his residence at Minari, where he had been in a large and gay circle of society. He was handsome, had excellent manners and address, and a vast fund of conversation and was, of course, a great favourite with the ladies. He had lately been half in love but fortunately his prudence was greater than his love and the lady was at time about to be united to another. He followed us to Jubbulpore with our surgeon. At Saugor we had a large society, at Jubbulpore a small one, but Jubbulpore, seemed to me more like my home than any other, and consequently I liked it better. Our boy had been very delicate at Saugor and I hoped the climate of Jubbulpore would agree with him. He was becoming more and more interesting every day and I more and more fond of him, but I had determined that if he were not stronger the next cold season than he had been, I should send him to England and confide him to the care of my sister, Mary Furse. I learnt that Mary's eyes were failing as indeed were mine, so that I had had to forgo reading by candlelight and to play cards or chess of an evening.'

As the cold weather receded and the hot months advanced

Thuggee's health began to decline. It is obvious from the speeding up of the tempo at which he worked that he was pressing himself with all his determination to bring to a solution every problem concerning violent crime which was piling in upon him. For months, right through the depressing heat and the rains, he pushed himself along despite attacks of malaria and a fine crop of boils, till by early August the doctors forced a decision upon him: it must either be sick leave or retirement. Obviously, with the calls on his purse, he could not retire. Obviously, with the governor-general and everyone else so dependent on him in the campaign, he could not sail away to England for a couple of years. But how else could he regain his health? The patient Amélie came to his rescue, pointing out that there was one place in India which he could reach easily, where the climate would cure him and where he would be within reach of those who wished to consult him. That place was Mussoorie, the little hill station, 7,000 feet up in the Himalaya, where British soldiers were sent to convalesce; it lay on a great ridge which faced the eternal snows away out towards Tibet. Thuggee jumped at the idea. From there he could keep in touch with his officers and would be near a corps of troops, the Sirmoor Battalion of Gurkhas, which had its home under the hills at Dehra Doon. He never could bear being far away from the soldiers. So in went his application for leave on medical certificate, to be readily and speedily granted by the Government of India.

In due course came a letter from the Court of Directors in London approving the grant and adding a comforting word or two, regretting 'that Captain Sleeman to whose able direction so much of the success of the operations against Thuggee is to be attributed, has been compelled by the state of his health to proceed to the Hills for a Year.'

Brother George had arrived in India with his regiment and there was a short reunion in the family, immensely enjoyed by the two brothers and nephew James, before Williams, Amélie and the boy Henry set forth in November to journey the seven hundred miles from Jubbulpore to Mussoorie, travelling through Damoh, the Saugor districts, through the Native States of Orchha, Dattia, Gwalior and other smaller territories, entering Agra on 1st January 1836, and on to Delhi and Mussoorie.

Thuggee wrote the fullest of letters to Mary Furse throughout the journey and from these entrancing messages he published in 1844 his classic of Indian country life, *Rambles and Recollections.* Only a few of his more entertaining experiences during the long trek can be accommodated here. Those who have wandered the Indian countryside as did Thuggee will find his rural discussions interesting and enjoyable, but too few have had this privilege. Visitors to India who pass from urban England to urban Calcutta, Delhi or Bombay without a knowledge of the peasants' tongue, may find congenial companionship in their limited 'intellectual' circle. Most of them, whatever the immediate purpose of their visit, intend to write or speak of India on their return and do not realize that Bloomsbury of India is more foreign to Indian cultivators than Bloomsbury of England is to their Delhi friends. Is it possible that mutual admiration may arise from a common dullness? Sleeman and his not always so simple rustic friends would not hold their interest for long.

Of all things he delighted most in debating on every conceivable topic as he passed through the country. Those who attacked him most, who slated the British Government and all its doings and who were not afraid to say what they thought of him, were his most congenial company. To keep himself in practice he took the little Sureemunt part of the way. This polished man was his constant companion. 'As I have said, his face is extremely beautiful—quite a model for a painter or a statuary; and his figure, though small, is handsome. He dresses with great elegance, mostly in azure-coloured satin surmounted by a rose-coloured turban and a waistband of the same colour. A greater master of all the convenances I have never seen, though he is of slender capacity and, as I have said, in stature less than five feet high.'

His first quest was to the mango groves which had been planted seven years before at his instigation by local farmers. He found that some trees were already fruiting and that nearly all had been married, 'Among the Hindus, neither the man who plants the grove nor his wife can taste of the fruit until he has married one of the mango-trees to some other tree (commonly the tamarind-tree) that grows near it in the same grove.' One of the proprietors had spent so much money on wells and irrigation that he could not afford the marriage ceremony. One tree was already in fruit but neither he nor his old wife could possibly eat it, so they sold all their silver and gold ornaments, borrowed all they could and had the grove married with fine pomp and ceremony before the fruit season of 1834. The more Brahmins that are fed on the occasion of the marriage, the greater the glory of the owner of the grove.

When Thuggee asked old Berjore Sing, during a visit to his grove, how many he had feasted, he replied with a heavy sigh that he had managed to feast only one hundred and fifty. He showed his visitor the mango-tree which had acted the part of bridegroom on the occasion, but the bride had disappeared from his side.

'And where is the bride, the tamarind?'

'The only tamarind I had in the grove died,' said the old man, 'before we could bring about the wedding, and I was obliged to get a jasmine as a wife for my mango. I planted it here so that we might, as required, cover both bride and bridegroom under one canopy during the ceremonies, but after the marriage was over the gardener neglected her and she pined away and died.'

'And what made you prefer the jasmine to all other trees after the tamarind?'

'Because it is the most celebrated of all trees save the rose.'

'And why not have chosen the rose for a wife?'

'Because no sane person ever heard of a marriage between the rose and the mango, while they take place every day between the mango and the *chumbaele* [jasmine].'

Sleeman's immense procession continued on its march: bullock carts, elephants, silver stick officials, a troop of mounted policemen, palanquins and the more lowly *tonjons, ekkas* for the servants pulled by a single nag, and so on. The General Superintendent and Principal Assistant to the Agent-General was in progress through the Company's territories and the treaty States. The governor-general ordained that his great servants should travel in some circumstance. So the obedient Thuggee journeyed in the manner required, casting a sardonic grin at the great cloud of dust that he was raising and the tenuous tail that stretched to the horizon behind him.

With him came his boon companion, the Maulvi, whose ideas on astronomy were vastly diverting. As they left the mango grove they discussed the mango weddings. The Maulvi scoffed and asked what else you could expect from Hindus who believed that the lightening was nothing more than the glittering arrows shot but the god Indur upon his foe, the formidable Rajah Bali. From this the conversation passed to shooting stars, and Sleeman demanded from the Maulvi an explanation of this phenomenon.

'You remember,' he answered, 'that the Prophet declared: "God has created stars for three uses: one of them as cause of ornament of the regions; the second to pelt the devils with; the third to direct people going through forests and on the sea." Therefore whoever shall explain them otherwise does wrong and loses his time and speaks from his own invention and embellishes.'

The shooting star was in the second category.

Like the Canterbury pilgrims, discussing and story-telling as they rode, they came to the town of Ludora, where the rajah, having spent most of his money on the ceremonies to the great satisfaction of his subjects, was just returned from the solemn celebration of yet another annual marriage—that between the Saligram, a rounded pebble, and the Tulsi, a small sacred shrub. All the ceremonies of a regular marriage had been fulfilled, with 'eight elephants, 1200 camels, 4000 horses, all mounted and elegantly furnished.' On the leading elephants, most sumptuously decorated, the pebble god had been taken to pay his bridal visit to the little shrub goddess. The rajah had entertained and feasted over a hundred thousand guests, an annual fixture for which he screwed the money out of those same guests, who now seemed happy that all had been well spent by their chief.

At Orchha the procession was greeted with a salute from the rajah's two brass cannon. This rajah had an ingenious method of enriching himself which others might well copy. He would appoint a prime minister and at once begin an intrigue with this man's known rival to ensure that in due course the rival would kill the minister, whose estates would then be forfeited to the ruler for misconduct—that is, for the murder of his predecessor. As the new prime minister acquired fresh possessions and extorted more wealth, the rajah would intrigue in turn with the new servant's rival, and so it went on very satisfactorily and there seemed to be no drying up of the source of expectant prime ministers.

In 1833 the then pirme minister, 'who was a most atrocious villain and employed the public establishments of his Chief to plunder travellers on the high road,' chanced to rob four men carrying treasure from Saugor to Jhansi. The attempt to murder them was indeed foiled by one of them escaping to Saugor and complaining to Sleeman, but the party had none the less been robbed of the treasure. When Sleeman brought the crime home to the minister, the rajah, anxious to take advantage of the occasion to fill his coffers, had him assassinated.

The Rajah was then about eighty years of age and his minister was a strong, athletic and brave man. One morning while he was sitting with him in private conversation, the Rajah pretended a wish to drink of the water in which his household god had been washed (the *Charanmrit)* and begged the minister fetch it from the place where it stood by the side of the idol in the court of the palace. As a man cannot take a sword before the idol, the minister put his down, as the Rajah knew he would, and, going to the idol, prostrated himself before taking the water. In that state he was cut down by Biari, another feudal Rajput baron who aspired to the seals, and by some of the latter's friends who had been placed there by the Rajah. He obtained the seals by this service. Since he was able to place one brother in command of the forces and make another chamberlain, he hoped to retain office longer than any of his predecessors.

At Jhansi, Thuggee stumbled into a first-class quarrel in the palace, where the young prince had died leaving two uncles, a regent and a son by a junior wife to fight over the succession. The only point on which most of them agreed was that Uncle Ragunath Rau should not succeed because he was an honest and resolute man and was bound to examine the accounts. The governor-general was determined that Ragunath should succeed and Sleeman, while pouring oil on troubled waters, made it quite clear to all concerned that he was treating this man as the future ruler despite the fact that he, Sleeman, had noticed that the unlucky Ragunath had the first signs of leprosy. And so it turned out that the only honest one of them became for a short time their ruler. In accordance with custom he drowned himself in the Ganges when the leprosy became apparent.

The cavalcade passed on to Dattia where the rajah had arranged for his visitor a magnificent shoot in a great walled hunting reserve. It seemed that the wall had kept the wild animals out instead of in, for Thuggee and his assistant were vouchsafed only one shot at a hoary old boar. However, he found another interest, that of the underworld of Dattia.

The then minister of Dattia, Ganesh, was a very great knave who encouraged all kinds of thieves and robbers to bring back from distant districts every season vast quantities of booty which they shared with him.

The chief himself was a mild old gentleman who would not suffer violence to be offered by any of his nobles, though he would not, perhaps, quarrel with his minister for getting for him a little addition to his revenue from without by affording a sanctuary to such kinds of people. As in Tehri, so here the pickpockets constituted the entire population of several villages and carried their depredations northward to the banks of the Indus and southward to Bombay and Madras. But colonies of thieves and robbers like these at that time abounded no less in our own territories than in those of native states; there were more than a thousand families of them in our district of Mazaffarnagar, Saharanpore and Meerut, in the upper Doab, all well enough known to the local authorities, who could do nothing with them.

These local operators worked remote districts and the plunder they brought home with them they shared liberally with their protectors among the native police and bigwigs of Dattia.

For some unexplained reason one of his rare fits of homesickness darkened his short stay at Dattia. He wrote to Mary:

'In my evening ramble on the bank of the river, which was flowing against the wind and rising into waves, my mind wandered back to the hours of infancy and boyhood, when I sat with my brothers watching our little vessels as they scudded over the ponds and streams of my native land, and then of my poor brothers, John and Lewis, whose bones now lie beneath the ocean. As we advance in age the dearest scenes of early days must necessarily become more and more associated in our recollection with painful feelings, for they who enjoyed such scenes with us must by degrees pass away and be remembered with sorrow even by those who are conscious of having fulfilled all their duties in life towards them; but with how much more by those who can never remember them without thinking of occasions of kindness and assistance neglected or disregarded! Many of them perhaps left behind them widows and children struggling with adversity and soliciting from us aid we strive in vain to give.'

Perhaps it was that he knew that his next stage would take him along the road to Gwalior where the great red fort topped the precipitous ridge and menaced the town below. 'One cannot but feel that he approaches the capital of a dynasty of barbarian princes who, like Attila, would choose their places of residence as devils choose their pandemonia, for their ugliness, and would rather reside in the dreary wastes of Tartary than on the shores of the Bosphorus!' Gwalior affronted him as no other State of India, not even the Kingdom of Oudh where he was to spend five precious years. Perhaps in retrospect he bethought him that even before he had reached his camp a gang of thieves had stolen one of his best carpets, all the brass brackets of his tent-poles and the brass hour bell that the sentries struck at the guard over his camp. They had filched all his assistant's cooking-pots, as well as the contents of a heavy box of Thuggee's geological specimens! The tents of a minor rajah who had come to pay his respects to his liege lord of Gwalior, which were pitched hard by, had been rifled of plate, jewels and valuable clothes. This rajah had also lost five horses, so he sent along to warn Sleeman that he must cut off the tails of all his horses or else they would certainly be panicked and ridden off that night. Thuggee promptly shifted his camp to a grove near the British residency and kept both tails and horses. He then rose to great eloquence about Gwalior:

'As a citizen of the world, I could not help thinking that it would be an immense blessing upon a large portion of our species if an earthquake were to swallow up this court of Gwalior and the army that surrounded it. Nothing worse could possibly succeed and something better might. It was lamentable to think how much of evil this court and camp inflicted upon the people who were subject to them. In January 1828 I was passing with a party of gentlemen through the town of Bhilsa, which belongs to this chief and lies between Saugor and Bhopal, when we found lying bleeding in one of the streets, twelve men belonging to a merchant at Mirzapore, who had the day before been wounded and plundered by a gang of robbers close outside the walls of the town. Those who were able ran in to the Amil, or chief of the district, who resides in the town and begged him to send some horsemen after the bandits and intercept them as they passed over the great plains. 'Send your own people,' said he, 'or hire men to send! Am I here to look after the private affairs of merchants and travellers, or to collect the revenues of the Prince?' Neither he nor the Prince himself, nor any other officer of the public establishment, ever dreamed that it was their duty to protect the life, property or character of travellers, or indeed of any other human beings save the members of their own families. In this pithy question, the Amil of Bhilsa described the nature and character of the government.'

All Sleeman's friends knew that the mere mention of the Gwalior army was the instantaneous fuse to a violent explosion. 'Robbers and murderers' was the least offensive expression he used for this gallant body. 'However,' said he with relish one day, 'after all a Dacoit leader once told a friend of mine that he and his men never committed murder, and to explain his point he observed: "God forbid that we should ever commit murder; but you British do the same. I hear that there is now a large assemblage of your troops in the upper provinces going to take foreign countries; if they are opposed, they will kill people. We only do the same!" 'So,' Thuggee went on, 'there are, it seems, two sides to even the Gwalior army.'

After this uncomfortable sojourn in the hated land he went on his way to Dholpore, meeting on the road one of the Company's Indian revenue officers who had been into Dholpore to obtain settlement of boundaries between some yeomen in British territory and subjects of that State. He had lost his case because the Dholpore chief had summoned all the witnesses on his side and had made them a little speech. 'You are of course expected to speak the truth regarding the land in dispute, but by the sacred stream of the Ganges, if you speak so as to lose this estate one inch of it you lose both your ears!'

'And most assuredly would they lose them,' commented the officer, 'if they were not to swear most resolutely that all the land in question belonged to Dholpore. Had I the same power to cut them off they would laugh in my face.'

The Rajah of Dholpore for all his efficient means of obtaining a favourable verdict in the lawcourts, ruled a prosperous and happy State and was very well disposed towards the British because they had interposed and protected him from greedy Gwalior. Despite this, 'and though he has never had anything and never can have or can hope to have anything, from the poor pageant of the house of Timur who now sits on the throne of Delhi, yet on his seal of office he declares himself to be the slave and creature of that imperial "warrior for the faith of Islam." This was no matter for surprise for every one of the old Mogul provinces had to keep one foot in each camp.

On 1st January 1836 the great procession wound its way into Agra. Many of us can remember with what doubtings we visited that city, for never did we imagine that the Taj Mahal could ever approach in beauty what we had so often heard of it from all and sundry, from the cultured and the uncultured and from those in all classes and pursuits. So it was with Thuggee and Amélie.

'After my quarter of a century of anticipated pleasure, I went on from part to part in the expectation that I must by and by come to something that would disappoint me, but no. The emotion which one feels at first is never impaired; on the contrary, it goes on improving from the first *coup d'ceil* of the dome in the distance to the minute inspection of the last flower upon the screen round the tomb.' He asked his wife what she thought of the building. 'I can't,' said she, 'tell you what I think for I don't know how to criticize such a building, but I can tell you what I feel. I would die tomorrow to have one like it built over me! Other women may have felt the same about the Taj. He and Amélie protested against the quadrille and tiffin parties which were sometimes given by Europeans of the station at this imperial which were sometimes given by Europeans of the station at this imperial tomb. 'Drinking and dancing are, no doubt, very good things in their season, even in a hot climate, but they are sadly out of place in a sepulchre and never fail to shock the good feelings of sober-minded people when given there. Good church music gives us great pleasure without exciting us to dancing or drinking; the Taj does the some, at least to the soberminded.'

After a few days, having crossed the great Jumma river, he visited the magnificent mausoleum raised by the Emperor Jehangir over his famous father, the Emperor Akbar, at Sikandar. Others beside Sleeman have been struck by the scale and beauty of this memorial and, in contrast, by the rude simplicity of the tomb itself which lies in a roughcast vault many feet below the fine marble slab in the main hall of the building. Thuggee has compared Akbar among sovereigns with Shakespeare among poets. We have to remember that this ruler's greatness lay to some extent in the contrast of his more stable ignore the cruelty of the punishments of his day and the frequent rebellions of his lifetime.

Before Sleeman left Agra he looked in on Father Gregory, the Roman Catholic priest, who had the care of a Christian Community which had already existed there for two hundred years. One evening the old priest came to dine with him when Major Godby, another guest, took occasion to ask the priest what progress Christianity was making amongst the people.

'Progress!' said he, "Why, what progress can we ever hope to make among a people who, the moment we begin to talk to them about the miracles performed by Christ, begin to tell us of those infinitely more wonderful performed by Krishna, who lifted a mountain upon his little finger as an umbrella to defend his shepherdess at Gobarham from a shower of rain.'

Thuggee supports the old priest's refreshing views:

'The Hindus never doubt any part of the miracles and prophecies of our scripture. They believe every word of them—and the only thing that surprises them is that they should be so much less wonderful than those of their own scriptures, in which they also implicitly believe. Men who believe that the histories of the wars and armours of Ram and Krishna, two of the incarnations of Vishnu, were written some fifty thousand years before these wars and armours actually took place upon the earth, would of course easily believe in the fulfilment of any prophecy that might be related to them out of any other book and, as to miracles, there is absolutely nothing too extraordinary for their belief. If a Christian of respectability were to tell a Hindu that, to satisfy some scruples of the Corinthians, St Paul had brought the sun and moon down upon the earth and made them rebound off again to their places, like tennis balls, without the slightest injury to any of the three planets, I do not think that he would feel the slightest doubt of the truth of it, but he would immediately be put in mind of something still more extraordinary that Krishna did to amuse the milkmaids, or to satisfy some sceptics of his day, and relate it with all the naivete imaginable.'

In mid January they reached Kosi where Sleeman was guided on the road to his camp by a local cultivator. While walking along the two fell into conversation, as one can well imagine, knowing William Sleeman. He asked his companion what life had been like under the Jats and Mahrattas, and was told that most of the country was a wild jungle. 'I remember,' said the old man, 'when you could not have got out of the road hereabouts without a good deal of risk. I could not have ventured a hundred yards from the village without the chance of having my clothes stripped off my back. Now the whole face of the country is under cultivation and the roads are safe. Formerly the government kept no faith with the landholders and cultivators, exacting ten rupees where they had bargained for five whenever they found the crops good, but in spite of all this *zulm* {oppression},' said the old man, 'there was then more *barkat* [blessing from above] than now. The lands yielded more returns to the cultivator and he could maintain his little family better upon five acres than he can now upon ten.'

Sleeman asked why this was so.

'A man cannot, sir, venture to tell the truth at all times and in all places,' he said.

'You may tell it now with safety, old friend, I am a mere traveller (*mosafir*)'.

'Here, sir, we all attribute these evils to the dreadful system of perjury which the practices of your judicial courts have brought among the people. You perpetually put the Ganges water into the hands of the Hindus, and the Koran into those of the Mahomedans, and all kinds of lies are every day told upon them. God almighty can stand this no longer and the lands have ceased to be blessed with that fertility which they had before this sad practice began. This, sir, is almost the only fault we have any of us to find with your government. By this system of perjury men are able to cheat each other out of their rights and bring down sterility upon the land, by which the innocent are made to suffer for the guilty.'

On reaching camp he asked a farmer who came to pay his respects to the commissioner of the division Mr. Fraser, what he thought of the matter, telling him what he had heard from his friend on the road. 'The diminished fertility,' said the farmer, 'owing no doubt to the want of those salutary fallows which the fields got under former governments, when invasion and civil wars were things of common occurrence and kept at least two-thirds of the land waste, but there is, on the other hand, no doubt that you have encouraged perjury a good deal in your courts of justice and this perjury must have some effect in depriving the land of the blessings of God! Every man now who has a cause in your civil courts seems to think it necessary either to swear falsely himself or to get others to do it for him. The European gentlemen, no doubt, do all they can to secure every man his rights but, surrounded as they are by perjured witnesses and corrupt native officers, they commonly labour in the dark.' Thuggee had to profess himself content with such unanimous evidence!

From Kosi the travellers made their way on to Delhi where they spent some days, as well all do, sightseeing about the seven cities and the old tombs and fortresses. Sleeman, during his journey and here at Delhi, made a number of careful architectural drawings of all those buildings that took his fancy. These he was later to include in his two volumes of *Rambles and Recollections.*

CHAPTER 16

Return to Jubbulpore

The Sleemans, having cast their ceremonial procession, arrived in Meerut in simple fashion. Here they stayed for two months, until the end of March. In his next letter home he writes:

'Meerut is a large station for military and civil establishments; it is the residence of a civil commissioner, a judge, a magistrate, a collector of land revenue and all their assistants and establishments. There are the major-general commanding the division; the brigadier commanding the station; four troops of horse and company of foot artillery. One regiment of European cavalry, one of European infantry, one of native cavalry and three of native infantry. It is justly considered the healthiest station in India for both Europeans and natives and I visited it in the latter end of the cold weather which is the healthiest season of the year, yet the European ladies were looking as if they had all come out of their graves and talking of the necessity of going off to the mountains to renovate as soon as the hot weather should set in. They had literally been fagging themselves to death with gaiety, at this the gayest and most delightful of all Indian stations, during the cold months, when they ought to have been laying in a store of strength to carry them through the trying seasons of the hot winds and rains. Up every night and all night, at balls and suppers, they could never go out to breathe the fresh air of the morning and were looking wretchedly ill, while the European soldiers from the barracks seemed as fresh as if they had never left their native land! There is no doubt that sitting up late at nights is extremely prejudicial to the health of Europeans in India. I have never seen the European, male or female, who could stand it long, however temperate in habits; and an old friend of mine once told me that if he went to bed a little exhilarated every night at ten o'clock and took his ride in the morning, he found himself much better than if he sat up till twelve or one o'clock with drinking and lay in bed in the mornings. Almost all the gay pleasures of society in India are enjoyed at night, and as ladies here, as everywhere else in Christian societies, are the life and soul of all good parties, as of all good novels, they often, to oblige others, sit up late, much against their own inclinations and even their judgments, aware as they are that they are gradually sinking under undue exertions.

'In India officers have much better opportunities, in time of peace, to learn how to handle troops than in England, from having them more concentrated in large stations, with fine open plaints to exercise upon. During the whole of the cold season, from the beginning of November to the end of February, the troops are at large stations exercised in brigades, and the artillery, cavalry and infantry together.' W.H.S.

At Meerut great fortune befell the family they had brought with them from Agra an excellent European nurse and there they met Dr. Pennington, an old friend of Thuggee's cousin, Dr. Henry Spry. On 24th February husband and wife were sitting together at breakfast at nine o'clock. Before eleven Dr. Pennington called William in to greet Louise Josephine, their eldest daughter. With this happy arrival came other good things, for brother George wrote that he would be coming up for a visit to Jubbulpore when his regiment moved to Hyderabad in 1836. Furthermore, James reported that he had been appointed as an assistant in the Thuggee Department.

During his time at Meerut Sleeman, while continuing his war against his pet abominations of the high roads, took advantage of the occasion to make friends with still another wide circle of country people. He travelled about the villages in his buggy. One day he stopped at a small village to rest his horse and, while it was being rubbed down and baited, walked into the bazaar. He bought some parched gram (pulse) and was lent a brass jug which an old woman filled with good cold water from the well. Thuggee sat himself down, munching his gram and taking great draughts of water, with a cheerful little crowd gathered about him. He picked an old man, the head landlord of the village, on whom to sharpen his wit.

'You are a Rajput?' The old man nodded. 'Then you have gone on subdividing your inheritance until hardly any of you have anything to eat?'

'True, we have hardly any of us enought to eat, but that's the fault of the government that doesn't leave us enough—that takes from us as much when the season is bad as when it's good!'

'And if the sky were to shower down upon you pearls and diamonds, instead of water, the Government would never demand more from you than the rate fixed upon?'

'No'.

'Then why should you expect remissions in bad season?'

'It just can't be disputed that the *barkat* [blessing from above] is less under you than it used to be formerly, and the land yields less to our labour.'

'True, my old friend, and this is the reason. Forty or fifty years ago, in what you call the times of the *barkat,* the cavalry of Sikh Freebooters from the Punjab used to sweep over this fine plain and massacre the whole population of some villages and a certain portion of that of every other village, and the lands of those killed used to lie waste for want of cultivators. Is not this all true?'

'Yes, quite true.'

'And the fine groves which had been planted over this plain by your ancestors were all swept away and destroyed by the same hordes of freebooters from whom your poor imbecile emperors, cooped up in yonder large city of Delhi, were utterly unable to defend you?'

'Quite true,' said the old man with a sigh. 'I remember when all this fine plain was as thickly studded with fine groves of mango-trees as Rohilkhand or any other part of India.'

'You know that the land requires rest from labour, as well as men and bullocks, and that if you go on sowing wheat and other exhausting crops it will go on yielding less and less return and at last will not be worth the tilling?'

'Quite well.'

'Then why don't you give the land rest by leaving it longer fallow or by a more frequent alternation of crops to relieve it?'

'Because we have increased so much that we shouldn't get enough to eat were we to leave it to fallow, and unless we tilled it with exhausting crops we shouldn't get the means of paying our rents to the Government.'

'The Sikh hordes in former days prevented this. They killed off a certain portion of your families and gave the land the rest which you now refuse it. When you'd exhausted one part you found another recovered by a long fallow, so that you had better returns; but now that we neither kill you nor suffer you to be killed by others you've broght all the cultivable lands into tillage and, under the old system of cropping to exhaustion, it's not surprising that they yield you less return.

By this time he had a crowd of people around him squatting on the ground. He went on munching his gram and talking to the old patriarch. They all laughed at the old man at the conclusion of this last speech and he confessed Sleeman was right.

'That is all true, sir, but still your government isn't considerate and goes on taking kingdom after kingdom and adding to its dominions without diminishing the burtden upon us, its old subjects. Here you have had armies taking away Afghanistan, but we shall not have one rupee less to pay!'

'True, my friend, nor would you demand a rupee less from those honest cultivators around us if we were to leave you all your lands untaxed. You complain of the Government—they compain of you.' (Here the circle around laughed at the old man again.)

'True, sir, very true—that is, no doubt, a very great evil.'

'And you know it is not an evil produced by us, but one arising out of your laws of inheritance. You have heard, no doubt, that with us the eldest son gets the whole of the land and the younger sons all go out in search of service, with such share as they can get of other property of their father?'

'Yes, sir. But where shall we get service? You have none to give us. I would serve tomorrow if you would take me a soldier,' said he, stroking his white whiskers.

The crowd laughed heartily and some observed that Sleeman would think him too old.

'Well,' said the old man, smiling, 'the gentleman is not himself very young and yet I dare say he is a good servant of his government!'

This paid Sleeman off for making the people laugh at the old man's expense. 'True, my old friend,' he said, 'but I began to serve when I was young and have been long learning.'

'Very well,' said the old man, 'but I should be glad to serve the rest of my life upon a smaller salary than you got when you began to learn.' That raised another laugh.

'Well, my friend, you complain of our government, but you must acknowledge that we do all we can to protect you, though it's true that we're often acting in the dark.' With a wink and a friendly grin Thuggee strolled off to his buggy.

On 12th April, by way of Saharanpore and Dehra Doon, as the heat was increasing in the plains, the family reached their bungalow high up at Mussoorie looking down on the magnificent broad green valley of the Doon with the silver ribbons of Ganges and Jumna winding out from the mountains on either side. Here they remained until late December, Amelie amusing herself within Mr. Webb's hotel on the fine billiard tables with slate beds, which had at that time newly arrived in India and had only lately been introduced in England. The whole family regained their health and spirits, Thuggee himself soon becoming the stalwart that he had been of old. In the autumn he went off with some friends on a walking tour of the Himalaya.

In October William applied to Calcutta for permission to return to the civil charge of Jubbulpore district, which he had left in 1830, and to resign from his position as Superintendent of the Thuggee Department. He felt that he might as Superintendent of the Thuggee Department, be getting out of touch with the administrative side of his profession. Everybody was most sympathetic. The governor-general noted the application and said that he must leave the decision to the Lieutenant-Governor of the North-Western Provinces. Still later on, the Court of Directors in London said that they could not 'allow the occasion of Major [he was promoted in February 1837] Sleeman's relinquishment of the important trust in which he has rendered so eminent a service to India and to human nature itself, to pass without directing Government to intimate to that Officer their warmest approbation of the manner in which that trust has been executed,' and 'their high appreciation of the qualities which have been manifested in planning and in conducting a system of operations which is in great measure of his creation.' The outcome of all the sympathy was that he did return to civil charge of Jubbulpore but retained, in addition, the post of Superintendent of the Thuggee Department, so his application, far from relieving him, simply increased the burden. He remarked rather wryly that was the result of applying for anything! Never again!

In January 1837 the family was back in Jubbulpore and Thuggee hard at work. His *Report on the System of Megpunnaism* was soon written, so he enjoyed his leisure hours by writing an *Analysis and Review of the Economic Doctrines of Ricardo* which he printed at the Serampore Press in India. Meanwhile little Henry was sick again. Amelie and William went into consultation and decided that she and the two children should sail for

England, so berths were booked on the East Indiaman, *Duke of Bedford,* sailing that autumn. Later, since Amelie was to have another baby early the next year, they arranged to send the five-year-old Henry home by himself to Mary Furse at Falmouth. In the autumn, therefore, they set off for Calcutta and there entrusted their small son to the captain of the ship and to their friends travelling with him. Poor old Salamat Ali, the head native Collector of Jubbulpore, who had been 'labouring in Sleeman's vineyard' for the past fifteen years and had known the boy since birth, wept bitterly when saying goodbye to little Henry. 'His two nice boys, without exactly knowing why, began to do the same; and little Henry caught the infection and wept louder than any of them.' William was obliged to hurry over the interview lest he should feel disposed to do likewise. In May 1838 Mary met the child in London and, of all things, asked him: 'Have you seen your father?' There was no reply, so she repeated it when they were in the carriage, when, she wrote afterwards, 'the burst of agony which shook his whole frame was a fearful answer and came like a mountain of misery on my mind.' Only too well do the many parents in a similar position know the price to be paid in such unhappiness.

There is in Thuggee's own hand a list of articles that he sent with Henry. Amelie's English was not yet so adept that she could readily write such a detailed document, so the devoted Thuggee undertook the labour of love. Some of the items packed in the seven large trunks were these:

15	Coloured trousers and coats	58	Eggs
21	Flannel *banians* or vests	58	Shirts
10	Pairs long white stockings	36	Pairs coloured stockings
40	Pinafores	18	Pairs of boots
16	Pairs of gloves	56	Dusters
1	Horsehair hat	5	Pairs Pashmina Stockings
6	Seers wax candles	20	Habitshers (*sic*)
1	Canister of barley	6	Seers Sago
17	Pairs of shoes	6	Seers sugar candy
1	Dozen worsted short stockings	1	Small sword
10	Dozen & 4 bottles of sweet Soda Water	1	Shovel for cabin
2	Spelling books	4	Boxes barley sugar
1	Birch for cabin	1	Pocket filter for water

Together with the large number of other items it made a formidable catalogue of needs for one little boy, albeit for six months.

No sooner had the parents returned forlorn to Jubbulpore than a message came that the governor-general had ordained that Major Sleeman should assume the appointment of Commissioner for the Suppression of Thuggee and Dacoity, whereby that officer now added to his Thug responsibilities those of wiping out the widespread and atrocious regiments to Badhak Dacoits which had ravaged, tortured and slaughtered in brutal fashion from the Nepalese border over Oudh and Bihar and had even penetrated to the Saugor district. It was not long before Sleeman 'got behind the scenes,' as he had sworn that he would long since, and found that he was slicing his way into the very band that had committed murder and violent robbery in Narsinghpore so many years ago.

On 10th February 1838 at Jubbulpore, Amelie presented him with a second daughter, whom they christened Henrietta. Soon after the Sleemans moved to Moradabad which was to be William's headquarters for the new campaign of suppression. Before they went he had the satisfaction of reading in the *Asiatic Journal* that he had been accorded the thanks of the Government for successfully establishing the Mauritius sugarcane in the Deccan. Amelie placed it on record that she considered that the thanks were due to her and demanded her reward. In Moradabad he advanced her to the charge of a bigger bungalow.

CHAPTER 17

Badhak Dacoits

For some months after Sleeman's arrival in Moradabad and his assumption of office from Hugh Fraser of the Bengal Civil Service nothing seemed to happen. The authorities were beginning to conclude that he had burnt himself out and lest this had occurred were casting round for a substitute. They were weary of the desultory campaigning which had been going on for over eight years, with no end in sight and the enemy's forays if anything on the increase. Already in Afghanistan the horizon was lowering: here at home in India British rule could not afford a hammering at its prestige. Did Sleeman imagine that his reputation would settle the affair without a struggle? The months of frustration moved slowly past. Then, in the spring of of 1839, the apparently sleeping Thuggee struck, falling like a tornado on the complacent Badhaks. They had had things all their own way, their guard was down and the effect was paralysing.

Sleeman had been studying his enemy and the area of operations, patiently moving into battle positions on a co-ordinated plan. All this was far more like soldiering than the pursuit of Thugs. He located around him several large bands of Dacoits, some numbering over a thousand strong in a system running into many thousands. They were well armed; they were well led; they were brave, cunning and cruel. It was necessary to develop a military operation, and that was a sheer joy to a man who never quite knew if he were soldier or civilian. His theatre of war lay from the Indus to the Jumna river, from the Nerbudda river to the Himalaya. His new intelligence network he linked on to his old Thug system, with information passing both ways. Now he looked over on to 'the other side of the hill,' his agents shadowing every Badhak gang. His plan was to harry all the gangs at the same time, concentrating against the two largest and best led. Having broken these two into disorganized pieces he would leave them no rest till they submitted or fled over the border into Nepal. Persons who attempted to succour or screen these murderous bandits would be dealt with as abettors of their crimes.

When he took over from Fraser in 1838 he found that the latter had recorded no information concerning these professional and hereditary robbers; indeed, all that was known was that four Badhaks had been arrested and were in jail. Fraser told Sleeeman that he had a most efficient agent who knew more about the Badhaks than anyone else in India. 'So you have,' agreed Thuggee, 'she is the sister of Chunda, a most notorious Badhak chieftain. I don't doubt she knows everything, but she hasn't told you much. However, she has seen that the Badhaks know everything you're doing.' All through 1838 Thuggee's energetic lieutenants had been combing the jails in British India and the States, and a remarkable haul they made of Badhaks who were inside for odd thefts and violence. Paton found fifty in Lucknow jail; Ramsay, Graham and Riddell sorted out a fair handful from Gwalior, Indore, Bhopal, and a few from British jails. All this fine catch came from the four whom Fraser had jailed and Thuggee had used as bait. He now turned them into what he termed 'intelligencers,' or spies.

The first targets were the companies of Mangal Sing on the far side of the Gogra river and of Gujraj, the Robin Hood of Gwalior.

For the former he allotted troops of the King of Oudh's army under a British captain, Hollings. To him Thuggee dispatched a party of his 'intelligencers,' among them a cracksman called Chandal whom Hollings at once sent in disguise across the Gogra to reconnoitre Mangal Sing's dispositions. On his return he made his report. As a pedlar he had mingled freely with the dacoits and had sold sugar to and been paid liberally by a 'fine young man of about thirty-five years of age, with large eyes, a shapely form and very courteous deportment'—Mangal Sing, Badhak robber. He moved about with a bodyguard of thiry well-armed men, feasting and celebrating and having a high old time on the proceeds of recent dacoities. Chandal located the whole force in three separate bodies.

Hollings started off well until an appeal from one of his flank parties that it was about to be beset by two thousand enemy sent him chasing uselessly off to its aid. However, even that waste of time was not fatal, but what was fatal was his entering into negotiations with Mangal Sing through some rascally women who turned out to be the wives of Mangal's subordinates. The dacoit gathered his scattered bands to fight. Hollings, coming in from all directions, soon had them penned and was looking forward to a decisive fight when they slid out of the ring through the forces of two local rajahs, who were obviously in their pay while supposedly supporting the British. Thuggee was really angry and more so because Oudh insisted on drawing off its forces from the hunt. He hurried to Lucknow and bullied and persuaded the court there to leave its troops in the field. The disorganized Badhaks, now left no opportunity to gather, were chased in famished and demoralized parties over the border into Nepal, whereupon Thuggee demanded that the Gurkha governor of Palpa should deliver up Mangal Sing and the remnants of his gangs. There was paltering, bargaining and delay but neither Brian Hodgson, the Resident at Kathmandu, nor William Sleeman were men to be balked of their prize. Hodgson brought pressure to bear on Bhim Sen, the Nepalese prime minister, while Sleeman kept watch on the border. It was the season of the deadly *awal,* the malarial scourge, in the Nepal Terai where Mangal Sing's followers were being slowly decimated. The history of the British in India is full of deeds of devotion and courage but perhaps Lieutenant MacDonough's name has not yet found a place in the record. This young officer volunteered to command the Oudh troops watching the border approaches, knowing full well that he was almost certainly signing his own death warrant. There he stood firm at his post despite everything, until the Nepalese Government handed over to him Mangal Singh and every single live dacoit of his gangs. He then delivered them into custody in Lucknow, was seized with this savage malaria and died. But he had done his duty and no one in those brave days expected more or less of him.

One large gang was thus broken. While this was in progress simultaneous heavy blows were being struck at the lesser gangs unitl they so disintegrated that Captain James Sleeman could take up the quarrel with his armed police. Further westward Sleeman had directed Birch and Graham from Rajputana and Agra to concentrate forces on the dangerous leader, Gujraj. He was so pressed for agents that it was not until later in 1839 that he could send these two officers suitable spies who knew the tangled ravines about the Chambal river, Alwar, Karauli and Gwalior States. Despite this the hunt had opened with an immediate success when one of Birch's patrols overtook a detached party of Badhaks and slew Belasa, Gujraj's son, his father's lieutenant and a cunnng resolute leader. Birch raced up to reinforce his patrol and he and Graham joined forces and smashed into Gujrarj's main body, breaking it into smithereens, then hunting the broken bits over the border into what they thought was sanctuary in Gwalior. Gujraj was among the fugitives. Sleeman's men now found a most unexpected obstacle, for the British agent for Rajputana, Colonel Sutherland, hereupon put his foot down, affirming with justice that it was illegal for Thuggee's men to hunt Gwalior subjects in the Gwalior State. Sleeman was already sadly dissatisfied at the lenient penalties dealt out to these criminals in the States, knew that they were protected by big-wigs whom they bribed, and was enraged that Birch, who had been persistently hunting Gujraj for eight years should be denied victory at this final stage by a British official, of all people. At once he demanded that Calcutta should order Colonel Sutherland to toe the line. Calcutta acted immediately.

With Birch and Graham vigorously chasing the Badhak leader, this man at length surrendered himself and all his subordinate leaders to the Gwalior army. Thuggee demanded that every one of these culprits be handed over, but the Regent of Gwalior, jealous of the success of Birch and Graham and fearing that Sleeman would certainly extract from the prisoners much information implicating the Gwalior rulers in the worst crimes of murder and robbery committed in British India, flatly refused to comply. Sleeman then ordered Graham into Gwalior to act as prosecutor in the trials and to secure every man convicted. Graham seized all those convicted on the first day, Gujraj luckily being among them. Then the Mama Sahib, the regent, blatantly swore that the rest of the twenty-five prisoners had escaped, as well as over a hundred other Badhak Dacoits whom Graham had already captured and put up for trial. Thuggee ordered Graham to bring the birds he had got and leave the rest. He then tried Gujraj and sentenced him to transportation for life.

Graham and Birch now set out after one Balkishan, another celebrated leader. In March 1841 Graham made a long trek by night and fell upon this man's bodyguard at dawn, hoping to catch him alive. Sepoy Debi Sing tried to seize him but the dacoit drew a knife, so the stout Debi dealt him a blow with his sword that severed the head from the body. He carried the head to Graham as proof of identity.

Thus it was that by 1842 Sleeman and his men had broken up every gang, both great and small, and scattered the robbers like thistledown over the borders into Nepal and into the Indian States. He conducted numerous other operations, all of much the same pattern, with the happy result that by 1848 the ominous word Badhak was forgotten.

That same year, after consideration of Lieutenant-Colonel Sleeman's final report on the Suppression of the Badhak Dacoits, the Court of Directors of the Honourable East India Company passed a resolution which included the words: '...never in the history of crime and its suppression has there been any other instance of so few arrests, compared with final convictions, or of so much security to the innocent in the pursuit of the guilty.'

While these fierce activities were still continuing, Colonel Low, Resident at the Court of Oudh, was facing a dangerous situation in Lucknow. The king had died and there was an attempt to usurp the throne by force. Low and his assistant, Paton, behaved with astonishing courage when they stood firm for the legitimate heir, surrounded as they were by a mob howling for their blood and a well-armed soldiery willing and ready to spill it, all egged on to kill them by the king's mother, who wanted her grandson on the throne and herself as regent. Indian troops of the Bengal Army arrived in the nick of time to save the lives of these two brave men. Sleeman always took a close interest in the affairs of Oudh, so he wrote to congratulate Low on his success. His interest was not wasted; there would come a day when he would be standing in Low's shoes.

However, it was only by coincidence that Lord Auckland now offered Sleeman the much coveted post of Resident at Lucknow. He readily accepted and started packing up his house and sending off his belongings to that station, eagerly looking forward to completing the task of cleaning up the Augean stable of the Kingdom of Oudh. Colonel Low, hearing that his father was dangerously ill, had tendered his resignation. As Thuggee was handing over charge at Moradabad another letter came from Lord Auckland enclosing one from Low to his lordship, saying that the house of Caunter & Co. of Calcutta, in which his brother was a partner, had failed; in consequence every farthing he had saved had been swept away. In this painful contingency he begged to place himself once more at the governor-general's disposal.

Amélie had been overjoyed at the news of her admirable William's advancement, knowing also that he longed for just this kind of employment in a Native State, where his endeavours would be rewarded by the immense satisfaction of knowing how much he was improving the sorry lot of its people. Lord Auckland's second letter arrived when she and her husband were sitting at breakfast in a half-packed bungalow. Thuggee read the note and turning to the servant behind him ordered all packing to stop.

'That is a pity on every score,' said he, handing her the letter. 'Firstly Low's poor old father will not see him, secondly poor Low will be in straits for money, and thirdly we would have enjoyed our time in Lucknow.'

Amélie read the letter and took his hand. 'It is no matter,' said she, 'as concerns us. It is poor Colonel Low we must think about, so write to him and tell him to go back to Lucknow. Now you can arrange the Bareilly race meetings, Will; everyone will be very glad you're staying on.'

'I expected that from you, my dear. I can't order Low back but I can tell him and Lord Auckland that I give up all claim to the Lucknow post.'

Thuggee walked into his office, took up his quill, wrote the two letters, stood up, stretched himself and walked off to his court-room.

A week or two later he had a personal letter from Lord Auckland, which surprised him more than any other he had ever received, for the governor-general said that, when he would leave India in February 1842, he would particularly recommend Sleeman to his successor, Lord Ellenborough. Thus it was that, when precisely the right opportunity offered, Ellenborough promoted him to the important position of his agent in Bundelkhand, with another thousand pounds a year. The additional salary was very acceptable, although brother Thomas was now no longer a drain, since he had prospered in business and become Mayor of Tenby.

During these years of which we are now speaking a British-Indian army had marched into Afghanistan to depose the Amir, who had been flirting with the Russians, and to place the British candidate on the throne. The Indian Government was for ever nervous of Russian plans in that country, not necessarily because a Russian army might march through the Khyber Pass but because Russian intrigue could easily stir the wild Pathan tribes who lay astraddle the western mountains and send them down to join hands with the great Sikh power of the Punjab. Until Britain was secure on these western mountains, the chance of a combination between the Pathans and the Indian States was a constant worry to our forbears.

Sleeman's martial ardour was raised to such a fever pitch when he heard of the disasters to our army in Afghanistan that he could not refrain from giving his opinion and advice to the governor-general, with whom he was in personal touch.

'We were ill-served by our officers in Afghanistan: of the soldiers, Elphinstone was a child and Shelton always had a character for a martinet and was detested by officers and men; Macnaghten's was the only head and he seems to have been unequal to the occasion, from his never having been sufficiently among men. As a cabinet minister or Governor, he would have been always what he had been—invaluable—but a man required more training among men for such scenes as those in which he had been engaged. His staff, moreover, were as much in the dark as he himself as to the feelings and designs of the people. Of our other soldiers, Nott, who came to the rescue after the disaster that followed our retreat from Kabul, has been of little service but has a mind, and a good deal of it—and mind goes a great way in military as in other matters: Pollock, another good soldier ....'

Allahabad 8 February 1842

. . .There is one thing I would urge for the fight with the mountaineers—you should have better arms for your light troops. All the good guns, rifles and other arms should be purchased at once and given to the light troops. I can assure you that the wretched things made in Rampore and sold at ten rupees a piece are better than what are served out in our Magazines. Fifty good rifles or good fowling pieces would be of more use in the hands of light infantry than five hundred of the others. . . . The Sikhs are doing well. The licking they have had in China [Thibet] has been useful and they think we are now fighting their battle. They will feel entirely dependent upon us during the rest of this fearful contest. We must occupy the Khyber Pass, *coûte que coûte*. And when we do, all will be well. . . . Send a whole steamer with good guns to be distributed to the best marksmen of the Light Infantry, European and Natives. Each officer of the Light Infantry should have Smith's double-barrel rifle to save his men by picking off these devils at a distance.

I see another letter of Avenger in the Delhi paper of the 2nd of this month. I think it must be old Richards, the best officer for Mountain warfare that we have had in any time. I wish he had been 20 years younger and at the head of the troops has ever been mentally weak. . . .

He toured his own areas and found all peaceful. He made his report to the governor-general.

Allahabad,
9th February 1842

My Lord,

. . . Tomorrow is the last day of the great Hindu Festival at the Junction of the Ganges and Jumna at this place, and the concourse of people is greater than it has been known for many years. I rode through the whole of this morning with the Judge, Mr. Lang, unattended, and everywhere the people made way for us with the same respectful attention as usual and were displaying their merchandize of all kinds with the same feeling of entire security as if they had heard nothing of what has occurred in the North West, though the merchants of Allahabad receive the news as quickly as we do. The Magistrate, Mr Montgomery, to whom all look up with confidence, sat upon his little bench in the midst of at least four hundred thousand persons, attended by only two or three persons and a couple of native writers. The European ladies go of an evening along the street that leads through the whole of this crowd in their chairs, making their purchases with as much security as they would in any street in London. A noble feeling towards us and our rule pervades the whole Hindu community and, I should, nine-tenths of the Mahomedans; as they, the Mahomedans, are not more than one-tenth of the whole, I may say that this feeling pervades ninety-nine hundred of our subjcts.

A vast deal of this is owing to the measures adopted within the last few years—the great moderation in our revenue settlements, the abolition of the transit duties and odious right of search involved in them, that of the pilgrim tax—the liberal share in the administration given to the educated classes—the formation of roads and the security given to travellers upon them—these and many others are giving us a firm hold upon the respect and affections of the people. . . .

CHAPTER 18

Rebellion

Three years earlier, on 28th July 1839, Amélie gave birth to a third daughter—Amelia. That was just one year after they reached Moradabad. Then nephew James was posted to Burhanpore as assistant in the Thuggee Department, and so became his uncle's right-hand man. But there was much on the debit side. A deep sorrow afflicted poor Thuggee when he learnt of the death of his dearly loved younger brother George, of the Queen's 39th Regiment. At the end of November, George had been ordered to meet a large detachment of new recruits who had arrived in Bombay from England. He accordingly set out for Joulna to take them over. On 28th November, he arrived at his camp in perfect health, complained the next morning that he was feeling unwell but rode through the march. At Joulna at eight o'clock that evening he was dead of cholera. On getting the news Thuggee ordered out his tents and went off alone on a short tour to pull himself together. Like so many of his time George was a most devout Christian and was not ashamed to express himself as such in conversation and letters, whereas William was broader based and less emotional but held his brother's genuine piety in deep respect.

Early in 1842 he learnt of the death of his lifelong friend Captain John Furse, husband of his sister Mary. John had died of wounds and hardships endured in his many actions at sea, leaving Mary a childless widow. So Amélie and William once more consulted about their children and decided to send the three little girls off from Calcutta to England to join Henry with sister Mary at Falmouth. In May came the anxiously awaited news of their arrival.

Perhaps it was as well, with all these partings so thick upon him and Amélie, that out of a blue and peaceful sky there should suddenly burst upon him rumour upon rumour of violence and insurrection in his old domain of Saugor and Bundelkhand. Although Thuggee was deeply plunged in his dacoit campaign, Lord Ellenborough summoned him post-haste to meet him at Allahabad. Off went Thuggee, pressing ahead by night and day. At Allahabad Ellenborough told him outright that he was the only man who could put matters straight and that he was to go off and do it at once. Like a cannon ball, Thuggee shot off again to his old stamping-ground at Saugor. Unable to find out from the governor-general or anyone else why this trouble had broken out, he dashed off a few messages to men whom he knew and trusted, asking for news. Major J.G. Drummond replied succinctly: 'I am decidedly of the opinion that our late Governor-General [Auckland] was most unfortunate in almost the whole of his appointments. They were generally speaking either hot-headed fools, or self-sufficient, overbearing blockheads: and it is well they are turned out to make way for better men.'

So Thuggee in a fine indignation descended upon the blockheads who had set his old friends by the ears.

In his report he said that the outbreak in Saugor, at least, had 'originated in the insolence of office. Had the country been full of troops, men would have submitted to it, however bitter the draught.' The two leading personages in this rebellion had flown to arms simply because one of them had lost a case in the Company's civil court, while the other considered that he was the victim of an unreasonable demand for the quit-rent. It was a most confused rising with no particular shape. One act of violence, in which a mob of armed Bundela cultivators had set upon and killed a few policemen near Jhansi, then plundered a village, led to unconnected and sporadic outbursts of violence all over these regions.

Thuggee found that not only were the British officials in fear of their lives, but even their Indian servants could not move outside their compounds and none could visit the bazaars to buy food. He was dumb founded at this strange state of affairs where all had been peace, trust and confidence. He summoned the British officials to meet him as he rode into each district, ordering them to send to him Indians whom he had known in former days. He himself, scorning to go about among his old friends with any sort of escort, rode openly through the countryside and was not only unchallenged, but welcomed with a most touching friendship as though he were indeed a deliverer.

The lieutenant-governor had already ordered troops into the area, so Sleeman, having interviewed and drawn to his side a large number of loyal Indian landholders, made back to Jhansi to receive the commanders and dispose the troops over the affected regions. He had also arranged to meet James in order to concert measures lest this lawlessness brought out of hiding any of the gangs that they hunted into the States. His headquarters were now located at Jhansi in a country of plains and woods, with hills, rivers and pools, and thither came Amélie.

On 1st May 1842, in the early morning, he had James rode out for their customary exercise. As they passed the gate of their house Sleeman noticed a native sitting with his back against the post. James also glanced down and, after they had ridden a little way, told Thuggee that this was a man he had dismissed from the service for grave misconduct when at Bareilly a few months ago: he supposed the man had come to appeal against dismissal. 'He's already appealed and I've refused it,' answered his uncle.

On their return the man was still there. As he said nothing they took no notice, and at six o'clock went to breakfast. Amélie was waiting for them but before she could sit down had to retire, and at eight o'clock she introduced Thuggee to his fourth daughter, Elizabeth. With such a large family Thuggee was now seriously considering settling in America, and particularly retiring to the Mississippi valley as the only field extensive enough for a family such as his was becoming. He wished that he had the means of settling there with twenty years less on his shoulders. 'It is a noble country, were it not deformed with that horrible system of slavery. It can only shake off that, its institutions will make it a model for the world. I read all I can find about America, among other works being de Tocqueville's magnificent work on Democracy in America.'

For a few days he stayed at his headquarters collecting reports from his officers and, as was now his custom, from his agents. Daily he and James rode out in the early morning and daily they passed the squatter at the gate. It happened that James had brought with him the native police officer who had reported this ex-sepoy for a criminal neglect of duty. So they all three knew he was there but thought he was only the usual importunate petitioner. Neither Thuggee nor James, out of pride, ever thought of mentioning to each other that whereas the man was at first in sackcloth and ashes he was by degrees arming himself with a knife, then a blunderbuss and then a sword. He seemed a little soft in the head.

After breakfast one day they went with the police inspector to walk round the Sleeman stables, along one side of which ran a low wall. The trio stood talking near this wall, the inspector with his back to it.

There was a shattering blast and a great gust of smoke. The inspector fell forward into Thuggee's arms. James leapt the wall and charged after a fleeing figure. He tripped and fell. The murderer turned with drawn sword and James lay at his mercy, as he was later to lie at the mercy of a wounded tiger.

He rose on one knee, grasping the handle of the axe over which he had fallen, and hurled it with all his strength, striking his attacker in the chest and sending him staggering aside. Thuggee's orderly, Tikaram, rushed in, receiving a cut on the wrist and throwing the man to the ground. The grooms joined in and bound the raging fanatic, the *Ghazi,* with ropes.

Thuggee was attending his policeman, who breathed his last in his arms. Four musket balls had lodged in the lungs from behind. He was distraught with grief, for those pellets had obviously been meant for him.

James ran to him. 'We were fools!' muttered Thuggee. 'We should have expected that from an Afghan.'

Later in court the assassin confessed that he had primed himself for this clumsy murder with the maddening hempen drug called *charras.* This was only one more lucky escape for the man who had earned the bitter enmity of every would-be murderer in central India.

The governor-general's agents parted with his nephew and resumed his personal tour of the districts. By 1st August he could report to Maddock, Secretary to the Government of India, that he had brought into submission every rebellious chief except three minor rajahs, some by the use of force but nearly all by persuasion and the ties of old friendship. In January 1843 he had travelled throughout the whole area and everywhere the people, as he passed on his way, flocked round him expressing their gratitude at what he had done to bring about 'this peaceful state of affairs' where all had so recently been plundering, strife and rapine. 'I was concerned to find that there was no longer that sympathy between the people and the agents now employed in these regions by our Government. The European officers no longer showed that courtesy towards the middle and higher classes and that kindness towards the humbler which characterized the officers of our day, while the native officers rather imitated or took advantage of this.'

He sent his soldiers after the three remaining recalcitrants and had the pleasure of accepting the surrender of the last of them mounted on his ceremonial elephant in the presence of the Rajah of Jhansi; an impressive ending only marred by one of the rajah's elephants going *musth* at a time when no one dared shoot it for fear of alarming the crowd and setting alight another civil war. It barged about, hurled over other beasts and trampled on sightseers, until its *mahout* was able to coax it out into the open country where it set off on a solitary steeple-chase, its galloping rump disappearing, almost zooming, round a mango grove in the distance.

Only one of the rebellious chiefs of Bundelkhand had shown any resistance. Sleeman always had a ready fellow feeling for a good rebel who rose in anger against inefficient, careless or oppressive rule, but he had nothing but scorn for the man who made rebellion serve as an excuse for plunder and murder. This prince had been ringleader in inciting the wild border tribes to ravage British districts, and to pillage and slaughter harmless peasants. This one man alone, despite his protestations to make of him an example. Infantry, cavalry and artillery marched on his capital town. He fled.

On the vacant *gaddi* Sleeman set a better-conditioned prince of the same family, at the same time offering the fugitive a sufficient pension for life. This the latter contemptuously refused, and assembled a considerable force in a strong position in the foothills. Here Sleeman's brigadier came upon him, and the brigade, incensed at the devastation they had witnessed across the countryside, roared into the attack as one man carrying the position in one assault. The rebels scattered to the four winds, their leader fleeing into the forests. Destitute, he in time came forth and gave himself up. Thuggee, generous to the defeated, conferred on him the pension he had originally offered.

Besides the unfortunate collection in one area of all the incompetents of the Company's civil service, there were other reasons for this outbreak. For one thing it had been predicted by astrologers that British rule would come to an end in this year, Sumbut 1890, and the resounding defeats in Afghanistan together with the successes of the rebels early on in the revolt had given colour to this unlucky prediction. Sleeman's report covered all points. The outcome of this report was harsher than he had liked. To some extent he blamed himself for the result because he had refused to give the names of the delinquents to the Government, being certain that he could himself restore them to a proper sense of their duty. Lord Ellenborough, having no particular names, adjudged all to be guilty. In Bundelkhand he removed the most culpable officers but in the Saugor district he swept the whole yard clean, placing Sleeman at the head of the government of the territory, as commissioner, remarking that he 'possessed to a degree the confidence of Chiefs and people,' and had 'that without which good Government is in India impossible—a real feeling of regard for the natives of the 'Country.' All the new officers whom Ellenborough appointed were men who had been on service in the field with the Indian Army and 'had had the opportunity of appreciating the many natural virtues of the native character.'

Sleeman, now as at other times, was too forbearing with those who failed him or fell down on their jobs in any capacity. Himself determined and of restless energy, intensely interested in every facet of the life about him, even in the failures themselves, he tardily accepted that there were some who by nature were incurably unenterprising, indolent, careless or selfish. For too long he suffered these men, always expecting that his own enthusiasm would work the improvement that sometimes never came. Here, on this occasion, he was persuaded that if matters were left to him he could deal with those who had failed the State and would see that they never failed again. He may have been right but he was not given the chance to make the attempt.

With the added authority, Sleeman moved about with added dignity. He says that he travelled in such princely style because the governor-general wished it, had given him the means, and it fell in with the tastes of the native chiefs among whom he represented the Government. He had a carriage and two pair and a half of fine mares of English breed, four fine saddle horses, three riding elephants, sixty camels for his tents and he knew not how many carts for table and kitchen gear, besides numerous porters of all descriptions. His escort consisted of a couple of companies of infantry and a troop of cavalry, with one captain and one subaltern. The two six-pounders he sent back.

The severe results of Sleeman's report at once set the press by the ears. The Delhi papers were filled with misrepresentations of the state of affairs in Bundelkhand, written by a certain colonel of the 8th Cavalry, merely because Sleeman would not agree to the spot he had chosen for encamping a Brigadier Young's force. A Captain H., who was annoyed because Sleeman had refused to accept him for a post in the Saugor territories, under the pseudonym of 'A Voice from Bundelcund' wrote a number of villainous letters to the *Delhi Gazette*, in which he slandered Sleeman and his administration. The Allahabad correspondent of the *Bombay Times* levelled serious charges against the efficient Thuggee. For once he was stung into replying to the charges in the columns of that paper and sent Lord Ellenborough a copy of his reply, saying that if he allowed these charges to pass it must reflect on the governor-general for employing such a dastard as his representative in Bundelkhand.

To his letter he received the following from Lord Ellenborough himself, not much to his liking and certainly a caution to him to let the attacks of the press go unheeded.

Barrackpore, August 14, 1843.
'Sir,

I only received today your letter of the 3rd enclosing a copy of your letter to the *Bombay Times* in refutation of certain customary falsehoods which had been published. The refutation is certainly perfect and I can have no objection to anything except to your having transmitted for publication in a newspaper an official document. It is not that in the present instance the publication of documents which came before you officially and of the letter which accompanied these when they were transmitted to you can do any harm, but the principle is important that no public officer has, without the previous permission of his Government, any power over the documents of which he comes into possession by means of his office or even over the official letters he himself writes. In this country, where precedent is so much adhered to, it is essential to guard against the creation of a bad one. Another public officer without your judgement might, deeming himself permitted to do so by this precedent, publish documents or letters of which the publication might be very injurious to the service of his Government . . . unless I have been greatly misinformed your character in India would have enabled you to allow such falsehoods as these which you have repelled to pass in contemptuous silence, and I must advise you to trust to your character and not, unless under most extreme and extraordinary circumstances, to descend into the arena with the anonymous slanders of the press. . . .

It was now that Sleeman, having settled Thuggee and Dacoity in a campaign of years and seeing the disturbing effects on the minds of all people, from the highest to the lowest, of the continuing fear that the Company would annex those Indian States on its borders, launched himself on the final campaign of his career. His object was, at all costs to himself, to persuade the British power from any further appropriation of territory. It was a noble end but one feels that he was only one small vessel plying helplessly against the whole flood of history. Day in and day out he strove with pen and voice and by the example he himself set to render it unnecessary and inexpedient to encroach further upon the possessions of the Indian rajahs and other rulers. Had he, here and at Saugor and later at Gwalior and Oudh, adopted the doctrines of the absorbing school he considered that he might have become one of the most popular and influential men in India; but he would, he said, at the same time have rendered our rule and character odious to the people of India and so far have injured our permanent interest in the country. The people see that these annexations and confiscations go on and that rewards and honorary distinctions are given for them, and for the victories which lead to them, and for little else. *The Native States I consider to be breakwaters and when they are all swept away, we shall be left at the mercy of our native army, which may not always be sufficiently under our control.* Such a feeling as that which pervaded Bundelkhand and Gwalior in 1842 must, sooner or later, pervade all India—if these doctrines are carried out to their full extent: and our rule could not, probably, exist under it.

Discussing the expansion of Rome, in *A History of Europe,* H.A.L. Fisher writes: 'The successive stages of her conquest of Italy were forced upon her because, as Britain afterwards experienced in India, an orderly power ringed round by turbulence always finds itself compelled to establish peace and security upon its frontiers.'

The italics are mine: they relate to events in 1857.

While riding about during this insurrection, Thuggee would gather the local people around him and hold a pow-vow on the causes and conditions that had led to the disturbances. Most of these farmers and peasants had been mercilessly plundered by the landed aristocracy from the jungles on the borders of the Indian States. These jungle barons were the very people who had in the past protected Thugs and Dacoits. On one occasion Sleeman had some fifty of the local people seated about him in his tent. After remonstrating with them for the want of support on their part of the government officers, he turned to Umrai Sing, whom he had known for twenty-five years on the banks of the Nerbudda. 'Why did you withhold from the local officers the information which you must have had of the movements and positions of the rebels and their followers who were laying the country waste? In no part of India have the farmers and cultivators been more favoured in fight assessments and protection of life and property; but there are some men who never can be satisfied; give them what you will, they will always be craving for more.'

'True, sahib,' said Umrai Sing, looking him steadily in the face and with the greatest possible gravity, 'there are some people who never can be satisfied, give them what you will. Give them the whole of Hindustan, and they will go off to Kabul and take more!'

There was a pause, during which all except Sleeman, who was enjoying himself, looked somewhat embarrassed at the old man's strictures. He continued: 'After the Mahratta war, in 1817, you prohibited the people of your newly acquired districts from carrying arms, not dreaming that the only persons who would obey or regard your order were the peaceful landholders and peasantry of the plains who were satisfied with your government and anxious for its duration, but were exposed to the envy and hatred of the Gond and Lodhi chiefs who occupied the hills and jungles on their borders.

'When they came down upon us, you had no means left to protect us; and, having no longer any arms or any experience of the use of them after a quarter of a century of peace, we were unable to defend our villages, our houses or our families; if we attempted to defend them we and our families were killed; if we did not we were robbed and threatened with death if we gave you information to their prejudice. We saw that they could carry their threats into execution, for your local officers had not the means to protect us from their vengeance, and we suffered in silence. But you must not infer from this that we were tired of your rule or pleased with their depredations; all here can testify that we longed for the return of your strength and their downfall. It is true, however, that the new European officers placed over us did not treat us with the same courtesy and consideration as the old ones, or seem to entertain the same kindly feeling towards us, and our communion with them was less free and cordial.'

Sleeman comments: 'All approved, as did I, of my old friend's speech and declared that he had given expression to the thoughts and feelings of all present, and of all the people of the plains, who lived happily under our rule and prayed earnestly for its duration.'

The insurrection was over and the peace of Sleeman spread over the land. This latest *tour de force* of William Sleeman was a triumph of personality, probably the greatest of his life. In the modern democratic fold, where virtue is scorned as prejudice, self-control mocked at as narrow-minded and exhibitionism made to do for leadership, it is seldom that honest personality or leadership can register itself in a great cause until the terror-stricken sheep come bleating for a shepherd. There is dire risk that one day the sheep will have baa'ed our available shepherds into withdrawal from public life, no leader will arise and wolves will take charge of the fold. Therefore it is good to look back to a country and an age where a sterling personality could so decisively prevail. There is a great full fixed between those who think and write and talk and those who can do these things but also must act. The latter—the Sleeman, the rare birds—can visit either side of the gulf at will: the former can seldom cross.

CHAPTER 19

The Battle of Maharajpore

In Chapter 10 mention is made of the seizure of the throne of the Mahratta State of Gwalior by the ill-natured young prince, Jankoji. In 1842 his maharani became pregnant. One of the ministers on the maharajah's personal staff was a man called 'the Khasji.' This rogue wished his chief to have a son and heir, and prepared to ensure the event. Sleeman's report to Lord Ellenborough told the whole story. Other authorities have questioned the truth of the report, but in view of its author's well-known integrity the strange story must be accepted. Khasji smuggled in from outside several women expected to be confined at the same time, hoping that at least one would give birth to a boy whom he could substitute for a daughter if the maharani were not fortunate enough to bear a son. His intention was then to poison the chief and to have himself proclaimed as regent during the boy's minority. It so happened that none of the ladies met his wishes: not a boy was born. There was no male heir.

The poor maharani and her infant both died. Jankoji, anxious for an heir, married late in 1842 a little girl of twelve years old. However, early in 1843 this prince died without heir, unmourned and unwept, whereupon the little maharani, as was customary, adopted a nine-year-old relative, one Jyoji, as her son and as heir to Gwalior. It happened that in May 1843 Sleeman was in that territory on Dacoit business when a court intrigue overthrew the regent, the Mama Sahib. The Gwalior army, the real power behind the scenes as usual, was heavily implicated. The person most active in deposing the Mama Sahib was this same Dada Khasji Wala, who promptly obtained for himself a position in Gwalior little less influential than that of the now vacant regency. On this the Resident, Spiers, was withdrawn to Dholpore, outside Gwalior territory, as a mark of the governor-general's displeasure with the court. Being on the spot, Thuggee included in his dispatches to the governor-general an account of the new turn of events, stressing again the danger to the State and to all its neighbours of the lawlessness of the Gwalior army.

In June Sleeman read that he had been gazetted to the rank of lieutenant-colonel on 26th May, the rank that is so often the hurdle of officers of the army.

It happened that at this time the Sikh state at Lahore was in alarmingly confused condition following the death of its great Ranah, Ranjit Singh. The Government of India feared that the Sikh army might break out, cross the border into our territory and enter into a confederation with the truculent Gwalior forces. The Gwalior durbar, with its little thirteen-year-old maharani as regent and its child of nine as maharajah, was thrown into utter disorder by all these activities, and lawlessness and anarchy widely prevailed. The governor-general wrote to Sleeman predicting the necessity of moving a strong force into Gwalior. He had already decided that the Gwalior army was a menace that he must confront and had accordingly directed the commander-in-chief to place his headquarters at Cawnpore and to assemble a considerable force there for exercises.

For a time after the expulsion of the Mama Sahib the new regency had some control of the troops and kept a firm hand on the treasury, so that the troops found that they could get their pay, this being about all they cared for. However, by the autumn national feeling in Gwalior was uniting all factions against the Company and the position of the maharani and the little maharajah was becoming precarious, the latter's life being at the whim of the army. On 27th October, Lord Ellenborough suddenly added the Dominions of Scindhia (Gwalior) to Sleeman's already extensive territory, so that the whole problem of the Gwalior Native State was imposed upon him and he superseded Spiers as Resident. The charge now committed to him was an immense one, that of Bundelkhand, Saugor and the Nerbudda territories, the Dominions of Scindhia and, still, the duties of the General Superintendent for the Suppression of Thuggee and Dacoity. This addition was flattering but onerous.

He took a rapid survey of all his duties and territory, called in his officers for consultation and, after a visit to Saugor to make certain that there could be no more trouble from there, rode the two hundred miles into Gwalior, where he arrived in mid November. Here he found such a threatening state of affairs and so turbulent an army that he sent word to the governor-general. He was thereupon instructed to attempt, by negotiation at the court and by using a firm hand with the army, to obtain the surrender of the Khasji. In this he succeeded, expecting that that would be the end of the matter. Doubtless he was aided by a threatening gesture of the Company's army, for on 11th December the governor-general, who was by now at Agra, put the army into motion towards Gwalior. On 18th December Lord Ellenborough wrote to him.

'The Governor-General is gratified by the delivery of the Dada Khasji Wala to the charge of the British Government, as indicating, on the part of Her Highness and the Durbar of Gwalior, a disposition to restore the accustomed relations of friendship between the two states. But Her Highness is already informed that the movement of the British armies cannot be arrested until the Governor-General has full security for the future maintenance of tranquillity upon the common frontier; nor until there shall be stablised at Gwalior a Government willing and able to coerce its own subjects, and to maintain permanently the relations of amity with the British Government and its allies.'

He then went on to insist on the expediency of increasing the proportion of the Gwalior forces under the control of British officers.

On his part Thuggee Sleeman unceasingly and desperately urged upon the Government the need for moderation and patience, but his plea went unheeded. The issue, after the surrender of the Khasji, soon became for him simply one of whether the little maharajah, now summoned to a conference, should meet the governor-general on the other side of the River Chambal outside his own territory, as was the inviolable custom, or whether the governor-general should cross the Chambal to meet him inside the Gwalior borders, and so gravely offend the susceptibilities of the population and army of Gwalior.

On 21st December Thuggee again wrote urgently to the Government: 'When I mentioned his Lordship's intention to cross the Chambal on the 22nd, Sacharan Rao, the brother of Ram Rao Phalkea, and Balwant Rao, who had come to meet me, expressed a very earnest desire that this might not take place, as it was usual for His Highness to pay the first visit to the Governor-General on the other side of the river. They seemed to have this very much at heart, and I think it my duty to mention it.' He followed this with a statement of the ceremonies observed in 1832, when the chief first crossed the Chambal to visit the governor-general and the latter crossed to the Gwalior side the following day to return the visit, hoping that protocol might prevail where good sense was failing.

On 22nd December he visited the maharajah and the maharani and told them that he had been commanded to report to the governor-general's camp and then to return and to accompany the young chief. He thereafter again reported to the secretary that 'they were exceedingly earnest in the expression of their hope that his Lordship would remain to receive the young chief's visit on the other side of the Chambal'.

On the 24th, near despair, he once more wrote to the secretary, who was still with the governor-general. 'The soldiers talk largely to my people of the army crossing the Chambal as a hostile movement on the part of our Government.'

On the 25th he described the absolute disorganization of the Gwalior army, the violent feeling against the passage of the Chambal and the impossibility of averting a collision if British troops were brought into contact with the Gwalior forces.

He then quitted Gwalior to visit the governor-general and pitched his camp at Dhunaila, whence he entreated the durbar to persuade the maharajah to meet him and accompany him to the governor-general. His continued presence in Gwalior was, he found, only embittering feeling against his government and was achieving nothing towards a settlement of the differences. At Dhunaila it became apparent to him that if he were again to visit the maharajah it must be without a single soldier, horse or foot, for it would be impossible to prevent a violent incident if any of them accompanied him; and among such a licentious soldiery, without any competent commanding officers, he decided that it was unsafe for any European or native officer to go with him. An untoward incident would precipitate a general conflict. There was a large park of Gwalior artillery on each side of the river at Dhunaila and the troops boasted to him and to those in his camp that they were come to throw the British back over the Chambal.

The fatal step had, however, been taken; the British army had passed over the Chambal river.

By now the sentiments of everyone in Gwalior, from the court to the meanest soldier, were hostile to the British, and Sleeman's position at Dhunaila was one of extreme hazard. On 28th December, learning that British forces were approaching Maharajpore, he rode out by little-known tracks towards that place. All about him were Maharatta soldiers hurrying forward and he had to use the utmost discretion to avoid clashing with them. A solitary rider with only a groom riding by him luckily attracted little attention among the already preoccupied and excited soldiery. He satisfied himself that a battle must ensue soon after daylight, unless he could do something to persuade the maharajah's encourage to bring the prince early the next day to meet Lord Ellenborough. In great haste he galloped back to his camp to find out the whereabouts of the maharajah, fearing that he might even now be in the field with his army, but learned to his relief that, as far as was known, he was daily at his camp though spending the nights at his great fort in Gwalior. Thuggee determined to make a last bid for peace, no matter what the consequences might be to himself.

Before dawn on 29th December he left his camp accompanied only by a native mounted orderly, both of them unarmed.

According to his reckonings, the British and Mahrattas would clash near Maharajpore but the main battle would be fought about Seondah, nearer to Gwalior. He had seen the Gwalior army marching from its cantonments towards the fortified village of Seondah and there taking position, throwing out artillery and infantry outposts in some strength towards Maharajpore. He knew full well that while he talked with the prince, General Gough would be advancing his army in battle order and that he might never see the light of the sun again. As dawn broke he looked at the brightening sky with a new feeling of wonder at the beauty that he had seen almost daily throughout his life in India.

Word of his visit had been sent before him to the maharajah. He prayed now that the very crops and the broken ravines of the wide plains about Seondah would so delay Gough's advance that he would yet have time to persuade the prince to come at once with him to the British camp, and to send word to his army that he was on his way and that it should withdraw to a safe distance from the British while Sleeman galloped on to meet his lordship.

He clattered over the stones to the vast walls of the fort, through the heavy gates before the sleepy sentries could realize the need to question his presence, and up the twelve hundred steps he rode with his single attendant into Gwalior fort, the strongest prison in India. The place was full of Mahratta soldiers, their attitude to him, particularly that of the officers at the main guard, truculent if not hostile. He feigned to see nothing unusual in his visit and was admitted to the courtyard. As he approached the audience hall he dismounted and threw the reins to his groom, telling him to take both horses to the foot of the steps and to await him by a tank outside the fort where there was shade for man and beast.

Following the durbar officer he walked into the audience hall. Here he was met by the new minister, Ram Rao Phalkea, until lately a staunch friend of the British and, fortunately for him, a personal friend of his own. They conversed for a short while until the chief, a mere boy, entered, attended by members of his household, when Sleeman paid his compliments to His Highness and asked for what reason his entourage appeared fully armed. The chamberlain replied that in these troubled times men must care for their own lives. Sleeman pointed to his riding whip and said that the British force had no wish to fight, the Gwalior authorities could ensure that their army had no such intention either.

He now implored the maharajah and his minister to accompany him to the governor-general's camp at once, so as to assure him of Scindhia's wish to find a peaceful settlement and of his intention to purge army and court of its violent and hostile members. His requests were met with great politeness, but nothing he could say would overcome the feeling of insult and grief at the violation of Gwalior territory by the Company's army.. Without this he might have succeeded.

The discussion dragged on for an hour, the minister for ever demanding the withdrawal at once of the British forces over the Chambal before any negotiations could take place. Sleeman knew that it was too late to effect this but that there was just time for a meeting between the chief and the governor-general, at which there would be some faint hope that the British army might be halted and the Gwalior army drawn back on Gwalior. As he was repeating his appeal with great earnestness, an officer of the household entered and sought the prime minister's ear. Turning to Sleeman the latter said: 'I should tell you, sir, that your army is advancing on Gwalior and that there is fighting about Maharajpore. You had better leave here before it is too late.'

'There is time yet,' said Sleeman, 'to avoid a general action. If the maharajah will let himself be seen riding with me on the high road towards the British and send word to his army that he is to negotiate for peace all is not yet lost.'

Thuggee remained talking for a little, anxious not to show any doubt of his safety, and then, unhurried, expressed his profound regrets that his visit was fruitless, paid his compliments and bade the chief and the minister farewell. Stepping slowly out into the sunlight, he strained his ears for the sound of guns but could hear none. Across the courtyard he went unconcernedly, wending his way past the main guard and down those long twelve hundred steps. To hurry would have cost him his life. He had refused an escort, as he thought it unworthy that he should be protected as he walked from the house of his friends. This he had told the minister before the prince, and the point was understood.

All about him was a crowd of soldiers, coming and going in haste and mostly in excitement. They regarded him with suspicion and surprise and many cast a backward glance at him. It would have been so easy and so readily excused to cut him down. At the guard on the gate the officer ordered him to halt. Thuggee stopped and asked him if he usually halted the maharajah's visitors, for if he did his ears would not long be on his head. He passed on, out through the gate, but the horses were not in sight. He wondered how he would escape if he did not find them. If he ran he would be cut down at once. It might come to this, that he should have to face the enemy and dare them to kill him.

He walked on over the bridge in the blazing sunlight and there at last he found his orderly, fast asleep in the shade of a further grove of trees. In haste he mounted, set spurs to his horse and left the slumberer to follow as he might. Tightening girths as he rode he trotted steadily on, pulling rein to walk his horse through the town for fear of disturbing the already buzzing hive. As he reached the far end of the street his orderly caught up with him and the sound of a brisk cannonade broke on his ears. Here at last he could cast all discretion aside, and broke into a gallop, riding hard for his camp at Dhunaila to warn it and to set it on the move away from the Gwalior force hard by.

As he galloped over the plain he could see that his assistant was aware of the position and that all was in readiness and awaiting his arrival to get on the road. After all was over Sleeman confessed that he fervently hoped that he would never again find himself in such a pickle. It was one thing to face a stronger enemy and to fight it out and quite another to stand helplessly waiting to be hacked to bits by a ruthless mob.

General Gough had overstepped his mark, as Sleeman rather expected he would.

His army had forced its way through Maharajpore on to the dead level plain which extends from that village to Seondah. This immense plain, which spreads for miles on either side, is partially intersected with ravines, but for the most part is fertile and cultivated. The ravines had imposed delays on General Gough, which had enabled Sleeman to take his leave of Gwalior fort and to keep his life and his freedom, but must have enraged the bold general. The fine crops, in the absence of all reconnaissance on the part of Gough's leads, served to hide the Mahratta infantry and artillery from observation by the advancing columns, who only became aware of the enemy's position when finding themselves within range of their guns. The surprise was so complete that the governor-general and the ladies, who were attending as though for a social occasion, found themselves with the cannon balls bowling about their elephants' legs. No one seemed to expect a battle, despite the serious warnings that Sleeman had repeatedly sent to them of the extreme feelings of the Gwalior army and court.

Relying on the never-failing courage of the Europeans he commanded, the commander-in-chief put his favourite—or, as it might seem from his later campaigns on the Sutlej, his only—measure into execution and carried the Mahratta batteries at the point of the bayonet.

In less than three hours the Gwalior *finsi* (their famous artillery), ammunition and stores, etc., were in Gough's hands. But this success was dearly purchased. The loss of life, among both European and native troops, was very considerable.

The enemy had wisely taken up their positions among ravines, which were deep enough to prevent Gough's cavalry acting in force. The Mahratta cavalry 10,000 strong, made off at the opening of the action. The infantry maintained a resolute defence about the villages, but were at last driven to seek shelter within the enclosures; the villages catching fire, numbers were burnt and hundreds driven out to death under the musketry and bayonets of the Company's troops. Many others, as they returned in small bodies to Gwalior, were mercilessly butchered by the villagers, whom in their days of pride and power they had so mercilessly oppressed.

Thus despite Gough's plans the pestilence known as the Gwalior army ceased to be a political instrument in its native land. Lord Ellenborough himself had been under fire in the thick of the fighting and had distinguished himself by his coolness and courage. He was there by pure accident, for he had asked Gough where he should remain and was advised to stay at the rear of the reserve battery. Thither he went, but an unforeseen movement of the enemy brought him under fire. When he was advised to retire to a safer position he said 'Very good' and turned his horse in the direction indicated. It so chanced that he thus rode into the open within 350 yards of a Mahratta battery and was saluted with a shower of grape. Once in it his spirit was roused, he thoroughly enjoyed it and seemed utterly regardless of danger. This incident and his kindness to the wounded increased Lord Ellenborough's popularity with the troops.

As soon as possible after the battle the governor-general sent Sleeman to the regent to inform her and the minister and chiefs that, having by the test of battle asserted the authority of the Supreme Government, he had no intention of assuming the whole civil and military administration of the Dominions of Scindhia, but insisted that the Gwalior army, which had done such grievous harm to the State and had for so long been a menace to its neighbours, should be disbanded and in its place a Gwalior contingent be formed under European officers. At a full durbar he himself confirmed these conditions and many others, including the establishment of a council nominated by himself to administer the country under the eye of the Resident. Sleeman translated his speech to the audience at the time, for he had delivered it in English, a language with which the assembly was almost entirely unacquainted. Ellenborough's wise and liberal decision enabled his forces to enter the fort of Gwalior without conflict; otherwise its siege would have occupied them for many months. Furthermore, with the aid of the chiefs and the council the new Resident was able to secure the disbandment of the whole of the Gwalior army, cavalry, infantry and artillery without trouble, leaving only a bodyguard for the maharajah.

The reader already knows of Sleeman's strong opposition to the policy of absorbing Native States. Apart from any humanitarian feeling there was another reason which, he said, often escaped the 'school of absorption.'

The misrule of such states, situated in the midst of our dominions, is not without its use. There is, as Gibbon justly observes, 'a strong propensity in human nature to depreciate the advantages, and to magnify the evils of the present time,' and if the people had not before their eyes such specimens of native rule, to contrast with ours, they would think more highly than they do of that of their past Mahomedan and Hindu sovereigns and be much less disposed than they are to estimate fairly the advantages of being under ours. The native governments of the present day are fair specimens of what they have always been—grinding military despotisms—their whole history is that of 'Saul has killed his thousands, and David his tens of thousands'; as if rulers were made merely to slay and the ruled to be slain. In politics, as in landscape, 'Tis distance lends enchantments to the view,' and the past might be all *couleur de rose* in the imaginations of the people, were it not represented in these ill-governed states, where the 'lucky accident' of a good governor is not to be expected in a century and where the secret of the responsibility of the minister to the people is yet undiscovered.

After the battles of Maharajpore and Punniar, and the subjugation of the Gwalior State, he wrote to Sir Herbert Maddock, the secretary, and offered to resign; Maddock counselled him to remain at his post as Resident and remain he did, hoping that he might find the opportunity to restore to Gwalior its old dignity and much of its independence.

Henry Lawrence supported him, writing to the *Calcutta Review* in 1844 about the Kingdom of Oudh: 'Let not a rupee come into the Company's coffers. Let Oudh be at last governed, not for one man, the King, but for him and his people.'

Throughout all his dealings with the Native States Sleeman, while guiding the princes with the best advice he could give and helping them in every possible way, made every attempt, and saw that his officers did likewise, to keep the responsibility for all executive action in the hands of the rulers and their minister, rather than to usurp their power and to handle their revenue. He pursued this settled policy at Gwalior with success. His first concern was to aid the Gwalior authorities in the suppression of the bandit gangs which from time to time sprang up in their territory. For this he procured troops and lent them to the ruler.

He now added to his Nepal war medal the Maharajpore 'Star' for the battle he had striven to prevent!

In 1844 Lord Ellenborough was recalled, an event on which Thuggee observed:

'His recall was expected by hardly anybody but himself and the few who happened to be in the secret of the many angry letters which he wrote to the Court. I had a kind letter from him and replied expressing my thanks for much courtesy and kindness received from him, but, above all, for the confidence which had opened to me a field of usefulness wider than I might otherwise have had. The dismissal of the Saugor officials had been a harsh measure and adopted on insufficient grounds, but some of them deserved it, and with the old machinery it would have been difficult to carry out the measures necessary to restore good feeling. His annexation of Sind was the principal cause of his quarrel with the Directors. There was no justice in our conduct there.'

The Court of Directors sent out Sir Henry Hardinge in his place, though told by him that he approved of all Lord Ellenborough had done and that he should make no change in policy—but no change of policy meant nothing, for no one knew precisely what Lord Ellenborough's policy was. So far as Sind and Gwalior were concerned, it seemed to be simply to force a fight on those who could fight, and it would have been the same in the Punjab. In Gwalior he behaved magnanimously after the battle—not so in Sind.

It was unfortunate that aggression against Gwalior followed so quickly upon that against Sind.

On 31st October 1844 a fourth daughter was born to Amelie at Jhansi but died the same day. The Indian hot season had been too great a strain for Amelie; she remained in feeble health for months afterwards. A year later news came from England that Louisa had died of fever at the age of nine. Thuggee began to wonder if any of the rest of them would ever see the shores of England.

Towards the close of 1845 he sustained severe injuries from his horse falling with him. At the time he was not aware of the extent of the damage and it was only in later years that the stiffness and rheumatic pains in his right shoulder had begun to afflict him. He 'had on a villainous broadcloth cloak and was helpless and there I lay until a passing native found me and called to some gentlemen who were riding close by. I fractured my right collar bone and got badly shaken. It was the first time that I have ever been thoroughly stunned by a fall, though I had broken my collar bone 32 years before by hunting.' His horse must have turned over like a flash, for he remembered nothing of it except the grinding of the muscles in his back and neck as they stretched and almost burst when the back of his head struck the ground and his chin was buried in his breast. Thereafter all was black until, from a very long way away, as it seemed, he heard his native Samaritan calling 'Sahib!'

The horse was a very fine Arab for which he had paid 2,200 rupees, a large sum in those days. His arms were in braces for months afterwards, but he felt little from the bruises, though his back and neck troubled him very much.

As compensation for his ill fate, Amelie, two days after their arrival at Jubbulpore during a tour of his immense territory, presented him with a fifth daughter—Mary. 'Amelie suffered more after her confinement than on former occasions and could not move for some weeks. We were on tour in tents but managed to get home before the end of February, by which time the heat was becoming insufferable in camp.'

William Sleeman surveyed his vast realm and was able to report:

'All within my charge was quiet. All adherents of the Rajah of Jytpore, with the Rajah himself, had surrendered and every marauder had done the same or been seized in Bundelkhand or the Saugor territories, and the Gwalior State was no less quiet. All was beyond my hopes and almost equal to my wishes.'

He had to meet many thousands of his old native friends in these parts and every day saw him surrounded by a multitude who had something to ask or something to say, and so it went on day after day until he got back to Jhansi and out of his old territories. This, with his bodily condition after the fall, tried his strength to the utmost. Also, at this time he began to realize that he was at the beginning of a hard struggle in which he would be upholding the rights of the Native States against the plans of a strong party of his own countrymen, supported, he came to believe, by the highest in India. This was to be the theme of his life in India to the very end.

By now he had succeeded in disbanding the Gwalior army, that chronic threat to settled government, and had organized in its place a Gwalior contingent under a British brigadier, Wymer. On its colours it carried the one battle honour 'Punniar.' Thereafter matters began to run along more peacefully under a council friendly to the British and to himself—a council whose object was to keep the State at peace within itself and to restore order where none had existed for years. Troubles he had, but none so pressing or severe as those he had surmounted elsewhere. His assistant for the affairs of Scindhia's Dominions was Captain Sir Richmond Shakespear, an able and sensible official who had been General Gough's aide-de-camp at the Battle of Maharajpore (although a political officer and recently deputy commissioner at Saugor). For him Sleeman laid down the policy he had always followed in his dealings with Native States—the hardest for a political officer to pursue and therefore the most worth while.

'As a general rule, do all the good you can in your present position, but let it as far as possible appear to emanate from the durbar and not from yourself. The regency should be supported with a firm but delicate hand and guided where necessary, but there should be little appearance of this guidance, for our object is to set up the Government so that it may be able to perform its functions while retaining the respect of its subjects. Our interference with the internal administration should appear as little as possible ostensible and prominent. The people should be made to look to the constituted authorities should be made to feel that they are alone responsible for well governing.'

Blessed with such good diplomacy, their relationship with all in the State showed an improvement at once and none could have had more help from the council than he.

In the neighbouring Kingdom of Oudh matters were going from bad to worse until, in 1847, the governor-general, Lord Hardinge, pained by the suffering caused by the native maladministration in that territory and fearful that the confusion would spill across the Company's borders, issued a stern warning to the weakling who now ascended the throne. Wajid Ali Shah, the king, had succeeded on the death of his father on 13th February 1847. In a letter dated 24th July of that year, the Resident was told by the Supreme Government that 'it will be His Majesty's duty to establish such an administration to be carried out by his own officers as shall ensure the prosperity of the people; that any infringement of this essential principle will be an infringement of the treaty; that the Governor-General must, in the performance of his duty, require the King to fulfil his obligations to his subjects—that His Majesty must understand that, as a sovereign, he has duties to perform to, as well as claims to extract from the people committed to his care.'

In November 1847 Lord Hardinge himself visited Lucknow. He had drawn up a memorandum for his conference with the king, and this was read and carefully explained to Wajid Ali. The memorandum made it perfectly clear that, in the event of the King of Oudh failing to conduct the affairs of his kingdom in an humane and civilized manner for the benefit of his people, the Supreme Government would itself, under the treaties of 1801 and 1837, interfere in the country's affairs. So Oudh had been warned in 1847, ten years before the events of 1857.

CHAPTER 20

To Lucknow

Year after year colonel Sleeman's report on the state of his dominions showed the same tranquillity that he had already recorded, as well as a certain material progress in the development of the countryside. Now that the pestilential Gwalior army had been disbanded and a new force under British offices recruited, the noisy collisions round and about the court had come to an end. He always spoke in admiration of Ellenborough's tolerant policy towards the State after his virtually unprovoked onslaughts at Maharajpore and Punniar, for that statesman had returned the government to the hands of the little regent, having entrusted Sleeman with the selection of honest and upright men, friendly to the British, to form a Council of State.

Almost without exception, Ellenborough has been blamed for his high-handed treatment of Gwalior. It is, however , hard to see how else he could have eliminated the Gwalior army's pernicious influence in its country's affairs. Whatever policy he might have adopted that army had to be crushed by superior force.

The other wide territories of Bundelkhand and Saugor remained in Thuggee's hands. His official offices were 'Agent to the Governor-General in Bundelcund and In charge of the affairs of Scindhia's Dominions.' And still he was the General Superintendent for Suppression of Thuggee and Dacoity. He seems to have been altogether too willing a horse and so to have had every heavy load that was beyond the capacity of other men thrown on to his wagon. His headquarters were at Jhansi and from there he set out every autumn to tour among the people. His procession stretched from camp to camp and his main preoccupation was to find excuses to get away from the elephants, and to ride off in great detours among the villages. But when he crossed the borders of Gwalior he had to behave himself with the sober dignity required of the governor-general's representative accredited to the court.

During these peaceful years in a storm-tossed life he came to find himself in purgatory at the never-ending ceremonies of the brilliant court of Gwalior and of the large military station. On one tour through Gwalior he took James Sleeman and James's sister, Elizabeth, who had recently come out to India to keep house for her bachelor brother. James, a bold rider and a first-class performer with a spear, thoroughly enjoyed himself, off at dawn across the fields beating the high grass, sometimes for partridge and often for a warrantable boar. No one who has ridden after pig will ever acknowledge the danger of the sport. It is nevertheless a thoroughly risky feat to ride at full gallop over a country on the tail of a jinking boar, often across ravines, always among the pot-holes of tilled fields and rough country, and blind through the head-high grass. At some time the boar, armed with a fine pair of tusks, will turn and charge, to be faced by horse, rider and spear or by the erstwhile rider now on foot. Other animals may be roused and attack the hunter. Percy Marsh, the well-known district administrator and hog-hunter of recent times in the United Provinces, was once set upon by a leopard which clung to his horse's flank. By some miracle, horse and rider remained upright and Marsh killed for the devastation they wreak among the peasants' crops.

Elizabeth kept a full diary of the tour, from Jhansi right through the whole long journey over the months of the cold weather. She describes the constant visits and ceremonies, tiger and elephant fights, army parades, mounted tournaments, dinners and durbars that her uncle was compelled to attend, all of which duties he fulfilled in person, as well as receiving an unending stream of visitors, while attending to the daily administrative work of his districts.

She tells us something of the days they passed when they were back at his Jhansi headquarters.

'With infinite care and at great expense Col. Sleeman has made a beautiful garden and in this we are used to walk every evening, regarding ourselves with oranges and lquats, both of which fruits are now in great perfection.... There are, besides, numberless citron and lime trees, looking extremely pretty with their rich ripe fruit and dark green leaves. The pomegranate, with its bright scarlet flower and its beautiful fruit in every stage, and the vine, the fig, the custard apple and the pombello giving promise of delicious fruits during the next three intolerable months of heat, mosquitoes and monotony. Of a morning we used to ride on a high rocky common over which my uncle has cut a nice, wide road and covered it with sand and gravel. We were never early enough to accompany him in his ride, but we used to gallop out and meet him just as he turned homewards when, with the sun behind us and a delicious westerly breeze in our front, we cured not how long we lingered on our homeward path. We usually found our good Aunt and the children returned from their carriage airing, and the former seated at a small table outside the verandah, where we soon joined her and partook of a *chota hazri*, or literally, small breakfast. At this time the *dawk*, with its letters and papers (always doubly acceptable in India), used to arrive and, after chatting over their contents and gossiping for an hour or so, we used to retire to dress for breakfast at ten. Books, of which Colonel Sleeman has a greater number than I have ever seen in a private collection, work, chess, visitors agreeably occupied the rest of the day. Two or three small parties and one grand dinner at home and at the Mess was all the visiting we had.

Throughout the rest of his time in Jhansi the old Nathpore fever was upon him and Amelie's health too was a constant bother. It was hardly to be wondered at that when the Court of Directors in London complained to the Government in Calcutta of the long delay in the disposal of criminal cases against the Badhak Dacoits, Thuggee exploded to the governor-general's secretary.

His reply ended: 'You will soon get my Report, and it will be worth having and the last I shall make on crime in India.'

'If Hercules had not had better instruments he could not so easily have cleared out his stable, but he had no ''Honourable Court'' to find fault with his mode of doing the thing, I conclude. The fact is, however, that our prisoners are pretty well tried before they get into quod. . . .'

Others were not forgetful of his achievements. This same importunate Court of Directors highly commended his administration of justice when they did read his report. Additionally, Lord Hardinge in 1847 asked him to send in an account of his services during his career in India, obviously intending to send his name in to the Queen for a knighthood. Now Thuggee was very hard worked at this time and he was striving between other tasks and during the attacks of fever, to finish off his report on the Badhak Dacoits and to produce it as he always produced his reports as a full, reliable and interesting document. This he did and the well-printed, well-bound book that contains it remains for all to see. So he put aside for later attention the secretary's letter asking for his record of service. To him, as he pointed out in a letter to sister Mary, a K.C.B. or any other honour of the sort meant very little when set beside his military rank, of which he was very proud, or beside his work done for the good of India. Finally in March 1848 he wrote to Lord Hardinge:

'I am afraid that the narrative of my humble service will be found much longer than it ought to be, but I have written it hastily that it might go by this mail, and it is the first attempt I have ever thought of making at such a narrative, for I have gone on quietly 'through evil and through good report,' doing, to the best of my ability, the duties which it has pleased the Government of India, from time to time, to confide to me, in the manner which appeared to me most conformable to its wishes and its honour, satisfied and grateful for the trust and confidence which enabled me to do so much good for the people and to secure so much of their attachment and gratitude to their rulers.

Permit me to subscribe myself, with great respect,

Your Lordship's faithful and obedient humble servant,

W.H. Sleeman

It happened that he had delayed too long with this letter and he fully realized that this was so, but the thought never disturbed him in the least. It is here that one has a further insight into the character of this dedicated man, a man without personal ambition other than to achieve more and ever more good.

In the meanwhile, the long-wanted second son was born to Amelie—Charles Arthur—only to die in Mussoorie in 1849. It is little wonder that these two sent their children back to England whenever opportunity offered. In October 1848 Thuggee arranged for his wife and the children, Elizabeth, Mary and Charles, to go to the hills for their health's sake, to Mussoorie, their old haunt. There they stayed until after the boy's death, when, in 1850, the two girls were sent home to Mary Furse, now living at the Green Bank, Falmouth, overlooking the harbour where lay the West India packets, but never now the ship of Captain John Furse.

Sleeman had in 1848 applied to the governor-general, Lord Dalhousie, to be given an appointment which would admit of his dealing solely with the Indian States. He was finding that not only was his present command altogether too hybrid between British districts and the State of Gwalior, but also that the districts were well set upon steady development and needed little more of that creative drive without which life became to him drab and uneventful. His urge now was to lead on other backward States so that they would lever offer to the Company any well-founded reason for annexation. He therefore hoped that perhaps he might be sent as Resident to succeed Colonel Sutherland in Rajputana. Colonel Low left Lucknow and Colonel Richmond had succeeded him as Resident in Oudh, Calcutta having deemed to inopportune to take Sleeman off his vital task in Gwalior. To Thuggee's request for employment in the Native States came this reply from the Marquess of Dalhousie:

To Lucknow

Government House
Sept. 16, 1848

My dear Colonel Sleeman,

It was a matter of regret to me that I had not anticipated your desire to succeed Colonel Sutherland in Rajpootannah before I made arrangements which prevented my offering that appointment to you. I now regret it no longer, since the course of events has put it in my power to propose an arrangement which will, I apprehend, be more agreeable to you, and which will make your services more actively beneficial to the State.

Colonel Richmond has intimated his intention of immediately resigning the Residency at Lucknow. The communication made by the Governor-General to the King of Oudh, in October, 1847, gave His Majesty to understand that if the condition of Government was not very materially amended before two years had expired, the management for his behoof would be taken into the hands of the British Government.

There seems little reason to expect or to hope that in October 1849, any amendment whatever will have been effected. The reconstruction of the internal administration of a great, rich and oppressed country, is a noble as well as an arduous task for the officer to whom the duty is entrusted, and the Government have recourse to one of the best of its servants for that purpose.

The high reputation you have earned, your experience of civil administration, your knowledge of the people, and the qualifications you possess as a public man, have led me to submit your name to the Council of India as one to whom I could commit this important charge with entire confidence that its duties would be well performed. I do myself, therefore, the honour, of proposing to you to accept the office of Resident at Lucknow, with especial reference to the great changes which, in all probability, will take place. Retaining your superintendency of Thuggee affairs, it will be manifestly necessary that you should be relieved from the duty of the trials of Thugs usually condemned at Lucknow.

In the hope that you will not withhold from the Government your services in the capacity I have named, and in the further hope of finding an opportunity of personally making your acquaintance,

I have the honour to be,
Dear Colonel Sleeman,
Very faithfully yours,
Dalhousie'

When this letter actually arrived Sleeman, like so many of us in similar circumstances, felt a pang of regret that he would be finally leaving the places and the people that he knew so well. Compliments poured in on him for the valuable work that he had done since he had taken over Gwalior. It did seem, however, that his General Superintendency was to cling to him till the day of doom. There was an Irish irrationality in the situation in which the first straw on the camel's back looked like also becoming the last.

He replied and accepted, but could not refrain from adding a word of warning to his lordship about the risks and injustice of annexing even the chaotic Oudh.

Soon afterwards came another message from the Secretary to the Government of India, Elliott, in which was the note of warning about the Kingdom of Oudh which he had all along expected. His letter began with a reference to reports Sleeman had submitted on instances of violence and oppression in the State of Oudh, and instructed him to caution the king against continuing to neglect the duties of his high station. Lord Hardinge's minatory words to the king on his last visit to Lucknow were repeated. Ellott's letter ended:

'You are requested to refer to the papers connected with the late Governor-General's visit to Lucknow and communicate your opinions generally with reference to the subjects which then came under discussion.

Accustomed as you have long been to the details of civil administration, you will be able after a short time to state whether the necessity for the interference of the British Govt in the affairs of Oudh is in your opinion so urgent as it appeared to the late Governor-General to be.'

Richmond was to leave Lucknow on 25th November: Sleeman expected to enter officially in January. In the meantime he planned to travel as far as Agra in his cold season tour to meet Lord Dalhousie for the first time. All was so quiet within his charge that he had lent the commander-in-chief two regiments of infantry and a number of European officers who were in civil employment under him for service with their own regiments during the impending war with the Sikhs. At Agra in November 1848 he met Lord Dalhousie, a determined and forthright man who left him in little doubt as to his intentions. Sleeman's one apprehension was that he might make the mistake of thinking that because a Native State was in a condition of confusion it was inevitable that the Company should assume its government and its revenues. His own view had always been that we should seek ever to maintain the authority of the native princes and exert ourselves to improve their administrations: that assumption of this State would be unjust and would lead to trouble, as the fancied threat of annexation had caused the insurrections in Saugor and Bundelkhand. Lord Hardinge's warning in October 1847 may perhaps have led Dalhousie to conclude that the next step would be assumption, but Sleeman now dissuaded him from this course and Dalhousie at that time agreed with him.

He entered upon his appointment to Lucknow, the plum of the political appointments, with the firm intention of saving Oudh from assumption by the British power at whatever cost to himself. In this service he had to rescue the rulers of Oudh from themselves and he knew from all his experience that the task would tax him to the utmost and might prove to be beyond his powers. He realized and said at the time that this was the greatest task to which he had ever submitted himself and the one which he believed to be nearest to his heart. Yet history remembers him only as the inexorable agent in the extirpation of Thugs and not for this devoted endeavours on behalf of Oudh. It is not to flatter him to say that if he, with his abilities and knowledge, could not succeed, then no one else could, with the possible exception of Colonel James Outram.

His wife and children did not witness the impressive ceremonial entry of the new Resident into Lucknow. His processing was met outside the city by the minister and conducted to the royal park at Dilkusha where he was greeted by the king and invited into the royal *howdah*. Before him rose Lucknow, city of palaces, tall mosques, temples and fountains. Seated by the king to denote the quasi-equality on which Lord Hastings had long ago insisted, and escorted by the flank companies of three of the king's regiments under European officers, he rode past the extensive ice-pits and entered the city by wider and finer streets than in any other native city of India. Sleeman's own brilliant cortege consisted of upwards of three hundred elephants and camels lavishly decorated. The princes and nobles of the kingdom were blazing in jewels. The recent victory at Chillianwala lent to the procession the character of a triumph. The king's cortege was of equal size. Every roof was crowded with spectators and through streets lined with crowds for their whole length the Resident was escorted to the Shah Manzil palace for breakfast by the Gumti river among the orange-trees, roses, pools filled with brightly coloured fish, and bubbling fountains. At the residency he found waiting his 'own fine equipage, the carriage plain but of beautiful design and craftsmanship and the horses such as the Queen of England herself might envy,' four fine bays, the pair of wheelers alone having cost over 600 in Calcutta. Postilions and outriders accompanied the carriage and six troopers rode behind. Altogether a stylish turn-out.

That night Thuggee walked out upon the verandah of the residency, the building which was one day to become so famous in the bloody epoch of the great defence of 1857. If we pause to contemplate the stature of this man from a West Country village of England, and to imagine him in the company of those equally imposing but sincere personalities who came after him at Lucknow—Henry Lawrence, Inglis, Outram, Havelock—one can only hope and trust that the British race will ever continue so to match its men to the occasion. Such men are not bred from cynicism out of malice and jealousy. It has been rashly said that all power corrupts. As often as not it refines. It is not power that corrupts but a selfish use of it.

Sleeman looked round on the lawns and flower beds, the fountains and the statuary, and at the black elephantine bulk of the houses in the residency gardens standing hard against the ink-blue night, took a deep breath of the fragrance about him, turned slowly and went back to his candlelit study.

He had committed himself to the struggle for the freedom of Oudh.

CHAPTER 21

Resident at Lucknow

Wajid Ali Khan of Oudh was a monarch naturally intelligent but so soused in debauchery that he was seldom fit to conduct even minor affairs. He was superstitious and credulous to a degree. When he succeeded to the throne in 1847 the treasury was reasonably stocked: by the time Sleeman arrived in January 1849 it was bare. His flatterers, his eunuchs, his mistresses and wives, few of whom were faithful to him, and their paramours and chief singers, had made free with the treasury and passed most of it to their relatives outside the kingdom, in Rampore, Cawnpore and elsewhere. Whenever Sleeman sought an interview with the king he was told that His Majesty had taken medicine and would not be able to see anyone (except his fiddlers, singers, and so on) for ten days, or else that he was about to take medicine, or that he had palpitations from which his family had always suffered. Dr Bell, the residency surgeon, reported that there was nothing organically wrong with the king but that he was enfeebled by 'excessive indulgence in sexual pleasures' and 'that all the men and many of the women of the family have always been addicted to this kind of indulgence.' In due course Sleeman wrote to Dalhousie:

'. . . After much consideration I am therefore of opinion that the best plan would be to require the King to resign for a time, or during the minority of the heir apparent, all powers to a Board of three Commissioners to act with the advice of the Resident. These Commissioners to be nominated by the King but subject to the approval of the Governor-General.

. . . His Majesty may now be considered well in bodily health, though he hears with great difficulty and sometimes complains of palpitations of the heart. He frequently goes out to take the air in his carriage but he still secludes himself from his people, and is prevented from hearing anything of their sufferings. His children, the minister, his physicians, singers and eunuchs are alone admitted to his presence when at home and, while out, no one is permitted to approach him with their complaints, though the streets are crowded with people clamouring for a redress of the wrongs they suffer in the town or the Provinces. His Majesty persuades himself that he leaves all to the Minister and the Minister persuades him that all is every-where as it should be, while he—the Minister—complains to me and others that he is thwarted by His Majesty's personal favourites in all that he does to remedy the evils from which the people everywhere suffer. The King's time is given up entirely to singing and dancing and he has no pleasure in the society of any but singers, dancers and musicians. He has indulged in them from childhood and they are become inveterable. It is exceedingly irksome to him to hear anything of public affairs, for he has never given any attention to them.'

There can never have been a more gullible monarch than Wajid Ali Khan. It seems, as Sleeman tells the tale, that he could swallow anything. There are many examples of his childish superstitions. His Chief Singer once came to him and said that a renowned Dervish, who would cure him of the palpitations of the heart, had arrived in Lucknow. Wajid Ali of course put himself in the hands of these two tricksters and was accordingly guided to a certain house in the Lucknow bazaar. He was led to an empty darkened room. As the door shut behind him a harsh voice rang out, coming as it seemed from nowhere, for he was quite alone in the room. The voice told him that on condition that he placed on the table a considerable offering in money and jewels the King of the Fairies would cure him of his distressing affliction. His Majesty made many visits and regularly paid his fee, until one of his many wives who bore a grudge against the Chief Singer told him how the hoax was worked. The silly monarch had sufficient wit to have the 'Dervish' seized secretly one night and transported to the palace, where he was so handled that he confessed to being himself the King of the Fairies. Wajid Ali ordered him under pain of death to re-enact the whole play for his benefit at a definite time in a selected room of the palace. At that hour the king took the Chief Singer to this little room. It was darkened and the door closed behind them. All happened as before, the voice, the offer and the large donation. The king and the singer then left the room, but as they shut the door the same voice called to them from inside. They re-entered to see the self-styled King of the Fairies standing bowing in the middle of the room, having descended through a false ceiling made of canvas. The singer was aghast. The king turned on him and lashed him with his tongue but had not the courage to punish him as he deserved, so the tricks and antics of his courtiers went on as before.

Later the king fell in love with one of his mother's waiting-maids, and demanded her in marriage. She was his mother's favourite bedfellow and she would not part with her. The king became angry and to soothe him his mother in a rash moment told him that it was purely out of regard for him and his children that she refused to part with this young woman; that she had a *sampun,* or the coiled figure of a snake, in the hair on the back of her neck. No man would purchase even a horse with this mark or believe that any family could be safe in which was kept a horse or mare with such a mark! His mother told him that if he cohabited with a woman so blemished he and all his children must perish. The king said he feared that he might have among his many wives some with marks of this kind, and that this could account for his frequent attacks of palpitation of th heart, to which the queen dowager emphatically agreed. When the king went on to ascribe to this the recent death of the heir apparent, his mother again agreed most heartily. The chief eunuch, Bashir, was forthwith ordered to inspect the backs of the necks of all save that of the chief consort, the mother of the late and present heir apparent. He reported that he had found the fatal mark upon the necks of no less than eight of the king's wives. The high priest was summoned and divorce from the whole eight forthwith pronounced. The ladies were ordered to depart with whatever they had saved for themselves. Some of their friends suggested to His Majesty that the Muslims were but unskilful judges in these matters, and that a court of Brahmins should be assembled, as they had whole volumes devoted solely to this science. The most expert were accordingly collected, and they declared that though there were marks resembling in some ways the *sampun,* it was of no importance; the evil ladies were very indignant. Six of them, resenting the divorce, insisted upon leaving the palace. Two only consented to remain. Thus, for what they were worth, the king lost his wives.

Sleeman soon came to the conclusion that the king's sole ambition was the puerile one of becoming the finest drummer in Oudh. On the occasion of every Muslim festival he could be seen walking proudly at the head of the procession thumping with both hands at a *madal* (a two-ended drum) hung round his neck. He seemed to imagine that his skill with this simple instrument was admirable to his people, who stood dutifully lining both sides of the road. They, in fact, had the usual respect for dignity which most Indians evince and found his performances contemptible, while the gentry, nurtured in the polite manners customary to their class, found his performances contemptible, and behaviour incomprehensible. This was the man in whose hands lay the happiness of millions of men and women, both Muslim and Hindu. Furthermore, it was known throughout Lucknow that the king often tried his hand at somewhat risky verse and that he had also commissioned a long poem giving very exactly a history of the intrigues of his palace and the infidelity of his wives. Thuggee had not seen this poem, but some of his friends among the Lucknow gentry described it as most undignified and quite uninhibited!

It was little wonder that Sleeman, when he made his lengthy tour through Oudh in the winter of 1849, should have found the state of the country so terrible as to merit one of the most blistering reports that could ever have reached the Government of India. It was little wonder too, that he should have strongly urged Dalhousie to appoint a Council of Regency such as Ellenborough had appointed in Gwalior, which Sleeman had so successfully operated, to rule in the name of the king or of his son. Dalhousie does not seem to have commented on this useful suggestion. Sleeman thereupon wrote to say that if he were given the authority he would pick up three or four of the king's nearest relations and a regular regiment and forthwith proceed to the palace, where he would insist upon all the fiddlers, eunuchs and singers being surrendered to him and in consultation with the queen mother proclaim a regency pending Calcutta's decision concerning the Council of State. He intended to exile these rogues into the Company's keeping, explaining that as they were all of them nominally the commanding officers of the king's army, they would leave vacancies for the British to appoint reliable and active men who would not line their purses off the men's pay, off the equipment ammunition and the rations of their beasts.

It soon became patent that the new Resident's battle was to be waged against the sycophantic flock of fiddlers, singers and eunuchs who dominated the councils of the king, and that these were so deeply embedded in the whole administration of the country, both civil and military, that no less than surgical operation would ever suffice for this severe treatment. Thuggee would need all the support he could obtain from those British officers who served him and from the governor-general himself. From the latter he could be confident of help: among the former he was not so fortunate in the men whom Richmond had left to serve him. In the queen mother he had an ally, true and staunch so long as her own interests were not affected, but always ready to exploit her son's superstitions where her own inclinations were concerned. Under her late husband's rule she had known better days in Oudh: in so far as she felt able she ever tried to reinforce Sleeman's homilies and warnings to the young debauchee who unworthily sat on his father's throne.

Sleeman's predecessors, Low and Richmond, had not faced the problems that now presented themselves. Low, whose personal courage had saved the *gaddi* (royal seat) for the legitimate claimant, had thereafter found his prince to be honestly concerned to keep the State solvent. The coffers had been filled from year to year and a strict control set upon extravagance. Richmond had somewhat the same advantage for a few years but seems not to have concerned himself overmuch when the profligate Wajid Ali succeeded to power and to the riches hoarded up for him in the Lucknow treasury. The new prince dipped freely with both hands to the benefit of the greediest and most worthless gang of reprobates who ever clung to the hem of a monarch's robe. Those who do not know the East and who may never have been drawn to delve into contemporary records of Indian despotism cannot possibly conjure up in their imaginations the evil doings, cruelties, treacheries, tortures and horrors that were all too often the stock-in-trade of that rule. Much knowledge or reading on the subject habituates the mind to these fearful happenings; one's judgment of the chiefs under whom they occurred is then tempered by what one expected: which is not to say one condones them—only that one sees them against the oriental background of their time. Both Low and Richmond may well have viewed the conditions of Oudh in the 1840's in this manner, as must the historian. And so did Sleeman. But Sleeman was a man with a mission: where there was evil and oppression, there was Sleeman with his pen to expose it and the sword or the rope to destroy it. The Sleemans among us are in a tiny minority. They do not rest content with the easy way of pen and tongue; they pass to the far more hazardous and wearing way of acting offensively against the abuses they expose. However his fortunes may have swung, veered or backed, one thing must be remembered—that in all the great civil campaigns of his career he was the first to see the need of them and the first to undertake them, even the first in all recorded history.

It was his custom to go out and to see for himself. Having taken a cast round Lucknow, the king and his court, and having satisfied himself that he fully understood how affairs at the seat of government were misconducted, he sent his officers out to report to him on the highway robberies and murders that were rife on the main trade route between Lucknow and Cawnpore. While all these inquiries were proceeding he opened negotiations for permission to tour through the whole kingdom in the next cold season, to see for himself if all that Lords Hardinge and Dalhousie had heard was true and whether matters were really worse than in his young days when he went a hunting *Bhumeawatis* with his regiment. His request was unusual, for this was a sovereign State in all its internal affairs and no Resident had ever before ventured to claim such a privilege. Dalhousie was very agreeable to his project, so the young king, who had a wholesome fear of that determined proconsul, was soon brought to agree. Sleeman, who already knew personally some of the old vintage of ministers who had well served Saadat Ali, a former king and one of some merit, selected his companions for the tour. Among them was a trusted ex-prime minister, Hakim Mahnadi, well known to Thuggee as a sharp critic of the present regime. The tour was fixed for early December 1849, when Amélie and the children would be back again from Mussoorie.

This fixture came near to being cancelled when, in April, cantering in the early morning near the grandstand on the Lucknow racecourse, he took a heavy toss off his Arab. His horse put its foot in a hole and turned over, throwing Thuggee and breaking his thigh.

Apart from the temporary setback to his work, this fall compelled him for the rest of his time at Lucknow to abandon his morning exercise. From then onwards the days he spent at the residency followed a routine tedious to man of his active inclinations. He would rise early and take a walk about his gardens and then go to his desk. Breakfast and tiffin were light according to his long-standing habit: between them he would either visit the minister or the king, or else receive petitioners and visitors at his house. In the afternoon he was at his desk once more, the house being as a place of the dead, for Amélie, when in residence, insisted that all ladies staying with them should retire, as she did herself, from three to five o'clock. At the latter hour a dish of tea was served and then in the cool of the evening Amélie and he would drive three miles out along the Mall in their handsome barouche to the cantonments at Muriaon. They had an escort of two troopers in advance and three in rear, with the Muslim postboys all dressed in the English fashion. But this domesticity and gentle exercise galled her William, cripple that he then was. Muriaon had nothing to offer him save a regimental band, and a patient wait until the ladies should have talked out the station gossip. Back at the residency he returned to his desk until dark. Later on, in 1853, his eyesight worsening, he had to forsake all work by candlelight and would have been at a loss had he not by then acquired a thoroughly congenial set of officers on his staff. Most evenings Fletcher Hayes, the assistant resident, Fayrer, the surgeon, the A.D.C., the chaplain and the chief engineer forgathered at the residency for a talk or a game of whist or billiards. To join this group, whenever his duties allowed, came Weston, his most efficient police superintendent and close friend. Many of the outside servants were old friends of Thuggee's; in other words reformed Thugs from his Saugor establishment.

In March 1849, at long last, Dalhousie relieved Sleeman of all Thug duties, and apparently deeming it necessary that the appointment should remain in the family made James General Superindent in his uncle's place. So the two Sleemans saw much of each other in the next few years.

By June, Thuggee was improving from his accident and able to move about on crutches, but never again could he ride a horse. He had now arranged to go forth on 2nd December on his three months' ramble through Oudh. It had been borne in on him that he would have to start out in a *tonjon,* or litter, and try his best as time went on to change to an elephant. He was determined that somehow either *tonjon* or elephant would bear him away from the highway and among the villages where few officials penetrated and maladministration could be seen at its most typical. Before he went he had selected three tasks for settlement: to seek an interview with the king at which he would encourage and warn him; as a consequence of this to get the dismissal of the man whom he regarded as the biggest rogue in the State; and thirdly to beat out the covers that hid Bakhsh Ali and Ghulam Hazarat, two robber barons who were holding everyone in fee on the wide plains between Lucknow and Cawnpore. He started with the barons.

His officers reported to him that these two ruffians were robbing with violence on the highway, abducting every good-looking girl who ventured abroad, together with parents and husbands whenever they were too poor to purchase redress at court, and putting up the young women for sale as slaves. They were confident in their defiance of all authority because they were assured of the protection of the king's fiddlers. Thuggee's men informed him of the prisons where the unlucky slaves-to-be were kept both in Lucknow and outside. As usual he went straight to the target. Instead of seeking evidence for the State to bring these barons to trial, he set a price of two thousand rupees on each head and then requisitioned battalions in the Oudh service under British officers. On obtaining these he set his highly competent policeman, Weston, in charge of the operations. Thus, despite every obstacle placed in their way at the court, Captains Weston and Bunbury set hot on the quest, chased these brigands round the countryside, following the trial of the reward offered to the local inhibitants, and laid them by the heels, running Bakhsh Ali to ground in a low house in Lucknow and Ghulam Hazrat after storming his fort, covered by a six-pounder bombardment. Once these men were jailed, all the evidence needed came in hotfoot. These little operations started the ball rolling, so that when Thuggee demanded his interview with the king, the latter dared not refuse it. It was strange that Oudh had not till then realized what sort of a Resident Lord Dalhousie had wished upon it, nor that the whole tenor of palace life was about to suffer such a cleaning up as had not been known since the Moghul emperors first appointed a nawab of that province.

Having rendered life safe on the Cawnpore road and for forty miles round the capital, Thuggee then set for himself a task of herculean measure, which was to clear every single bamboo plantation for miles out from the city. He knew full well from earlier experience that the Oudh feudal lords, the *taluqdars,* lacking the ravines and mountains habitual to banditti, had recourse to protecting and concealing themselves in broad and impenetrable bamboo coverts of their own planting. Anyone who has tried to penetrate this forest in Assam or Burma will confirm the immense difficulties it presents to the movement of armed forces in attack. Every fort was ringed with bands of mature bamboo plantations, on which the six-pounder shell of that day would strike and either stick or bounce back. I recollect as a very young officer with an irregular corps on the Assam frontier having to leap nimbly from the path of a six-pound solid shot rebounding in this manner, catapulted back at the muzzle-loader that had discharged it. The occurrence was not uncommon.

Sleeman demanded great gangs of men and women from Lucknow to sally out, in return for the wood they cut, to raze to the ground every plantation over a wide area. By the time he went on tour the great labour was started. With confidence he now demanded to see the king and browbeat the *vakil* (agent) and the prime minister until they ceased to find excuses. Not even the plea that the king had taken purgative medicine and might therefore be a little nervous and preoccupied, as we might all be, stopped Thuggee from insisting on the appointment. Accordingly he set out for the palace in the Kaisar Bagh escorted by cavalry, with his residency officers by his side. He was received with 'God Save the Queen' played by the royal band and a royal salute by the guards. From his carriage he was borne in a golden palanquin into the audience hall with his officers walking on each side. At the door a 'very fat and short-winded man, though but thirty years of age,' gorgeously apparelled, embraced him and shook hands with his officers. This was the dose-tormented king, Wajid Ali. All then walked into an inner room and sat down, Sleeman at the king's right hand.

After the customary exchange of courtesies Thugee went straight to the point, which was that the king should instantly dismiss a man whom the Resident described as the greatest knave in all Oudh, Wasi Ali. This man, he insisted, and rightly, was the fountain of all evil at the court. For twenty years he had been worming his way into a postion of power over the minister by keeping a careful diary of every rupee that the latter had spent from the treasury, thereby attaining a firm position to blackmail that foolish servant of the king. We shall hear again of Wasi Ali. In addition, Sleeman demanded that all the regiments in Lucknow should be dispatched to the provinces so as to remove them from the evil influence of their worthless commanders, and that those commandrs should be at once relieved. He went on to insist that the king should remember Lord Hardinge's serious warning of two years before and should mend his ways. These admonitions lost some of their dignity by the fact that the monarch, through his ceaseless excesses, had become somewhat hard of hearing, so the Resident had to shout and the queen mother, who sat behind the screen to listen in on the conversation, had to raise her voice to a screaming approval of all he said. In time, warnings and approvals got through to the prince's understanding. His mother's pleadings reduced him to a tearful jelly and again and again he avowed his intention of fulfilling at once all that was demanded. But he never accepted the idea that he should show himself among his villages and investigate their many dire misfortunes. In his view they were there to serve his pleasures and desires, not to trouble him. Having obtained all the satisfaction that he could, the Resident and his staff took their leave. The king embraced him again at the door, placed a necklace about each neck, and presented them all with betelnut. Former kings would have returned the visit but Wajid Ali never left his own palace except to take part in religious or ceremonial processions with his drum.

The outcome was that the king sent Wasi Ali away from court to a distant city of Oudh and that after a few months, this indispensable scoundrel wheedled the king into having him back. Within a week or two, all the regiments and batteries were ordered away from Lucknow, but it was one thing to order them and still another to get them on the march. The order to move made an immense commotion, for not one of them had more than a small handful of the transport animals it was supposed to possess. There was no fodder in the stores, the cannon were short of wheels and lacked limbers, while ammunition for both infantry and artillery was only a symbol of what was shown to be on charge. Such was the condition of the corps commanded by the fiddlers, eunuchs and singers, for which they drew pay and all manner of stores. Their peculations were demonstrated to the whole of Lucknow by Sleeman's insisting on the order to march. Everything including the soldiers' pay had indeed been fiddled away. Most of the inhabitants of the city were only aggrieved that they had not themselves enjoyed the same opportunities. With the departure of Wasi Ali, Sleeman was under no illusions what he had done with this criminal.

His report on this interview gave the governor-general plainly to understand that King Wajid Ali was a wastrel and a feeble rake who cared nothing whatsoever for the welfare of his subjects.

In the autumn Amélie and the children arrived back from Mussoorie. Every evening the family would gather on the residency verandah while Thuggee drank his evening peg. As darkness fell they would re-enter the house, Thuggee to tidy up his study from the day's work and his wife to dress for their expected visitors. One evening they went in as usual after dusk, Amélie walking some paces ahead, William and little Elizabeth lingering to watch the red fade from the western sky. It was dark when they in turn stepped over the threshold into the hall. Thuggee turned aside to his lamplit study to fetch his spectacles and paused before the heavy curtains drawn across the high double windows. For no reason at all, alert, he whipped the curtains apart and faced a bearded Indian.

'Give me that knife,' said Sleeman in a low voice.

The man hestitatingly handed it to him, a Rajput dagger. Sleeman watched closely to see if the handle or blade came first. It was the handle.

'You are a Thug?'

'Yes, sahib.'

Sleeman stepped back and pointed to the door leading out to the verandah.

'Go before I call the guard.' Once more he spoke low. 'Never show your face in Oudh again!'

As he reached the door the man turned and made a *salaam* to the Resident. Thuggee strolled after him into the hall and took Elizabeth by the hand. 'Don't tell your mother,' said he. 'He'll never come back. James will see to that.'

It may very well be that during the twenty years of his campaign against Thuggee, Sleeman owed his immunity from assassination, in a country where the art was widely and skilfully practised, very largely to the intimidating effect of his strong personality, and to the fact that he inspired in Thugs a proper superstitious belief that he was for ever forewarned of his enemies intentions.

CHAPTER 22

The State of Oudh

On 2nd December 1849, William Sleeman and his family left Lucknow in regal style to do what no other Resident had done or been allowed to do, namely, to tour at will through the kingdom for three whole months inquiring as he pleased of the state of its administration, maladministration and lack of administration. His writers kept close note of all that he said and did and heard. On his return to the residency he printed up on his own press in the cellars below what was then his highly secret report. This report in years to come was copied into two closely printed volumes and must be the most valuable single document ever produced on the conditions prevailing in a Native State in the first half of the nineteenth century. It revealed a state of affairs at which imagination boggles. Unless a very great improvement could have been made, it is hard to see how Dalhousie could have kept his hands off the kingdom.

Having begun his work at the court, Sleeman now saw for himself what it entailed outside in the provinces. Those who wished to know what he discovered can still learn if they are fortunate enough to come across the two red volumes of Sleeman's *Tour through Oude.* In this present work one can only give a sketch of conditions and a few sordid examples.

When he left he handed over his duties at Lucknow to his assistant, Captain Wilberforce Bird, a young man who through his marriage had some influence at Simla and Calcutta and was not averse to using it. Thuggee was handicapped in his dealings with this rather unsatisfactory assistant by the fact that Colonel Richmond had strongly recommended him, in particular for his successes at the Lucknow court. Sleeman discovered before long that Bird was by no means the paragon that he had been represented. He used an overbearing manner at court to exact promises made only to keep him quiet, and seldom to be fulfilled. Sleeman remonstrated forcefully with Bird for having the effrontery to demand that the king should banish one of his sultans who had become the notorious mistress of his Chief Singer. As a result Wajid Ali did indeed send this wife on a pilgrimage to Mecca, chiefly because she was determined to be free to choose her own lovers. Nevertheless, however successful this negotiation, it was no part of the Resident's policy to interfere in the monarch's private affairs and Bird had to be told this once and for all. Matters were on a better footing with his assistant thereafter, but came to a head a year or two later when he became mixed up in a racing set on the Lucknow racecourse, consisting of those same fiddlers and singers whom Sleeman was trying to throw out of Oudh. Bird was fast becoming financially involved with these disreputable companions. However, it was not until early in 1853 that Sleeman rid himself of Captain Bird. It is inexplicable that he, so hard-pressed in his campaign to clean up the Augean stable, should not long before have sought a new broom. Thuggee was a patient man but this patience sometimes worked to his disadvantage and in this instance it contributed to his breakdown in 1854.

With his accidents and the recurring attacks of fever, his health was by no means what it ought to have been when he set out on his tour in December. He hoped to regain it in the sun and the sharp winter mornings of the countryside.

It might be expected that the unusual phenomenon of a British Resident in progress from Lucknow through the villages would excite some curiosity, but Sleeman had never anticipated that he would be plunged at once into the sea of petitioners and complainants that swamped him from the moment he left the bazaars of the city. It seemed that the new-found law and order that he had created in the vicinity had brought every man and woman out to converse with him and enjoy the unaccustomed security. This busy life began with his tour and continued until its very end at Chinhut, just outside Lucknow.

He says that it became painful for him to walk out of his tent of an evening to face every day 'the large crowds seeking redress in grievous wrongs' in which he saw no hope of redress: 'men and women whose dearest relatives had been murdered, their houses burnt down, their whole property taken away, their lands seized upon, their crops destroyed by ruffians residing in the same or neighbouring villages and sometimes even in the camp of the Amil, without the slightest fear of being punished or made to surrender any part of what they had stolen.' As the government authorities were too weak even to enforce the payment of the State's demands, there was no hope at all of their seizing or punishing offenders of any kind, even if they had wished to do so. Indeed, they not only acquiesced in many of the depredations of these gangs of robbers but acted in collusion with them in order to ensure their help in dealing with defaulting landholders. The brigandly *taluqdars* would gladly murder their rivals so that the State officials would make over to them the properties of the dead men.

Sleeman acknowledged that by himself he was never able to secure any substantial and permanent improvement in the administration, though he often managed to secure redress of individual wrongs and to relieve individual suffering. About this he has the following to say:

'The British character is, in consequence, respected in the remotest village and jungle in Oudh and there is, I believe, no part of India where a European officer is received among the people of all classes with more kindness and courtesy than in Oudh. There is certainly no city or town in any other Native State in India where he is treated in the crowded streets with more respect.

To refer such sufferers to the authorities at Lucknow would have been a cruel mockery. The present sovereign never hears a complaint or reads a petition or report of any kind.'

If only because so much and such severe censure has been levelled at Lord Dalhousie for annexing Oudh in 1856, it is necessary to consider the state of affairs which Sleeman so fully and honestly recorded for the governor-general. Thereupon one may make up one's own mind as to the necessity or desirability of substituting British for native rule in that kingdom. We know that William Sleeman was to the very end strongly opposed to any sort of absorption of this State and fought courageously against it, even risking his career in the struggle. There is space here only to touch on the main features of his report and that will be done. But before we go farther it is well to say that it was a pity that Dalhousie did not test Sleeman's plan for a Council of Regency before taking the ultimate step in 1856. He seems to have disregarded the advice of this very experienced political officer.

And now to the report. Here is a brief extract concerning the habits of the *taluqdars,* the barons of Oudh.

'The *taluqdars* were keeping the country in a perpetual state of disturbance and rendered life, property and industry everywhere insecure. Whenever they quarrelled with each other or with the local authorities of the Government from whatever cause, they look to indiscriminate plunder and murder over all lands not held by men of the same class; no road, town, village, or hamlet was secure from their merciless attacks; robbery and murder became their diversion—their sport; and they thought no more of taking the lives of men, women and children who never offended them, than those of deer or wild hogs. They not only robbed and murdered, but seized, confined and tortured all whom they seized and supposed to have money or credit, till they ransomed themselves with all they had, or could beg or borrow.'

Hardly a day went by during Sleeman's tour in which he had not abundant proof of numerous atrocities of this kind committed by landholders year by year within the district through which he was passing.

The same system was followed by landholders of smaller degrees and of this military class—some holders of single villages or co-sharers in a village. This class comprised Rajputs of all denominations, Mussulmans, and Pausies. Where one co-sharer in a village quarrelled with another or with the Government authorities, on whatever subject, he declared himself in a state of war and adopted the same system of indiscriminate plunder and reckless murder. He first robbed the house and murdered all he could of the family of the co-sharer with whom he had quarrelled, or whose tenement he wished to seize upon; and then got together all he could of the loose characters around, employed them in indiscriminate plunder and subsisted them upon the booty, without the slightest apprehension that he should thereby stand less high in the estimation of his neighbours, or that of the officers of Government; on the contrary, he expected, when his pastime was over, to be at least more feared and courted and more secure in the possession of increased lands held at lower rates.

There is no doubt that the evil system of 'farming out' the land was the root cause of much of the disorder in the body politic of Oudh. The State handed to a contractor for a settled sum the business of collecting the dues in a certain district, leaving the contractor to squeeze from the inhabitants what he liked provided that he fulfilled the agreed demand of the State. It was a pernicious way of running the country.

There was not a scoundrel of importance in the whole of Oudh with whom the new British Resident did not sooner or later come to grips. A short summary of the doings of two of the thousands of brutal ruffians who ranged the country may be condensed from his report. He had to rid the kingdom of both these men, Bhoori Khan and Mahepat Singh, together with a whole sheaf of other oppressors. For this work he could call on those units in Oudh that were commanded by British officers, and upon the armed police, a mere handful, with which he struck decisively at the brigands and their considerable armed bands, crushing them one by one, no matter how influential and how closely backed by local governors and courtiers heavily bribed from the proceeds of plunder.

Bhoori Khan's first recorded crime was to bring his gang down at night and seize a man called Bhowani, his two younger brothers, his sister-in-law and her son, along with other relations. He took them all to the jungles, tortured them with red-hot ramrods and put them in heavy fetters. He then demanded heavy ransoms. As none of them had the money he took Bhowani, flogged him until he was insensible, then thrust red-hot spikes in his eyes until he died. After more atrocities he kidnapped a man called Cheyn, a Brahmin, again demanding high ransom. The full sum not being paid, he hung cow's bones round his neck, thrust them into his mouth and drenched him in cow's blood to outcaste him for ever as a Hindu. When released Cheyn gave evidence that he had himself seen Bhoori Khan torture and murder many men and dishonour many respectable women. The brigand then seized three other men whom he beat senseless. One of them, a Brahmin, he took to a village pool and beside it forced a wretched low-caste man, under threat of his sword, to cut off his victim's nose with a blunt instrument right to the bone, taking with it all the upper lip. He then compelled his gang to rape a harmless cultivator's sister. Two travellers whom he caught he suspended from trees and first had their arms broken with bludgeons, then cut off their feet, and at last beat them over the head until they died.

During 1847 and 1848 this monster attacked and plundered the houses and property of a host more of harmless peasants, taking them to his fort and there torturing them by thrusting red-hot spikes under their finger-nails, pouring molten lead into mouths and noses, thrusting firebrands into their eyes, cutting off hands and arms, flogging them till they died and ravishing their women and inciting his men to do the same. He outcaste Rajputs and Brahmins by tying cows' bones about their necks, making his followers force open their mouths and spit down their throats, and by setting them on asses, dressed in the hides of pigs. One victim, Puroti, himself saw the noses of two victims cut off by Bhoori Khan, who put them on a plate and placed them in a recess in the wall. 'When Rampershad Tewari could not pay his demand, the robber forced a gram parcher to—in his father's face before releasing him.' And thus the tale of horror went on without interference from the State authorities.

There is space to depict only one more of these fiends and to tell the story of but two victims. When Mahepat Singh caught Ganga Ahir of Barauli and his friend Ramdhan, he stood Ramdhan in the middle of a circle of men with drawn swords. A man advanced and with one cut severed his right arm, which fell to the ground, another cut into the chest, under the stump, while a third cut him across the left side of the neck with a back-handed swipe. At this he fell dead. These braves then amused themselves by flogging Ganga Ahir with thorn bushes. Tiring of this, they put him aside for the day and brought him out on the morrow to be laid upon a bed of thorns and again beaten. One man then sat on his chest while others held his arms and legs and yet another cut off his nose and one of his hands at the wrist, and the fingers of the other hand. In this condition he was found unconscious that evening by a local villager who took him to his home and reported the matter to Captain Orr of the frontier police at Fyzabad. Orr had him taken to the hospital at Lucknow where he was put uner the care of the residency surgeon till he recovered. While he was still in hospital Orr laid the brutal Mahepat by the heels and brought him to Ganga to be recognized. 'As soon as he saw him all the terrible scene of Ramdhan's murder and his own torture came so vividly before him, that he trembled from head to foot like a man in an argue fit and was for some time unable to speak. At last, when he saw the fetters on Mahepat's legs and the handcuffs on his wrists and armed Government servants around him, he recovered his senses and, by degrees, recorded what he had witnessed and suffered at his hands.'

While mentioning the cutting off of noses, it is as well to remember that this was not an unusual form of brutality in the East. When in the 1760's Prithwi Narain captured Kirthipore in Nepal, he cut off the noses and lips of all those inhabitants who could not play a wind instrument, and checked the haul by having them weighed. In the 1930's there was a recrudescence of dacoity in Gwalior and the neighbourhood, one of its characteristics being the cutting off of noses, particularly of women, to extract ransom. An experienced superintendent of police named Young was sent to the area to suppress the outbreak. This he succeeded in doing, but it took several months.

It must be again stressed that the atrocities related above were only a tithe of those daily committed, and which the State authorities made no attempt whatsoever to restrain. While these cruelties were rife about them the Rajput gentry were continuing the horrible practice of female infanticide. Sleeman's inquiries showed that this evil had prevailed from the time of the first founder of the Rajput race. These high-born patricians, he writes, could not give 'their daughters in marriage to any but one of the Chauhan or Rathore clans of Rajputs, and they must give all their property with their daughters, while they can take nothing in return, as it is a great stain to take *kanya dam,* or virgin price, from anyone: mothers weep and scream when their first female infants are torn from them, but after two or three times giving birth to female infants, they become quiet and reconciled to the usage and say "Do as you like." It was the dread of sinking in substance from loss of property and in grade from loss of caste that alone led to the murder of female infants.'

The infant is destroyed in the room where it is born and there buried. The floor is then plastered over with cow dung and on the fifteenth day the family or village priest must cook and eat food in that room, as a *hom,* or burnt offering. I have been told that they put the milk of *mudar* shrub, asclepias gigantes, into the mouth of the infant to destroy it, and cover the mouth with the faeces which first pass from the infant's bowels. It soon dies; and, after the expiation, the parents again occupy the room and there receive the visits of their family and friends, and gossip as usual! Rajah Bakhtawar Sing told me that he had frequently heard the whole process described by midwives who have attended at the birth.

All the people I talked to said that, just as the crimes had been put down in British territory by honest and firm judicious measures, so could it be put down in Oudh, and that its suppression would do away with the scruples which one clan had for marriage with others, thus making it possible for all clans to intermarry and freely to contract for their daughters. I held that this barbarous and unhuman custom might be done away with as Mr Willoughby did away with it in Bombay, by making the abolition one of the conditions on which all Rajputs hold their lands and strictly enforcing that condition.

As time wore on Sleeman's influence brought him no little success in checking this scourge.

The Oudh army (that part not officered by the British) was dreaded and detested by the people, and despised by the transgressor barons. In the eyes of the State authorities the regiments were not there to protect the country and its people, but solely to enforce exactions from the wretched inhabitants. It has already been related in Chaper 5 how the local governors used the army to collect taxes. Consequently landholders who objected to paying taxes all kept numerous and undisciplined armed gangs of their own which they used in slack periods for fighting on another and for pillaging the peasantry. These armed gangs and the king's army moved over the face of the country like a swarm of locusts. The king's regiments stripped the thatch from the houses as fodder and bedding for horse and bullock, and the beams to cook their meals, fed their animals in the green crops and robbed the granaries for men and beast. As for the army, their colonels spent not one penny on rations or firewood for the sepoys and their animals, these sepoys had preforce to forage for them and to take them in liberal supply without payment because even their pay was months in arrear.

It has been shown that these regiments and batteries were so ill-equipped that it took weeks to prepare them to move out of Lucknow. During Sleeman's tour he visited and inspected certain of the king's regiments which he met on the route. Here is his report on one such inspection.

2nd January, 1850

'We halted at Rae Bareilly and I inspected the bullocks belonging to the guns of Sobha Singh's regiment and some guns belonging to the

Nazim. The bullocks have been starved, are hardly able to walk and quite unfit for any work. Some of the carriages of the guns are broken down and those that are still entire are so rotten that they could not bear a march. This regiment of Sobha Singh's was as good as any of those commanded by Captains Magness, Burnbury and Barlow, while commanded by the late Captain Buckley: and the native officers and sepoys trained under him are all still excellent, but they are not well provided. Like the others, this regiment was to have had guns permanently attached to it, but the want of Court influence has prevented this. They now have them only when sent on service from one or other of the batteries at Lucknow and the consequence is that they are good for nothing. Sobha Singh is at Court, in attendance on the Minister; and his adjutant, Bhopal Singh, a near relative of the Rajah of Mainpuri, commands. He seems to be a good soldier and an honest and respectable man.

'The Nazim has with him this one Kmaki, or auxiliary regiment, and half of three regiments of Najibs, amounting, according to the pay abstracts and muster-rolls, to fifteen hundred men. He has one hundred cavalry and seven guns, of which one only is fit for use, and for that one he has neither stores nor ammunition. He was obliged to purchase in the bazaar the power and cloth required to make up the cartridges for a salute for the Resident. Of the fifteen hundred Najibs, not two-thirds are present, and of these hardly one-half are efficient.'

At the end of February the Sleeman family was back at the residency, Amélie preparing and packing the belongings of little Elizebeth and Mary for the long journey to Falmouth and Mary Furse. Thuggee began rapidly organizing columns under his British officers to march out and do to all the robber chiefs, whom he had now identified, precisely as he had already done to the two near Lucknow before he left on tour. He busied himself to prepare urgently his report for Lord Dalhousie. He also had to arrange for the future career of his son Henry, who was now at school at Denmark Hill, near London. He and Amélie had wished that the boy should follow his father into the Indian Political Service, but this very suitable project had been knocked on the head by the death of the second boy. Henry was still the only son and must therefore stay in England to look after his sisters should anything happen to his father. So the ball was set rolling for his entry into the British cavalry. Lord

Fitzroy Somerest was brought to take an interest in him and through his good offices and those of Lords Ellenborough and Hardinge and the Duke of Wellington, Henry was in 1851 commissioned into the 16th (The Queen's) Light Dragons. Thuggee was longing for retirement so that he could be a companion to this only son and be near him to take a pride in his achievements.

CHAPTER 23

The Struggle for Oudh

In a Very Short time Sleeman's columns were on the march under Magness, Orr, Bunbury, Boileau and the indispensable Weston, making straight for the fortresses of Bhoori Khan, Mahepat and Prithipat. These were no mere dacoit skirmishes: they were military operations against a well-armed enemy in formidable defensive positions. The small columns drove them into these posts, there to pound them with light muzzle-loader cannon and mortars until they could effect a breach or scale the walls. They went at their task sometimes independently and again in concerted operations, but the rule was ever to march to the sound of the guns. Against the tight bamboo stockadings it was hard pounding indeed. As often as not the garrison slipped away at the last moment through the dense undergrowth, only to be hunted again and again until a starving remnant surrendered itself, or the leaders were slain in the open. It used to be said in India that a British officer could make a soldier out of the meekest of men. These young officers enlisted their sepoys from precisely the same sources as did the Amils of Oudh's provinces, but while the soldiers of the latter were derided as worthless cowards, those of the former proved themselves dauntless and skilled fighters. Weston and his friends marched with their men, confident in the heroic qualities of those they led, and as heroes their soldiers proved themselves.

None the less there was some mutual influence, never yet explained, binding the British officer and the Indian soldier. Through two hundred years of almost incessant fighting British officers and Indian soldiers came together in surely one of the strangest and most admirable fellowships-of-arms that can ever have been known in the history of armies. Much is heard of the Sepoy Mutiny of 1857. This short and unusual disturbance in one portion only of the Bengal Army had causes, political and military, peculiar to the time. Much also is heard of an Indian Army which bore an honoured name and took inspiring part in hard-fought battles from the first raising of its regiments to the final climax when the colours were borne through two world wars. The prestige of the Indian Army then stood second to none in the wide world. Some day the prodigious achievement of the handful of modest Britons who brought all this about will be recorded in a work befitting their deserts. Little is now remembered of those early Indian regiments and batteries who fought with such valour in eighteenth-century wars, at Buxar, Plassey, Seringapatam and on a score more of occasions. These and their young British leaders must not be ignored when the tale is told; nor must the valour and skill of the Indian officers and sepoys.

Out of Lucknow hastened Sleeman's punitive forces under their nonchalant young commanders and within a month or two a contrary stream of evil-looking miscreants flowed into the prisons of the capital. From the residency tower Sleeman could catch glimpses of the two streams, and watch the eager villagers clearing the bamboo plantations and ploughing and sowing where the wilderness and savagery had for so long reigned unchallenged. Thuggee's next preoccupation was to compel the Oudh magistrates to deal justly and hardly with his prisoners.

Before the rains broke in 1850 he cast up his account. On the credit side was the banishment of Wasi Ali and a solid band of the fiddling, singing courtiers; the capture of a number of robber barons and the destruction of their forces; the removal of the arrogant Oudh regiments from Lucknow to the provinces and the beginnings of furnishing them with a better cadre of officers. The ill-provided condition of the army had been exposed for all to see in Lucknow and was being made public in the field, where even now the batteries under native colonels had only three or four rounds of shot, and their gunners' first concern on firing was to retrieve the cannon-balls as soon as they cooled. On the debit side lay the fact that he himself could not adequately improve the administration and that the limit of his powers was to obtain redress for individuals who came to him. It was to provide himself with the authority to advise with every chance of acceptance that he begged Dalhousie to set up the Council of State, which, he assured his lordship, all responsible officials of Oudh were willing and glad to accept. But Dalhousie shelved the matter, so Sleeman could only struggle on using his own prestige, undoubtedly very great, to achieve his ends.

In 1851 he had again to report that the king was utterly unfit to handle the affairs of the State and showed no signs of ever being able to do so. Two years later he repeated the warning and added that the monarch was a hypochondriac suffering from delusions, though admittedly sane during long intervals. He was, he said, in constant dread of being poisoned by his chief wife so that her son should succeed, and so that she might restore her paramour whose banishment Sleeman had secured. This woman's uncle, the chief minister, would, the king thought, be glad to accept the regency after the poisoning. He feared to admonish his next wife for her infidelities with one of his court lest she should poison him and join her lover in Rampore.

Such was the lamentable state of affairs at the source of government in Lucknow.

From the sketch that has been given here of the abuses in Oudh administration, one may anticipate the explosive effect of Sleeman's report on the authorities in Calcutta. For years the affairs of Oudh had been regarded as scandalous and for years governors-general had been half minded to intervene physically in the government, yet their hand had been stayed by the expectation that warnings now backed by one of the most outstanding of their administrators would bring about a sufficient amelioration. No one had ever rendered so complete a record on the kingdom, so no one had ever rendered to the full the evils that prevailed. This report therefore struck the Government's conscience all the more sharply, yet nothing was done for the time being and only further periodic reports demanded. Thuggee realized the severe impact that this story must assuredly make and he at once set to work to mitigate its effect and to forestall any intention to assume the government of the country. To Lord Dalhousie he wrote:

'I believe that it is your Lordship's wish that the whole of the revenues of Oudh should be expended for the benefit of the royal family and people of Oudh, and that the British Government should disclaim any wish to derive any pecuniary advantages from assuming to itself the administration.'

He wrote to his friend, Sir James Weir Hogg, at the Court of Directors in London:

. . . If our Government interpose, it must not be by negotiation and treaty, but authoritatively on the ground of existing treaties and obligations to the people of Oudh. The treaty of 1837 gives our Government ample authority to take the whole administration on ourselves, in order to secure what we have often pledged ourselves to secure to the people; but if we do this we must, in order to stand well with the rest of India, honestly and distinctly disclaim all interested motives, and appropriate the whole of the revenues for the benefit of the people and royal family of Oudh.

Were we to take advantage of the occasion to annex or confiscate Oudh, or any part of it, our good name in India would inevitably suffer and that good name is more valuable to us than a dozen of Oudhs. We are now looked up to throughout India as the only impartial arbitrators that the people generally have ever had, or can ever hope to have, and from the time we cease to be so looked up to, we must begin to sink. . . . We must show ourselves to be high-minded and above taking advantage of its prostrate weakness, by appropriating its revenues exclusively to the benefit of the people and royal family of Oudh. We should soon make it the finest garden in India, with the people happy, prosperous, and attached to our rule and character.'

He told all in authority that to annex Oudh would lead to mutiny in the Bengal Army, for most of its recruits came from that kingdom.

Frustrated, he saw in the King of Oudh playing into the hands of the annexationists, the worst happening when the king was discovered by Sleeman and Dalhousie to be in communication with the Shah of Persia, who was advising him that before long Persia was to invade India and promising him 'in that event to do all he could for the stability of Oudh.' Sleeman's appeals, however, stayed the final act of assumption, but he could not live for ever and his health was failing.

Wasi Ali had meanwhile sneaked back to the court and renewed his old games. He soon recaptured his control of the minister and set to work, as he had always done in the past, to create misunderstandings and bad feeling between the British representative and the king. He would never rest till he had made the king believe that every bit of advice and every suggestion that the Resident might proffer him must arise from personal or material interest. At the same time he attempted to persuade and blackmail the Resident to take him into his confidence and to let all and sundry understand that he had decisive influence in that quarter. Had any Resident been so great a fool as to allow this man to worm himself in, he would have reduced himself to impotence and his name to mockery.

One of this courtier's close associates was a European scamp of the name of Brandon, a freelance merchant. Sleeman had Brandon thrown out of Oudh, but not till Brandon had put it about that the Resident fed out of Wasi Ali's hand. Earlier on Thuggee had forbidden this merchant ever to come near the residency, so the latter had some spite to work off on him. Both Wasi Ali and Brandon intrigued to get the stubborn Resident put out of the way by every possible means. It was unfortunate that the residency surgeon, Dr Bell, was little better than Brandon; having been forbidden by Sleeman to accept fees from the king and his courtiers, he teamed up with Brandon to oppose his master.

In March 1853 Sleeman exposed an intrigue by Wasi Ali in which he had forged the seals of certain honest noblemen to inculpate them in an attempt to drive out the king and enthrone a usurper. Later still he caught this same man broadcasting a charge that Amélie had been accepting costly presents from people at court. The arch-knave knew that it was Sleeman who had exposed these rascalities and it was not long before he acted.

As the Muharram festival of the night of 9th October 1853 would be as noisy an affair as most, crackers exploding about the streets and fireworks sizzling into the air, the Resident decided to sleep upstairs for a few nights, rather more remote from the celebrations than his bedroom on the ground floor. The blazing torches, the drums and rejoicings surged along the roads about the residency as the seasoned Thuggee made his way past the Oudh police sentry at the door of his former room and mounted the stairs. For one moment he thought of calling the N.C.O. to post the sentry on the upper landing, but 'No, I'll leave him there for tonight—tomorrow perhaps. After all, there is a sentry from the Bengal Army outside the house itself.' A few minutes later he rolled on to his bed, pulled up the sheet and dropped off to sleep.

Down below the policeman took a deep draught of the sherbet the servant had brought him, so refreshing on this hot night and so well deserved by one who was missing the night's entertainment. He yawned: it was a drowsy sort of night . . . Sleepy, he took another swig, stretched himself, yawned again, nodded and slumbered. It was about midnight when two Indians, scarves wrapped across their faces, stepped over the sleeper and quietly opened the bedroom door behind him. They crept to the bed, rose and together poised their swords and thrust and thrust, here, there, everywhere, again and again through the bed and through the pillows. With their hands they felt hurriedly over the bed. Whispering, they left the room, silently closed the door, stepped over the sentry and melted away into the shadows of the garden.

The Resident wakened at a louder explosion than usual, turned over, took a pull at a water bottle on the table by his bed and went to sleep again. At dawn his bearer roused him and told him the sentry was not to blame.

'What for?' demanded Thuggee.

'They got away, your Honour.'

'I dare say. Why were they?' asked his mystified sahib.

'Sahib not knowing'

'No. Come on!'

'You've always slept downstairs till now, sahib. You came up there last night because you didn't like the noise. Two men with pistols and knives got into the room below, couldn't find you there in the bed and went to the sentry and offered him thousands of rupees if he could say where you were. The soldier only had his bayonet with him so he told them to go to the backdoor and he would show them. He ran in and got his musket, then went to the backdoor, but they took fright and he only managed to fire one long shot in the dark. They got away.'

And where was the king's police sentry on the door downstaris?'

'He was asleep, sahib. Drugged.'

Rather against his own inclinations, Sleeman had to report this attempt to Calcutta. In reply Dalhousie wrote:

Government House
October 27th, 1853

My dear Colonel Sleeman,

Notwithstanding that you make light of the incident which you reported lately, I wish to congratulate you, as the Government has already congratulated itself, on your providential escape from a real danger of which we have had lately a fatal abundance.

We are all earnest in our desire that, whatever your own inclinations may be, you should not pass by this even with disregard, but on the contrary should prosecute any inquiries which may be suggested by your own suspicions to the furthest point to which they can be carried.

This is due to the whole body of Government servants throughout India not less than to yourself.

An official letter has been addressed to you to this effect. But I have been desirous to assure you of my indignation that such an occurrence should have come to pass and of my great satisfaction in your escape.

Believe me to be,
Yours very truly,
Dalhousie.

Lt. Colonel W.H. Sleeman etc. etc.
Lucknow.

Whatever may be said of the policies of the Marquess of Dalhousie, every man who served him had to acknowledge that, while he castigated those whom he found wanting, he was ever ready with a word to encourage those whom he trusted.

Despite his respect for Sleeman and fear of Dalhousie, the king, who was truly aghast at the attempted murder, was never able to bring the criminals to book. No one ever expected that he would.

By now Thuggee was weary of Assistant Bird, about whom Amelie caused some amusement at the table one day by exlaiming with her usual aplomb to all assembled: 'Ah, ha! he is no singing bird, he is one great fighting cock.' Thuggee dismissed him and in his place Calcutta sent him an excellent young man of the name of Flectcher Hayes. It was a year after Sleeman died that Bird wrote and published in England a pamphlet entitled "The Spoliation of Oudh," an attack on his former chief. Thus did Captain R.W. Bird take his revenge. Thuggee also rid himself of Dr Bell and was given a man who was later to become famous, a brilliant young surgeon, Fayrer, who gained a reputation as the residency surgeon during the siege of Lucknow in 1857. Fayrer's duties were varied. No doubt he discharged them well. He was residency surgeon, Superintendent of the King's Hospital, in medical charge of the Martiniere School, postmaster, Superintendent of the Khairat Khana, a pension establishment founded by King Nasir-ud-din, and Superintendent of the Char Bagh, a large public garden.

Later he also became Extra Assistant Resident. Now the family at the residency was a thoroughly happy one and Sleeman's position in Oudh very strong. Had Dalhousie fallen in with his advice, he could and would at one stroke have rid the court of all the human rubbish that encumbered it and at last have set the administration of Oudh on the path of progress.

In the Residency at Lucknow there now hung the portrait in oils by the well-known hand of Beechy. It showed the Resident as a somewhat remote official, unsmiling. Let that be the official portrait of Thuggee Sleeman. Those who knew him found him a warm and human person, self-disciplined and utterly forthright and honest in his dealings. He was a religious man but his religion was personal to himself and it never obtruded into the lives of others.

Among his visitors at this time were Dr and Mrs Login. Login had brought the Koh-i-Noor diamond out of Lahore in 1849 after the Sikh wars. The whole jewel-house had been handed over to him with no list whatsoever, to set in order, value and sell. There are few men outside the British Indian service who could ever have been so implicitly trusted. There before him was the Koh-i-Noor, Ranjit Singh's chair of state, silver pavilion, Shah Sujah's pavilion, relics of the Prophet, Kulgi plume of the Sikh Guru, sword of Holkar, sword of the Persian hero Rustum (taken from Shah Sujah), and immense colleciton of Cashmere shawls—rooms full of them—laid out on shelves and heaped up in bales, vast quantities of gold and silver and jewels beyond value—all handed to Login to be dealt with honestly and fairly.

Login told Sleeman with what relief he heard that the Koh-i-Noor had arrived in England. He had had it on his person from the day he took charge until Lord Dalhousie came to his quarters, bringing with him a small bag made personally by Lady Dalhousie. Into this Login placed the jewel and Dalhousie fastened the bag round his waist under his clothes.

A young officer of the name of Corbett, who on occasion commanded the residency guard, wrote to a friend in 1854: 'General Sleeman is, I believe, a Cornish man, and in his youthful days was an athlete, but when the meridian of life was past, his official duties were too onerous and important to admit of relaxation. Mentally he was in his prime at this period but physically he was far from that: short of stature though somewhat muscular and robust in frame he appeared shrunken and aged.' From this it was obvious that his physical appearance was now betrying the deterioration in his health.'

He was no longer in charge of Thuggee operations. But he felt that the time had come for him to send a last message to those devoted men who had helped him wipe out the scourge of the Yellow Scarf. So at the end of 1853 he had this final word for them:

'I do not say that there is no such thing as Thuggee at the present time in any part of the Company's dominions. It is probable still that an occasional traveller may, from time to time, be strangled by the wayside. But the cases are few in number and comparatively insignificant in character. The system is destroyed; the profession is ruined; the Guild is scattered, never again to be associated into a great corporate body. The craft and the mystery of Thuggee will no longer be handed down from father to son. A few English officers, acting under the orders of the supreme administrative authorities, have purged India of this great pollution. If we have done nothing else for the country, we have done this one good thing. It was a great achievement—a great victory. . . .

This was his very last report on his old enemies before he wrote finish to their story.

Sleeman's message was obviously a quotation from an article which must have been written by Kaye in a Calcutta paper, for Kaye, using similiar words, went on to write in his book, *The Administration of the East India Company,* published in 1853: 'It is an exploit worthy to be celebrated by every writer who undertakes to chronicle the achievements of the English in the East—one which it is impossible to dwell upon without pleasure and pride.'

Thus perished the Royal Profession.

In 1853 Sleeman was promoted to full colonel; in 1854, to major-general. He was heavily overworked and troubled at his ill success in Oudh; and worried too by his only son, Henry, in England. Henry Sleeman promised well in the army and became at one time A.D.C. to Lord Cardigan but his zeal failed him and he talked of leaving the service. It was a great blow to Thuggee that his son, once he had set his hand to the plough, should leave the furrow unfinished. It was not Thuggee's way and he took it hardly.

In the autumn of 1854 the following paragraph on Sleeman appeared in Allen's *Indian Mail:*

Forty-six years of incessant labour have had their influence even on his powerful frame; he has received one of those terrible warnings believed to indicate the approach of paralysis... With Colonel Sleeman will depart the last hope of any improvement in the condition of this unhappy country of Oudh. . . . He has appreciated the misery created by a native throne; he has sternly and even haughtily pointed to the King the miseries caused by his incapacity and has frequently extorted from his fears the mercy which it was in vain to hope from his humanity.

The great-hearted Thuggee had collapsed at his desk and revived to find Dr Fayrer by his bedside. In a few days he was back at work but knew it was indeed the end of his struggle. He applied to the Marquess of Dalhousie for leave to join Amelie in Mussoorie:

'Had your Lordship left the choice of a successor to me I should have pointed out Colonel Outram. . . . I hope he will come as soon as possible.'

Wasi Ali had won.

CHAPTER 24

The Last Defeat

In The Autuman of 1854 Thuggee came to Amelie in Mussoorie, to rest from his labours and to recover the strength that had so suddenly left him. He hoped to return to the work he loved and to the people for whom he had so great a sympathy, but the dice were loaded against him in this bitter struggle with declining health. Even now he still attempted more than his strength could sustain and the distress of it told upon him all the more heavily. He did not cease to take an interest in Oudh. He and Outram kept up a regular correspondence, for Outram, and Low who was now at headquarters in Calcutta, both set their faces with his against annexation.

Sleeman had tried gallantly: he had advanced the kingdom further towards order and good administration in the countryside than any other man of his time. In wide areas, where all had been confusion and plundering, peasants could safely tend their fields from seed to harvest. But the great abscess remained in the very heart of the State, in the court at Lucknow.

Soon it began to steal in one Thuggee that his active days were done. He looked hopefully to Outram to cure the fatal disease of Oudh. Where he had partly succeeded would Outram crown his work—the one man whom he deemed capable of doing so?

In November 1855 husband and wife set out from Mussoorie on the long road to his retirement in England. Thuggee was now a back number, a sick man in a palanquin, yet greeted by all as he passed. Through Dehra Doon they went to Meerut, Delhi and Cawnpore, thence, in the new river steamer bumping from sandbank to sandbank, past Benares; the *garrial*, long-nosed alligators sunning themselves on the sand by the Ganges, the villagers in their bamboo palisades in the water bathing, washing, fishing; so down to Calcutta. There they would stay a few days with friends before embarking on Messrs Green's East Indian ship *Monarch*, due to sail on 25th January 1856, with Captain Charles Wiltshire in command.

On 9th January there came a letter from Barrackpore, the governor-general's palace outside Calcutta:

Barrackpore Park
January 9th 1856

My dear General Sleeman,

I have heard today of your arrival in Calcutta, and have heard at the same time with sincere concern that you are still suffering in health. A desire to disturb you as little as possible induces me to have recourse to my pen, in order to convey to you a communication which I had hoped to be able to make in person.

Some time since, when adjusting the details connected with my retirement from the Government of India, I solicited permission to recommend to Her Majesty's gracious consideration the names of some who seemed to me to be worthy of Her Majesty's favour. My request was moderate. I asked only to be allowed to submit the name of one officer from each Presidency. The name which is selected from the Bengal Army was your own, and I ventured to express my hope that Her Majesty would be pleased to mark her sense of the long course of able, and honourable, and distinguished service through which you had passed, by conferring upon you the civil cross of a Knight Commander of the Bath.

As yet no reply has been received to my letter. But as you have now arrived at the Presidency, I lose no time in making known to you what has been done; in the hope that you will receive it as a proof of the high estimation in which your services and character are held, as well by myself as by the entire community of India.

I beg to remain,
My dear General,
Very truly yours,
DALHOUSIE

Thuggee replied to this letter:

11th January, 1856

My Lord,

I was yesterday evening favoured with your Lordship's most kind and flattering letter of the 9th instant from Barrackpore.

I cannot adequately express how highly honoured I feel by the mention that you have been pleased to make of my services to Her Majesty the Queen, and as much gratified I am by this crowning act of kindness from your Lordship in addition to the many favours I have received at your hands during the last eight years and whether it may, or may not be, my fate to live long enough to see the honourable for me, the letter now received from your Lordship will of itself be deemed by my family as a substantial honour, and it will be preserved, I trust, by my son, with feelings of honest pride, at the thought that his father had merited such a mark of distinction from so eminent a statesman as the Marquis of Dalhousie.

My right hand is so crippled by rheumatism that I am obliged to make use of an amanuensis to write this letter, and my bodily strength is so much reduced that I cannot hope before embarking for England to pay my personal respects to your Lordship.

Under these unfortunate circumstances, I now beg to take my leave of your Lordship; to offer my unfeigned and anxious wishes for your Lordship's health and happiness and with every sentiment of respect and gratitude, to subscribe myself,

Yours Lordship's most faithful and
Obedient Servant,
W.H. Sleeman.
Major General.

To the Most Noble
The Marquis of Dalhousie, K.T.
Governor General etc. etc.
Calcutta.

Friends from Government House now told him of the Queen's intention to confer a baronetcy on his arrival in England.

Pondering over the achievements of his life in India, he and Amelie turned to their scrapbook to see how others had assessed his work in the Thuggee campaign. On 17th July 1852 an anonymous correspondent had written to the *Bengal Chronicle* when he had gone far to win his battle with the Thugs: 'It is a greater exploit than the conquest of Sindh or the Punjab, or the annexation of Pegu; and the names of the commanders of that little army of Thughunters, Sleeman, and his unflinching Lieutenants, ought, in every history of India, to have honourable mention and to be held in grateful remembrance by every student of that history.'

He put the book down. He wondered if this were really true and if they would indeed be remembered. The baronetcy and the knighthood? Very great honours from the Queen he revered, but his military rank, major-general—what more in truth did he need?

Soldiering, Thuggee, Dacoity, revenue, land settlement, agricultural improvement and irrigation, insurrection in Bundelkhand and Saugor, Gwalior and all its troubles, and lastly the struggle to purge Oudh of its corruption, violence and lawlessness and to hold its government in place. He had led a full life, tense and strenuous. What else could a man desire? He had left a name too for his children.

Soon he became anxious and deeply concerned over reports that rusted friends had brought to him about Oudh. They said that the council had agreed to instructions being given to Outram to assume the government of that kingdom; that proclamations were ready to effect this purpose and that if the king did not accept the terms of a treaty which would leave him with 'no more sovereignty than the Baliff of Jersey,' he would be overpowered and the kingdom annexed. Our troops were ready to advance. Outram was said to be in Barrackpore conferring with the governor-general. Sleeman heard that the people of Oudh were in great excitement and that opinion among them was not unfavourable to this serious step. He wondered if they realized the full meaning of it—that is, if these reports were true.

Year after year he had warned the Government that to annex the Kingdom of Oudh would lead to grave trouble, to insurrection and to mutiny in the Bengal Army. God grant that he was wrong, for he was now powerless to influence these affairs.

24th January 1856, Calcutta

On the morrow Amelie and Thuggee were to go aboard the *Monarch.* He would be glad now to be gone.

Outram had left Calcutta for Lucknow.

Postscript.
The Log of the Monarch
A Journal of
East India Ship *"Monarch"*
Kept by Fleetwood John Williams, Midshipman,
from Calcutta towards, London

Remarks. *Sunday Feby* 10th 1856

Light and Fine. 3/45 a.m. Departed this life Major Gen. William Henry Sleeman

Let by Obs	*Long by Obs*
S	E
2.22	82.51

No. 1658

Fort William, Foreign Department
The 20th March 1856

The governor-General in Council directs the republicaiton of the following extract from the *London Gazette* of the 5th February 1856.

'The Queen has been graciously pleased to give orders for the folloiwng appointments to the Most Honourable Order of the Bath:

To be... Knights Commander of the said Most Honourable Order, viz:

Major General William Henry Sleeman, of the Bengal Army.

Major General James Outram, C.B. of the Bombay Army.'

12th May, 1856
20 miles to the Start

My dearest Beloved Sister,

It is with such a broken heart that I take up my pen to write to you, and to tell you that it has pleased God to deprive me of my ever lamented and dearest Husband. ... The very day he came on board he was suffering much all the morning, but all his friends were telling him that they were sure that the sea air would do him good and with that idea, in the hopes that God would be merciful to him to allow his reaching England, he came. After we had been on board a few days he looked a little better and we used to go on deck together, and he told me his appetite was good and I used to get anything he wished for and then in looking at me, he used to say, 'I feel very happy, happy to know you are with me, and to look at you makes me feel so happy that I should not like to leave you in this world, but I feel that I shall soon leave you unprotectd and that I shall not see my poor Sister Mary, and if you wish for anything, write to Lord Dalhousie.'

The day after this conversaitn which was Wednesday, we went on the deck in the evening, and after this he never left his cabin, and began to suffer a great deal; on Friday he was a little better, but on Saturday evening he did not know me, and could not speak, and he expired at 4 o' clock on Sunday morning, the 10th February, when the ship ''Monarch'' was in latitude 2-22 South, and longitude 82-51 East.....

Amelie

Allen's Indian Mail, June 3rd 1856.

His career of Indian service was long, and his labours most meritorious. They will cause him to be long remembered with honour; and if his services in the suppression of Thuggee were alone to grace his memory, he would have left behind him a name never to be forgotten. He was one of those men whom the Indian service has never failed to produce whenever an emergency called for them. Had his lot been cast under ordinary circumstances, he would have discharged his duties, whatever they might have been, well and satisfactorily; but India was the proper field for him, and he adds one more to the number of distinguished men, who, from Clive downwards, have there gained a reputation which, as long as either India or England has a place in history, may well be pronounced immoral.

Years before, Thuggee Sleeman had written his own epitaph:

Jhansi,
4th March 1856

To Lord Gardinge,

'I have gone on quietly, through evil and through good report, doing, to the best of my ability, the duties which it has pleased the Government of India, from time to time, to confide to me, in the manner which appeared to be most conformable to its wishes and its honour, satisfied and grateful for the trust and confidence which enabled me to do so much good for the people, and to secure so much of their attachment and gratitude to their rulers. . . .'

W.H. Sleeman.

Let those be the last words of this man who loved all that was fine in art, letters, poetry and in human achievement, and who stood positively and squarely for the decent things of life.

Happenings Post Death of Sleeman:

1856, Annexation of Oudh

1857, The Sepoy Mutiny

Lucknow Residency besieged: Cawnpore attacked by Gwalior Contingent

1858

Pax Britannica

APPENDIX I

The Newswriters

Sleeman explains:

'The news department in the Kingdom of Oude was under a Superintendent-general, who sometimes contracted for it, as for the revenues of a district, but more commonly held it in *amanee*, as a manager. When he contracted for it he paid a certain sum to the public treasury, over and above what he paid to the influential officers and Court favourites in gratuities. When he held it in *amanee*, he paid only gratuities, and the public treasury got nothing. His payments amounted to about the same in either case. He nominated his subordinates and appointed them to their several offices taking from each a present gratuity and a pledge for such monthly payments as he thought the post would enable him to make. They received from four to fifteen rupees a month each, and had each to pay to their President, for distribution among his patrons or patronesses at Court, from one hundred to give hundred rupees a month in ordinary times. Those to whom they were accredited had to pay them, under ordinary circumstances, certain sums monthly, to prevent their inventing or exaggerating cases of abuse of power or neglect of duty on their part; but when they happened to be really guilty of great acts of atrocity, or great neglect of duty, they were required to pay extraordinary sums, not only to the news-writers, who were especially accredited to them, but to all others who happened to be in the neighbourhood at the time. There were six hundred and fifty news-writers of this kind employed by the King, and paid monthly three thousand one hundred and ninety-four rupees, or on an average, between four and five rupees a month each; and the sums paid by them to their President for distribution among influential officers and Court favourites averaged above one hundred and fifty thousand rupees a year. Many, whose avowed salary was from four to ten rupees a month, received each, from the person to whom they were accredited, more than five hundred, three-fourths of which they must send for distribution among Court favourites or they could not retain their places a week, nor could their President retain his.

'Such were the reporters of the circumstances in all the cases on which the Sovereign and his ministers had to pass orders every day in Oude. Some of those who derived part of their incomes from this source were "persons behind the throne, who were greater than the throne itself." The mother of the heir-apparent got twelve thousand rupees a year from it.

'But their exactions were not confined to Government officers of all grades and denominations; they were extended to contractors of all kinds and denominations, to him who contracted for the supply of the public cattle with grain, as well as to him who contracted for the revenue and undivided government of whole provinces; and indeed, to every person who had anything to do under, or anything to apprehend from, government and its officers and favourites, and, in such a country, who has not? The European magistrate of one of our neighbouring districts one day, before the Oude Frontier Police was raised, entered the Oude territory at the head of his police in pursuit of some robbers who had found asylum in one of the King's villages. In the attempt to secure them some lives were lost; and, apprehensive of the consequences, he sent for the official news-writer and gratified him in the usual way. No report of the circumstances was made to the Oude Durbar; and neither the King, the Resident, nor the British Government ever heard anything about it. On the practical working of the system, many illustrations will be found in my Diary of a journey through the Kingdom of Oude.'

APPENDIX 2

Thug Approvers

Extracts from captain W.H. Sleeman's investigations into the customs and beliefs of Thuggee.

Sleeman: Do you ever recollect any misfortune arising from going on when a hare crossed the road before you?

Nasir: Yes. When General Deveton commanded the troops at Jhalna we were advancing towards his camp; a hare crossed the road; we disregarded the omen, though the hare actually screamed in crossing and went on. The very next day, I, with seventeen of our gang, were seized; and it was with great difficulty and delay that we got our release. We had killed some people belonging to the troops, but fortunately none of their property was found upon us.

S : And you think these signs are all mandates from the deity, and, if properly attended to, no harm can befall you.

N: Certainly, no one doubts it; ask anybody. How could Thugs have otherwise prospered? Have they not everywhere been protected as long as they have attended religiously to their rules?

S : But if there was such a deity as Bhowani, and she were your patroness, how could she allow me and others to seize and punish so many Thugs?

N : I have a hundred times heard my father and other old and wise men say, when we had killed a sweeper and otherwise infringed their rules, that we should be some day punished for it; that the European rulers would be made the instruments to chastise us for our disregard of omens and neglect of the rules laid down for our guidance.

S : The pickaxe is supposed to be possessed of supernatural powers and to fly at call to the hand of the Thug initiate. You have heard this from your fathers, who heard it from their fathers; who heard it from their fathers; but none of you have ever seen it, nor is it true?

N : It is true; quite true. And though we have not seen this, we have all of us seen the sacred pickaxe spring in the morning from the well into which it had been thrown overnight, and come to the hands of the man who carried it as his call. Nay, we have seen the pickaxes of different gangs all come up of themselves from the same well at the same time, and go to their several bearers.

S : (To Sahib Khan) You are a Muslim?

Yes; and the greater part of the Thugs of the South are Mussulmans.

S : And you still marry, inherit, pray, eat and drink according to the Koran? And your Paradise is to be the Paradise promised by Mahomed?

Yes, all, all!

S : Has Bhowani been anywhere named in the Koran?

Nowhere.

(Here a Muslim Thug from Hindustan interposed, and said he thought Bhowani and Fatima, the daughter of Mahomed, and wife of Ali, were one and the same person; and that it was Fatima who invented the use of *rumal* to strangle the great demon, Rukt Bijdana; which led to a discussion between him and some of my Muslim native officers, who did not like to find the amiable Fatima made a goddess of Thuggee, —an "Iphigenia in Tauris." The Thug was a sturdy wrangler and in the estimation of his associate Thugs had, I think, the best of the argument.)

S : Then has Bhowani anything to do with your Paradise?

Nothing.

S : She has no influence on your future state?

None.

S : Does Mahomed, your prophet, anywhere sanction crimes like your; the murder in cold blood of your fellow creatures for the sake of their money?

No.

S : Then do you never feel any dread of punishment hereafter?

Never. We never murder unless the omens are favourable; and we consider favourable omens as the mandate of the Deity.

S : What Deity?

Bhowani.

S : Bhowani, you say, has no influence upon the welfare, or otherwise, of your soul hereafter?

None, we believe; but she influences our fates in this world, and what she orders in this world, we believe that God will not punish in the next.

[Here Sleeman gave up the hopeless argument.]

S : And do you never feel any sympathy for the persons murdered—never any pity or compunction?

Never.

S : How can you murder old men and young children without some motions of pity—calmly and deliberately as they sit with you and converse with you and tell you of their private affairs, of their hopes and fears, of the wives and children they are going to meet after years of absence, toil and suffering?

From the time that the omens have been favourable, we consider them as victims thrown into our hands by the deity to be killed, and that we are the mere instruments in her hands to destroy them: that if we do not kill them, she will never be again propitious to us, and we and our families will be involved in misery and want.

S : And you can sleep as soundly by the bodies and over the graves of those whom you have murdered, and eat your meals with as much appetitie as ever?

Just the same; we sleep and eat just the same unless we are afraid of being discovered.

S : Do your wives never reproach you with your deeds?

In the South we never tell our wives what we do lest they should disclose our secrets.

S : And your children too reverence their Thug fathers like other sons, even after they have become acquainted with their trade?

The same. We love them and they love us.

S : At what age do you initiate them?

I was initiated by my father when I was only thirteen years of age.

S : Do they not become frightened?

Not after the second or third expedition.

Feringheea (a noted thug leader) : About twelve years ago my cousin, Aman Subadar, took out with us my cousin, Kurhora, brother of Umrao, a lad of fourteen, for the first time. He was mounted upon a pretty pony, and Harsuka, who had been already on three expeditions, an adopted son of Aman's, was appointed to take charge of the boy. We fell in with five Sikhs and, when we set out before daylight in the morning, Harsuka was ordered to take the bridle and keep the boy in the rear out of sight and hearing.

The boy became alarmed and impatient and got away from Harsuka and galloped up at the instant the *Jhirni*, or signal for murder was given. He heard the screams of the men and saw them all strangled. He was seized with a trembling and fell from his pony. He became immediately delirious, was dreadfully alarmed at the sight of the turbans of the murdered men, and when anyone touched or spoke to him, talked about the murders and screamed exactly like boy talks in his sleep, and trembled violently if anyone touched or spoke to him. We could not get him on and, after burying the bodies, Aman and I and a few others sat by him while the gang went on; we tried to tranquillize him, but he never recovered his senses and before evening he died. I have seen many instances of people greatly shocked at the first murder, but never one so strong as this. Kurhora was a very fine boy, and Harsuka took his death much to heart, and turned Byragi [monk]; he is now at some temple on the bank of the Nerbudda river.

S : Was not Jharhu, who was taken with your gang after the Bhilsa murders and hung at Jubbulpore, a brother of his?

Feringheea: Yes, poor Jharhu! You ought not to have hung him; he never strangled or assisted in strangling any man!

(Here the tears ran down over Feringheea's face. Strange as it may seem, I have never heard him speak of his young cousin Jharhu's fate without weeping, and yet all the males of his family have been Thugs for generations and neither he nor any of them would shed one tear for any man or woman whom they had done to death. Another brother of this Jharhu was a very noted Thug leader, at that time still at large, of the name of Phulsa.)

S : But you worship at Devi's temples? [Devi being the Hindu goddess, consort of the god Siva.}

Yes, of course. All men worship at her temple.

S : No. We sahib *log* [folk] never do.

I mean all Hindus and Muslims.

(Here my Mahomedan officers again interposed and declared that they never did: that it was only the very lowest orders of Muslims who did. But, unfortunately, these keen observers of passing events had seen the wives of some very respectable Muslims at Jubbulpore, during the time the smallpox was raging, take their children to her temples and prostrate them before the images of the Goddess of Destruction. The officers admitted this to be sometimes the case, but pretended that it was unknown to their husbands.)

S : Tell me frankly which oath, now while you are in custody, you who are Muslims deem the strongest—that upon the Koran or that upon the pickaxes?

If we could be allowed to consecrate the pickaxe in the prescribed form, neither the Koran nor anything else on earth could be so binding; but without consecration it would be of no avail.

S : Above the Nerbudda, chiefs have never had the same dread of punishing Thugs as below it, have they?

They had formerly, and have still in many parts.

S : Why should they fear? Have there been any instances of suffering from it?

A great many. Was not Nanha, the Rajah of Jalaun, made leprous by Devi for putting them to death?

Durgha: He was quite sensible of it.

S : Did he do anything to appease her?

Everything. Budhu had begun a well in Jalaun. The Rajah built it up in a magnificent style: he had a *chabutra* (tomb) raised to their name, fed Brahmins and consecrated it and had worship instituted upon it but all in vain. The disease was incurable and the Rajah died in a few months, a miserable death. The tombs and well are both kept up and visited by hundreds to this day and no one doubts that the Rajah was punished for putting these two Thugs to death.

Nasir: Ah, Devi took care of them, and why? Was it not that you were more attentive to her orders?

Durgha: The Company's *iqbal* (good fortune) is such that before the sound of your drums, sorcerers, witches and demons take flight, and how can Thuggee stand?

Devi Din: Thuggee! Why it is gone. There are not fifty *Asal* (Thugs of good birth) left between the Ganges and Jumna.

Choti, Brahman: And not more than that number of all our old clans of Gwalior and Bundelkhand. But the Suseas of Rajputana have been untouched, and much is to be done about Delhi and Patiala.

S : But Nasir and Sahib Khan think it can never be suppressed in the Deccan?

Nasir: I think it never can.

S : Then by whose killing have all the Thugs who have been hung at Saugor and Jubbulpore been killed?

God's, of course.

S : You think that we could never have caught and executed them but by the aid of God?

Certainly not.

S : Then you think that so far we have been assisted by God in what we have done?

Yes.

S : And you are satisfied that we should not have ventured to do what we have done unless we were assured that our God was working with us, or rather that we were the mere instruments of his hands?

Yes, I am.

S : Then do you not think that we may go on with the same assurance till the work we have in hand is done; till, in short, the system of Thuggee is suppressed?

God is almighty.

And there is but one God?

One God above all gods.

And if that God above all gods supports us, we shall succeed?

Certainly.

Then we are all satisfied that he is assisting us, and therefore hope to succeed even in the Deccan?

God only knows.

S : Sahib Khan: If God assists, you will succeed, but the country is large and favourable and the gangs are numerous and well organized.

S : How is it you Hindustan Thugs kill women with less scruple than the Deccan Thugs?

Feringheea: To that we owe much of our misfortunes. It began with the murder of the Kali Bibi.

S : Who was the Kali Bibi?

Durgha: I was not present but I have heard that she was on her way from Elichpore to Hyderabad with a gold *chadar* or sheet for the tomb of Daula Khan Nawab, the brother of Salabat Khan of Hyderabad, who had died just before. Shamsher Khan and Ghulab Khan strangled her, I believe.

S : Did any calamity befall you after the murder of the Kali Bibi?

I think not.

S : And therefore you continued to kill them?

Feringheea: For five years no misfortune befell us and they continued to kill women. But then the misfortunes of my family began.

S : And you are worse than the Deccan Thugs, for you murder handsome young women as well as the old and ugly?

Not always. I and my cousin Aman Subadar were with a gang of one hundred and fifty Thugs on an expedition through Rajputana about thirteen years ago when we met a hand some maiden of the Peshwa's, Baji Rau's, on her way from Poona to Cawnpore. We intended to kill her and her followers, but we found her very beautiful and, after having her and her party three days within our grasp, and knowing that they had a lac and a half of rupees worth of property in jewels and other things with them, we let her and all her party go. We had talked to her and felt love towards her, for she was very beautiful.

S : And how come you killed the Moghulani? She also is said to have been very handsome?

We none of us ventured near her palankeen. The Muslims were the only men who approached her before the murder. Madar Bakhsh strangled her.

S : And you think killing women has been one of the chief causes of your misfortunes?

Yes.

S : How did you preserve the infant daughter of Banda Ali Munshi for adoption?

Chattar: Ghubbu Khan strangled the mother while her infant was in her arms, and he determined to keep and adopt the child. But, after the bodies had all been put into the grave, Dhanni Khan urged him to kill the child also, or we should be seized on crossing the Nerbudda valley. He threw the child living in upon the dead bodies, and the grave was filled up over it.

S : And the child was buried alive?

Yes.

S : How was that affair managed?

We fell in with the Munshi and his family at Chapra, between Nagpore and Jubbulpore, and and they came on with us to Lucknadaun, where we found that some Companies of a Native Regiment under European officers were expected the next morning. It was determined to put all of the Munshi's party to death that evening, as he seemed likely to keep with the Companies. Our encampment was near the village, and the Munshi's tent was pitched close to us. In the afternoon some of the officers's tents came on in advance, and were pitched on the other side, leaving us between them and the village. The *Khalasis* (coolies) were all busily occupied in pitching them. Nur Khan and his son, Sadi Khan, and a few others went as soon as it became dark to the Munshi's tent and began to sing and play upon a sitar, as they had been accustomed to do. During this time some of them took up the Munshi's sword on pretence of wishing to look at it. His wife and children were inside listening to the music. The Jhirni, or signal, was given, but at this moment the Munshi saw his danger, called out 'Murder!' and attempted to rush through, but was seized and strangled. His wife, hearing him, ran out with the infant in her arms, but was seized by Ghubbu Khan, who strangled her and took the infant. The *Saises* (grooms) were at the time cleaning their horses and one of them seeing his danger, ran under the belly of his horse and called out 'Murder!' but he was soon seized and strangled, as well as all the rest.

S : How did not the *Khalasis* and others who were pitching the tents close by hear these calls for help?

As soon as the signal was given, those of the gang who were idle began to play and sing as loud as they could, and two vicious horses were let loose and many ran after them calling out as loudly as they could, so that the cries of the Munshi and his party were drowned.

S : Do you Thugs from Bihar ever murder women?

Bhidda: How could we do so? We do not even murder a person that has a cow with him, for we regard the cow as sacred and his master immune.

S : Did not the Hindus assist in strangling the women in the Sutrooh and Chalisrooh affairs?

Punna: God forbid! They sinned enough in consenting to share in the booty, but they never assisted in the murder.

S : Are you never afraid of the spirits of the persons you murder?

Nasir: Never, they cannot trouble us.

S : Why? Do they not trouble other men when they commit a murder?

Of course they do. The man who commits a murder is always haunted by spirits. He has sometimes fifty at a time upon him, and they drive him mad.

S : And how do they not trouble you?

Are not the people whom we kill, killed by the orders of Devi?

Kalyan: Yes. It is by the blessing of Devi that we escape evil.

Durgha: Do not all whom we kill go to Paradise, and why should their spirits stay to trouble us?

Inaent: A good deal of our security from spirits is to be attributed to the *rumal* with which we strangle.

S : I did not know that there was any virtue in the *rumal*?

Inaent: Is it not our sikka (ensign) as the pickaxe is our *nishan* (standard)?

Feringheea: More is attributable to the pickaxe. Do we not worship it every seventh day? Is it not our standard? Is its sound ever heard when digging the grave by any but a Thug? And can any man even swear to a falsehood upon it?

S : And no other instrument would answer, you think, for making the graves?

Nasir: How could we dig graves with any other instruments! This is the one appointed by Devi, and consecrated, and we should never have survived the attempt to use any other.

Feringheea: No man but a Thug who has been a strangler, and is remarkable for his cleanliness and decorum is permitted to carry it.

S : Are the usages of the River Thugs the same as yours?

Moradun: In worship, the same. They strangle in boats and throw the bodies into the river. If they see blood, they must go back and open the expedition anew. They give the Jhirni by first striking on the deck of the boat three times, when the man appointed to give it sees all clear.

S : Have the River Thugs the same Ramasi (dialect) as you?

Imam Bakhsh: No, totally different. They neither understand our Ramasi, nor do we theirs.

(I then sent for Buktawar.)

S : You are said to have occasionally gone with the River Thugs. What do you call them?

We call them Pungus. On one occasion only have I ever served with them.

S : Where do they live?

They live about Beerbohm, Bankua, Kulna-Kutwa, Seori and other places in the district of Burdwan, which is a very large district. Thugs do not live in these or any other towns, as they are there always liable to be a good deal annoyed by police questions, but live in small villages round about them. Annoying police questions are such as, Who's come? Who's gone? Who's born? Who's died? What's your occupation? Whence your income? and so forth. These questions annoy Thugs a good deal, and oblige them to share their incomes with the policemen as well as with the *zumeendars* (landowners).

S : When you have a poor traveller with you, or a party of travellers who appear to have little property about them, and you hear or see a very good omen, do you not let them go, in the hope that the virtue of the women will guide you to better prey?

Durgha: Let them go! never, never!—*kabhi nahin, kabhi nahin!*

Nasir: How could we let them go? Is not the good omen the order from Heaven to kill them, and would it not be a disobedience to let them go? If we did not kill them, should we ever get any more travellers?

Feringheea: I have known the experiment tried with good effect. I have known travellers who promised little, let go, and the virtue of the omen brought better.

Inaent: Yes. The virtue of the omen remains, but the traveller who has little should be let go, for you are sure to get a better.

Sahib Khan: Never, never! This is one of your Hindustani heresies. You could never let him go without losing all the fruits of your expedition. You might get property, but it could never do you any good. No success could result from your disobedience!

Morlee: Certainly not! The travellers who are in our hands when we have a good omen must never be let go, whether they promise little or much. The omen is unquestionably the order, as Nasir says.

Nasir: The idea of securing the good will of Devi by disobeying her order, is quite monstrous. We deccan Thugs do not understand how you got hold of this. Our ancestors were never guilty of such folly.

Feringheea: You do not mean to say that we of Murnai and Sindause were not as well instructed as you of Telingana?

Nasir and Sahib Khan: We only mean to say that you have clearly mistaken the nature of a good omen in this case. It is the order of Devi to take what she has put in your way—at least, so we in the Deccan understand it.

S : You told Mr. Johnstone, the traveller, while he was at Saugor, that the operations of your trade were to be seen in the caves at Ellora?[1]

Feringheea: All! Every one of the operations is to be seen there. In one place you see men strangling: in another burying the bodies: in another carrying them off to the graves. There is not one operation in Thuggee that is not exhibited in the caves of Ellora.

Durgha: In those caves are to be seen the operations of every trade in the world.

Choti: Whenever we passed near, we used to go and see these caves. Every man will there find his trade described, however secret he may think it; and they were all made in one night.

S : Does any person beside yourself consider that any of these figures represent Thugs?

Feringheea: Nobody else, but all Thugs know they do. We never told anyone else what we thought about them. Everybody there can see the secret operations of his trade, but he does not tell others of them, and no other person can understand what they mean. They are the works of God. No human hands were employed upon them. That everybody admits.

S : What particular operations are there described in figures?

Sahib Khan: I have seen the *Sotha* (inveigler) sitting upon the same carpet with the traveller, and in close conversation with him, just as well are when we are worming out their secrets. In another place, the strangler (*Bhartote*) has got his *rumal* over his neck and is strangling him; while another, the *Chamochi*, is holding him by the legs. These are the only two operations that I have seen described.

Nasir: These I have also seen, and there is no mistaking them. The *Chamochi* has a close hold of the legs and is pulling at them, thus, while the Bhartote is tightening the *rumal* round his neck, *thus*.

S : Have you seen no others?

Feringheea: I have seen these two, and also the *Lughas* carrying away the bodies to the graves, in this manner, and the sextons digging the grave with the sacred pickaxe. All is done just as if we had done it ourselves; nothing could be more exact.

S : And who do you think could have executed this work?

Feringheea: It could not have been done by Thugs because they would never have exposed the secrets of their trade, and no other human being could have done it. It must be the work of the gods; human hands could never have performed it.

S : And, supposing so, you go and worship it?

Sahib Khan: No. We go to gratify curiosity, and not to worship. We look upon it as a mausoleum, a collection of curious figures cut by some Demons, who knew the secrets of all mankind, and amused themselves in describing them.

Harnagar: We Hindus go for the same purpose. We never go to worship. We consider it as a Pantheon of unknown Gods.

S : But where did you fall in with Feringheea and the Moghulani?

Durgha: We fell in with them at Lalsont and came on with them to Somp. She had with her an old female servant, mounted upon a pony, one man-servant and six bearers for her palankeen. From Somp we sent on men to select a place for the murder, and set out with her before daylight; but the Thug who selects the place of murder, the *bele*, lost the road in the dark, and we were trying to find it when the young woman became alarmed and began to reproach us for taking her into the jungle in the dark. We told Feringheea to come up and quieten her but, dreading that some of her party might make off, the signal was given and they were all strangled. We got six hundred rupees worth of property from them.

S : And was this enough to tempt so large a gang to murder a beautiful young woman?

We were very adverse to it, and often said that we should not get two rupees apiece, and that she ought to be let go. But Feringheea insisted upon taking her.

S : How come you advised the murder of this young woman?

Feringheea: It was her fate to die by our hands. I had several times tried to shake them off before we met the Muslims, and when we came to Lalsont, I told her to go on, as I had joined some old friends and would be delayed. She then told me that I must go to her home near Agra, or she would get me into trouble; and being a Brahmin while she was a Muslim, I was afraid that I should be accused of improper intercourse and turned out of caste.

S : You were then a young man and she was a beautiful young woman. Have you no pity?

Madar Bakhsh: I had. But I had undertaken the duty and we must all have food. I have never known any other means of gaining it.

(It was this last statement that showed me that there might be a gleam of hope in trying to redeem these men, or at least some of them.)

Feringheea: We all feel pity sometimes, but the *goor* (sugar) of the Tuponi[1] changes our nature. It would change the nature of a horse. Let any man once taste of that *goor*, and he will be a Thug, though he knows all the trades and have all the wealth in the world. I never wanted food; my mother's family was opulent, her relations in high office. I have been in high office myself, and became so great a favourite wherever I went that I was sure of promotion, yet I was always miserable while absent from my gang, and obliged to return to Thuggee. My father made me taste of that fatal *goor* when I was yet a mere boy, and, if I were to live a thousand years, I should never be able to follow any other trade.

Kalyan Sing: When our gang was arrested at Hoshungabad, was there not a scramble among the Hill Chiefs and Zamindars to get us released upon their security? Did not many, both there and at Jubbulpore, who had never seen us in their lives, make their agents offer any security that could be demanded for our future good behaviour?

S : And why did they do this? They no doubt throught you very innocent and respectable men under misfortune?

Not at all. We managed to persuade them that we could by being allowed to follow our old trade under their protection, be made a new source of revenue to them. We told them that we would pay for the little land we might cultivate in their villages more than fifty times its value.

Choti: Did not the Khairo chief stand a long siege from his master, the Jhansi Rajah, before he would give up eight or ten of us?

Qaim Khan: And was not the Maharajah of Gwalior obliged to send two large guns and a great force against Bhume Zamindar of Bahmanpore before he would give us up; and were not several lives lost in the action which continued from daylight till nine in the morning? Bhume was very fond of us, particularly of our Jemadar Ghulab Khan, whose father had been hung the year before at Saugor, and who is now an approver with Mr. Thomas, and he said that he would rather die than give us up. But, poor man, he had only sixteen muskets to fight with, and had got into disgrace at Court by not paying his rents! The Lord Sahib (Lord William Bentinck) must have heard the guns, for he and the Rai Sahib were encamped only a few miles off at the time.

---

[1] *Tuponi,* or *Tupounee,* sacrifice of *goor* to Bhowani (Kali). The *good* or coarse sugar is placed on a clean cloth close to the consecrated pickaxe and a piece of silver. The leader of the gang sits beside these, places come *goor* in a hole in the ground, raises hands and eyes to heaven and prays.

S : How was it that this lad's father, an old and noted Thug, did not initiate him himself?

Buktawar: His father used to drink very hard, and in his fits of intoxication he used to neglect his prayers, and his days of fast. All days were the same to him. This lad, Shamshera, was always sober and religiously disposed, and separated from his father, living always with his uncle Dundi, who was a very worthy and good man.

S : But he was a Thug also?

Yes, he was, but he did not tell this boy so.

APPENDIX 3

Memorials

FALMOUTH

Church of King Charles Martyr

Sacred to the memory of Major General Sir W.H. Sleeman, K.C.B. who after an uninterrupted service of forty-seven years, died at sea on his passage to England on board the "Monarch" East Indiaman on the 10th Feb., 1856, aged 67 years.

He originated, organised, and successfully carried out the system for the suppression of Thuggee throughout India, and his experience of civil administration and knowledge of the people united to amenity of manner gained for him not only the confidence of the Government of India, but the love of the natives, who always regarded him as their friend and by whom his equity was profoundly appreciated.

Sacred also to the memory of Mrs Mary Furse. Relict of Captain John Furse, late of this place, and the only and dearly-loved Sister of the above, who after a long life devoted to acts of charity died at Penwerris Terrace, Falmouth, in the 77th year of her age, Sept. 7th 1863. She laboured to testify her faith in the truth as it is in Jesus, by the piety, obedience and charity of a Christian life, and to manifest a dependant and thankful sense of the riches of His mercy and grace.

JUBBULPORE

Christ Church

Sacred to the memory of Major General Sir William Sleeman, K.C.B. who, after an unbroken service of 47 years, during which he held some of the highest civil and political appointments in India, died at sea while on his return to England, February 10th 1856, Age 67. Amelie Sleeman died at 13 Soth Parade, Southsea, on 19th October 1882.

GLOSSARY

Amil, collector of revenue, comptroller of finances, ruler, administrator *Bowlee,* a large well.

Bunji, Buniji, Ramasi for merchandise.

Byragi, a follower of the god Vishnu.

Calee, Cali or Kali, Consort of the god Siva.

Chireya, Ramasi for the chirping of a small owlet, conisdered by Thugs to be a bad omen, whether the bird is sitting or flying.

Cotwall, Cootwal, Kotwal, the chief native police officer of a town.

Dussehra, Dessehra, or Dussehra festival, held in early October; it marks the close of the rainy season and the start of the cold season.

Datiya or Dutteea, a small state west of Jhansi district.

Daturias, dutooreeas, poisoners using datura (dutoora) plant seed, a powerful narcotic.

Devi, consort of the God Siva.

Doah or Dooah, Persian word for a tract of land between two rivers; here, specially, between the Ganges and the Jumna.

Filose or Filoze, Jean Baptiste, an Italian military adventurer in the service of Scindia.

Gaddi, cushion. To ascent the gaddi is to ascend the throne.

Goor, coarse sugar.

Gram, a pulse; also termed chick-pea.

Gwalior, The old city encirlces the north end of the fortress. The new city is called Lashkar, or camp of the army, and is south and a mile distant.

Hindostan, Hindustan, This term is used in two senses by Sleeman and his associates in this book: (a) the land of the Hindus; India; (b) that part of India under British rule or control which lay north of the Nerbudda river, and exclusive of Bengal and Bihar. The latter provinces were regarded as Purab (the East) or Dekhan (Deccan; the South). The Thugs used the term in this latter sense.

Ice pits (of the royal household), pits used for storing ice before its manufacture was introduced to India by the British. On winter nights, water was poured into shallow, porous, earthenware saucers, which were then placed where cold air could circulate around them (straw was used in this technique). By dawn discs of ice would have formed, and these would be stored underground for use in the hot weather.

Isle of France, the Mauritius. Captured by Rowley and Abercrombie in November 1810.

Kali, consort of the god Siva.

Kos, Koss, Coss, usually about 2 miles, but varies.

Kotwal, Cotwall, chief police officer of a town.

Kukri, the curved Gurkha knife.

Maulvi, a Muslim professor, a learned man.

Moira, Lord, afterwards Lord Hastings, Governor-General of India 1813 to 1823.

Mujarram, Mohurram, annual commemoration in October of the defeat of Ali at the Battle of Kerbala in A.D. 680.

Mutiny of November 1824, the 47th Native Infantry, ordered to Rangoon from Barrackpore, refused to leave India to cross the seas and broke out into open mutiny.

Nerbudda River, boundary between Hindustan, or Northern India, and the Deccan (Dakhan) or Southern India.

North West Province, the seat of the Government of the N.W. Province was at Agra from 1833-1868.

Nujeeb, Najib, noble or worthy; here means 'a volunteer', or 'irregular'.

Pariah, a Tamil term meaning 'outcaste'.

Patel, a village proprietor.

Pipal tree, sacred to Vishnu.

Rupee, in Sleeman's day it was worth two shillings.

Saligram, a fossil ammonite.

Sarae or Sarai, an inn of eastern type.

Suttee, sati, a virtuous woman (especially one who burns herself with her husband). Sut, or sat, is the masculine form of sati.

Sikh, a disciple (of Nanak Shah).

Siva, god of destruction; Parvati or Devi is his wife.

Sheristhadar, sheriff's officer.

Sipahee, armed follower (sepoy).

Sureemant (correctly *srimant*—pron. Shreemunt), a title given to any exalted or venerable person.

Talookdar, Taluqdar, baronial lord.

Thevenot, Fean de, author of *Travels,* 1684.

Thug pron. T'ug, means a deceiver.

Toolsee, or Tulsi, plant, the basil shrub, sacred to Vishnu.

Vishnu, the second of the Hindu Trinity, representing a principle of stability. Sometimes deemed to be the creator of the world.

Yug (sanskrit *yuga*), originally a yoke; an age, an epoch, a cycle. In mythology an age of the world, a long mundane period of years, of which there are four: *Krit* or *Satya-yug, Treta, Dwapar,* and *Kali,* of which the first three have already elapsed, while the Kali is that in which we are supposed to live, comprising 432,000 years, of which nearly 5000 have elapsed.

Wakeel, Wokeel, Vakil, attorney, agent, administrator.

Zamindar, Zemmendar, etc., landlord.

Index

O

P

Q

R

S

T

U

W

Y